Safe House

Explorations in Creative Nonfiction

"A promising tradition of creative nonfiction is nascent in Africa. Fresh ways of writing African experiences are afoot. This publication signals the gestation of something enormously exciting and genuinely new."
— Jonny Steinberg, author of *A Man of Good Hope*

"Not so much timely as long overdue, this collection of essays and short memoirs directs the focus inward, leaping from blade-sharp observations of contemporary life around the African continent to a striking consideration of the continent's cultural and political future. *Safe House* transports the reader beyond the tired narrative of news reports through individual stories and into worlds of hidden complexities. Stimulating reading."
— Aminatta Forna

"The stories in this anthology provide a form of connective tissue to contemporary life on the African continent in Cape Town, Nairobi, Dakar, and Kano. As a whole, it is both microscopic and panoramic, and strongly argues for an annual take of the same. As an Editor who regularly commissions nonfiction I am full of envy."
— Billy Kahora, Editor of *Kwani?*

Safe House

Explorations in Creative Nonfiction

Edited by Ellah Wakatama Allfrey

DUNDURN

TORONTO

Design: Janette Thompson (Jansom)
Cover design: Robin Farrow
Cover image: © Msingi Sasis/Nairobi Noir www.nairobinoir.com
Printer: Webcom

Library and Archives Canada Cataloguing in Publication

Safe house : explorations in creative nonfiction / edited by Ellah Wakatama Allfrey.

Issued in print and electronic formats.
ISBN 978-1-4597-3547-7 (paperback).--ISBN 978-1-4597-3548-4 (pdf).-- ISBN 978-1-4597-3549-1 (epub)

1. African literature (English)--21st century. 2. Africa--In literature.
I. Allfrey, Ellah Wakatama, 1966-, editor

PR9348.S24 2016   820.8'096   C2016-900864-9
                                             C2016-900865-7

1   2   3   4   5   20   19   18   17   16

Conseil des Arts du Canada   Canada Council for the Arts   Canada   ONTARIO ARTS COUNCIL / CONSEIL DES ARTS DE L'ONTARIO / an Ontario government agency / un organisme du gouvernement de l'Ontario

We acknowledge the support of the **Canada Council for the Arts** and the **Ontario Arts Council** for our publishing program. We also acknowledge the financial support of the **Government of Canada** through the **Canada Book Fund** and **Livres Canada Books**, and the **Government of Ontario** through the **Ontario Book Publishing Tax Credit** and the **Ontario Media Development Corporation**.

VISIT US AT
Dundurn.com | @dundurnpress | Facebook.com/dundurnpress | Pinterest.com/dundurnpress

Dundurn
3 Church Street, Suite 500
Toronto, Ontario, Canada
M5E 1M2

The Commonwealth Foundation and Commonwealth Writers acknowledge the support of the Miles Morland Foundation.

MILES MORLAND FOUNDATION   Commonwealth Foundation   COMMONWEALTH WRITERS

CONTENTS

III. THEN AND NOW

COMMONWEALTH WRITERS

Commonwealth Writers, the cultural initiative of the Commonwealth Foundation, develops and connects writers across the world. It believes that well-told stories can help people make sense of events, engage with others, and take action to bring about change. Responsive and proactive, it is committed to tackling the challenges faced by writers in different regions and working with local and international partners to identify and deliver projects. Its activities take place in Commonwealth countries, but its community is global.

The Commonwealth Foundation is an intergovernmental development organization with an international remit and reach, uniquely situated at the interface between government and civil society.

We would like to thank the Miles Morland Foundation for additional support, which made this anthology possible, and the team at Dundurn Press for all their hard work and enthusiasm.

www.commonwealthwriters.org

ABOUT THE EDITORS

ELLAH WAKATAMA ALLFREY is a Zimbabwean-born editor and critic. Based in London, she is the former deputy editor of *Granta* magazine and has also held positions as senior editor at Jonathan Cape and assistant editor at Penguin. In 2015 she served as a judge for the Man Booker Prize. She is series editor of the Kwani? Manuscript Project and the editor of *Africa39* (Bloomsbury, 2014), and *Let's Tell this Story Properly* (Commonwealth Writers/Dundurn Press, 2015). She sits on the boards of Art for Amnesty, the Caine Prize for African Writing, Jalada Trust, and the Writers Centre Norwich and is a patron of the Etisalat Literature Prize. Her introduction to *Woman of the Aeroplanes* by Kojo Laing was published by Pearson in 2012. In 2011 she was awarded an OBE for services to the publishing industry.

OTIENO OWINO lives in Nairobi, Kenya. He was selected for the 2014 African Writers Trust's Editorial Skills Training Workshop, organized in collaboration with Commonwealth Writers. Since 2015, he has worked as an assistant editor at Kwani Trust, East Africa's leading literary network and publisher, where he has been part of the editorial teams on the Kwani? Manuscript Project, and *Kwani?*, a journal of short fiction, nonfiction, and poetry.

INTRODUCTION

Nineteen seventy-seven was life-changing. That year, my parents bought a house in the suburb of Tynwald, in what was then still Rhodesia. The Second Chimurenga* was at its zenith, and independence was only three years away. Tynwald was zoned for white residents only, but, in an act of wilful defiance carried out with affected but determined nonchalance, my parents declared their own UDI** and integrated the neighbourhood, aided and abetted by their estate agent, Peggy Healy.

My family had returned from the United States two years prior, and we had been living first with relatives and then in rented accommodation. The house at Tynwald, a sprawling L-shape with five acres of grounds, a long driveway, and a guava orchard, seemed like paradise. Of course, the move attracted attention. There must have been legal wrangling to which we children were oblivious, but I do remember a camera crew arriving to take pictures of us all (my parents, my brothers, my little sister, Mavhu, and me) in our new home for a magazine feature on examples of the country's gradual shift towards racial equality.

Despite all this, the real event of the year, at least for me and my brothers, was the release of the first *Star Wars* movie. My father

---

* (also known as the Zimbabwe War of Liberation)
** Unilateral Declaration of Independence

dropped us off at the Kine 1 in town, and for the next two hours, along with audiences across the globe, we journeyed to a galaxy far, far away ... It was the first time I had been to the cinema, and though my father was late picking us up, we hardly noticed. As we waited, my younger brother, Nhamu, and I re-enacted scenes from the film (leaping from the pavement with imaginary lightsabers, summoning the Force) while first-born Richard tried, with little success, to contain our exuberance.

In December 2015 I was back in Harare for a holiday visit, and, along with my husband, daughter, and Richard's two children, Farai and Tariro, I watched the latest installment in the *Star Wars* saga, whooping with joy as John Boyega made his appearance as Finn, the *black* Stormtrooper. By then, both my brothers were deceased. Every moment of the film (from the reunion between Han Solo and Princess Leia to C3PO's familiar wittering in indignation) had me consumed with longing for their company. Afterwards, we went home to the new house in Marlborough where my parents had moved after selling the property in Tynwald, our family home for thirty-seven years. What had been a bucolic semi-rural suburb (complete with a fishing stream and anthills heaving with ishkwa, the flying ants that are a rainy-season delicacy) was now surrounded by high-density townships and cut through by a major highway. When a neighbour, a Chinese expatriate who sold light-industrial equipment from the yard of his own property, made an offer, my parents were finally persuaded to move.

In the years between, Rhodesia had become Zimbabwe. A lot has changed. While my country remains blessed with temperate weather and a people whose dignity and forbearance inspire me every day, the political aspirations of 1977 seem as distant a possibility as the hope Nhamu and I had then of Han Solo turning up at our doorstep with an invitation to join the crew of the *Millennium Falcon*. For most of the population, it is a struggle to meet basic needs, and my parents' generation, whose defiance and determination won the nation's freedom, find their pensions worthless as a result of economic collapse. Many endure the loneliness that is a consequence of the massive exodus of the young to seek fortune elsewhere, as I have done.

In his memoir, *Black Gold of the Sun*, the Ghanaian writer Ekow Eshun writes of his love of comic books, speculating that African children of the diaspora especially have a unique affinity with superheroes. It is a sense of belonging elsewhere, a longing for a special power that will both set them apart from the society they live in and ensure them admiration and acceptance. His memoir evokes a particular African childhood that inspired me to think of my own — as preoccupied and influenced by a fictional Empire as it was by the political turmoil of those formative years. I devoured it, along with Binyavanga Wainaina's *One Day I Will Write about this Place* and Aminatta Forna's *The Devil that Danced on the Water.* Yet I found I wanted still more: more stories about the events — big and small — that form my continent's recent past and present.

My thirst has been slaked, somewhat, by the extraordinary publishing that has emerged out of Africa in the past decade, such as has appeared in the journals *Kwani?* and *Chimurenga*. But as a reader and publisher I still find myself longing for a wider range of choices. Perhaps because of our turbulent struggle against colonialism, the well-wrought polemic is well-developed in Africa and, from Achebe to Adichie, our fiction has achieved renown for decades. But African creative nonfiction, from the personal essay to the travelogue to the forensic investigation, seems, to me, to be in a germinal phase. This must have, in part, to do with resources. You have to leave your study to write compelling nonfiction. It takes time and money.

Safe House is an expression of my confidence that we are long past the time when readers — both in Africa and across the world — will respond only to African stories told by Western "experts." We know, from the critical and commercial successes of Africa's contemporary literary greats, that there is a huge appetite for our

stories. But this confidence has to be tempered by the acknow-
ledgement that without the creation of a marketplace to sustain
the writers and the practical support (an editorial team and a publisher) to ensure the work finds an audience, there is a limit to any
such explorations in creative nonfiction.

When the team at Commonwealth Writers approached me with
the idea for an anthology of non-fiction from African countries,
I wanted to invite writers to tell me what these stories would be
and how they wanted to write them. Rather than focusing on a
theme inspired by news or current affairs, I was curious to find out
what subjects would come up if writers were given the freedom of
choice, the incentive of payment and publication, and the security
of editorial support. We sent out a public call for submissions and
selected the proposals that most stood out in terms of subject matter and approach.

I also directly commissioned several pieces on subjects I felt
merited exploration from an African perspective, most particularly
an account of the Ebola crisis and several pieces on the lives of
gay Africans. While the former was reported extensively in Western
media, I wondered about the experience of those who had had to
live in the midst of the epidemic. The latter has become a bell-
wether, in that expression of sexuality seems to articulate a particular tension between tradition and modernity on the African
continent. But for the most part the "gay debate" is dismissed, in
Africa, as a Western issue imposed on us. On this topic, and indeed
others, I wanted to hear from voices that could bring a different
perspective: writers interrogating subjects with the advantage of
a shared culture and geographic space; writers journeying internationally *within* Africa, bringing home the news from elsewhere on
the continent and relating it to their own experience.

Too often, writing about Africa has been at a distance, a view to
a place far away. What I hoped to encourage, as we developed the
pieces in this collection, was, in each instance, a personal voice that
allowed the writer to become a part of the story. The expression of

such subjectivity requires a particular combination of confidence and vulnerability. In their individual expressions of this combination, the contributors begin to define a specifically African genre of creative nonfiction, one inflected by the geography and politics, the cultures and histories, of this continent.

The writers selected here represent as wide a range in experience as they do in subject and form. There are seasoned nonfiction practitioners, writers who are beginning to make their mark in their home countries, and those established in other genres who are trying nonfiction for the first time.

Some have chosen to explore themes through the prism of their own life experiences: Kofi Akpabli's family history of an Accra neighbourhood; Isaac Otidi Amuke and his memoir of student activism and exile; Chike Frankie Edozien writing of a lost love and the burden of silence; novelist Hawa Jande Golakai's diary written during the Ebola crisis in Liberia; Beatrice Lamwaka's memoir of conflict in northern Uganda; and activist Sarita Ranchod's episodic account of growing up in Cape Town's Indian community.

There are reports of the lives of others: Kevin Eze on Chinese migrants living in Senegal's capital; Mark Gevisser as he chronicles the travails of a young gay Ugandan man living as a refugee in Kenya; Simone Haysom on the life of a Cape Town petty criminal; Elnathan John's visits to a community facing social exile in northern Nigeria; and Bongani Kona's account of a South African murder.

And there are the travellers: poet Neema Komba visits an ancestral landmark in Tanzania; photographer Msingi Sasis traverses Nairobi at night; while Barbara Wanjala journeys from Kenya to Senegal to meet with LGBT activists in Dakar.

In 2014, Commonwealth Writers facilitated two workshops that I ran in Kampala, Uganda. The first was an Editorial Training and Skills Development workshop in partnership with African Writers' Trust, the second a Creative Non-Fiction workshop that I taught with Mark Gevisser. Both laid the groundwork for this collection, and I am deeply grateful to the team at Commonwealth Writers for that early support and for providing the impetus and the resources that have made this collection possible. I am also grateful to Mark Gevisser for his continued support and advice.

Finally, I want to express thanks and admiration to my assistant editor, Otieno Owino, a participant in that Kampala editors' workshop, for his hard work, insight, and general brilliance.

Ellah Wakatama Allfrey
January 2016

Part I

AT HOME AND AWAY

FUGEE

Hawa Jande Golakai

There's a saying that goes, "You can't go home again." It offers no direction as to where you're supposed to go. It's meant to be poignant: some manner of existential examination of how things once lost can't be retrieved, relived, at least not from the same perspective. I think. I've always been a little too literal for the deepness of sayings.

MARCH 16–22, 2014
DURBAN, SOUTH AFRICA

"Ja, but where are you from originally?" the journalist presses me.

Ah. This again. I'm one of the featured authors at Durban's seventeenth *Time of the Writer* arts festival, and at these events, being grilled about "otherness" is a train that's never late. "You can't be unoriginally from somewhere. I don't think that's a thing."

She waves her hand. "But you know what I mean. You're quite accomplished, considering." She catches herself and flinches at the "considering." I let it slide. "You've lived in South Africa for years, right? You've gotten most of your education here?"

I smile. She's doing that cherry-pick thing people feel obliged to do with foreigners, timeline the best of your attributes so their country can take credit for it. "Postgrad education," I correct. But I'm tired and cranky, not exactly shipshape for interviews. It's not going to matter anyway. No one reads articles about writers, and we don't much care — just buy the book.

"So. West Africa. There's that virus scare starting up at the moment."

I sit up. "It's across the border. In Guinea." Is she putting this in the piece? Why do I keep clarifying where the reported cases are from whenever I'm asked? It's not like viruses need visas to travel.

"You mentioned you moved home two years ago. Why'd you decide to go back?"

I want to say it was less a deliberate decision and more a quest for closure, a need to tie up a loose end that had dangled, frayed and fraught, for too long. But I've stopped saying this. I morph into a mumbling cretin when I do, as if afraid the *real*-real reasons (*frustration much? drifter*) will seem ridiculous. People then feel the need to tilt their heads and nod, like it's noble and they get it, or they don't but won't be rude enough to admit it.

Instead I beauty-queen my reply: it was time to move on, to help my recovering country. To revert fully to my native state, which, aside from the odd visit, I haven't done in over two decades. To see how much it's changed, the land that small me took for granted she'd grow up in, get a job, marry, have piccaninnies, likely grow old and die. Life has taken me down brighter, more meandering lanes, for which I'm very grateful. The journalist nods to my words, scribbling away.

When the article comes out, it says I went home because it's where I'd always wanted to get married and have children, as if finally I can stop being a loser and make it happen. My best friend calls me to laugh; she's just learned something new about me. I sigh. No one reads articles about writers anyway.

MARCH 23–APRIL 12
JOHANNESBURG, SOUTH AFRICA

My friend Fran laughs like a bawdy barmaid in a Chaucer tale, a comforting sound. I've decided to round out my stay to a month, so I'm staying at her flat, plotting insidious ways of never leaving. Our mouths run all day, about shoes and sex, politics and career changes, original versus fusion curry recipes, TV content. The meaningful mindlessness that any red-blooded woman who lives in a male-dominated household doesn't know she misses until the tap is turned back on. Her spare bedroom is a cloud of amenities. SuperSpar is five minutes away, full of strawberries, peaches, and other edible exotica that I never see or can't afford in Monrovia. The guy behind the counter at the Clicks pharmacy is so delicious he's practically a food group. I trawl the malls, stoked to be back in Jozi, home of posh cars and cinched-waist lovelies with awesome hair. Feeling uncouth, I get a Zimbabwean hairdresser to braid me; her price is a blip on my radar. I'm balling in dollars.

On rare occasions, Fran gets serious. "Ebola's making the news online. You know it's getting serious when it makes the news." She glances at me. I stay quiet. "Are you considering going back to your job?"

"I'm at my job," I answer tersely. "National Health Coordinator at Ministry of Health" is a title I've buried, along with career dissatisfaction. After all those years studying to be, then working as, a medical immunologist, I'm now an author, a career switcher, trying to fade out the former as I find my feet in the latter. The irony is I left a tough profession that involved essays and articles that few understood to do "what anyone who knows the alphabet could manage," my critics say. Writing isn't respectable, not in Africa anyway. I'm considered a sufferer of "Me Disease," an unrepentant member of the selfish generation, we who shirk duty to follow pipe dreams. There's little consideration for how hard it's been to let go — which I still haven't done fully — for how much I question myself.

"Do you think they'll be able to contain it?" Fran asks.

"No." Snip. Snarl. I cringe at my tone. She means well. We drop it, switch back to safe terrain. A guy back home has thrown his hat into the ring for my affection. I don't know. Men are dicks ... but then again, men *have* dicks, so. I'm vacillating between uncertainty and blushes. We've spent more time talking and texting now that I'm on the other side of the continent than we did when I was home; social media makes Bravehearts out of us all. Fran does her laugh: please give Contender a whirl. Hhmmm.

At night, though, on my laptop, I'm stealth-surfing the web. Numbers are climbing in Guinea, and now Sierra Leone, but I know the true figures are understated. Through the grapevine at my old job, I hear they're not really doing anything or mobilizing forces to stop it leaking through the borders. Immobile. Do we even have forces? The Neglected Tropical Diseases Unit — they contend with elephantiasis and yellow fever, last of the unicorn afflictions. Is Ebola not contemporary enough, and if so, will it get an upgrade fast enough to make us take it seriously? Because hemorrhagic viruses are the last word in seriousness. And we don't have testing centres. We won't know what measures to take. We don't have anywhere near enough doctors. On a normal day our one major hospital, John F. Kennedy Medical, is heaving with humanity, all waiting for hours on end for treatment.

"But it's across the border mostly," says my ex-colleague. "And we weren't really *infectious*-infectious. You were one of the few real disease scientists we had. And you left." Pause. "Anyway, you know our government. These old guys move slow. Let's see."

Guilt bites a chunk out of me. I kick it in the teeth. It goes away. Well, retreats. Into a dark corner, where it squats, eyeing me, gnawing on something I didn't give it permission to eat. I don't lock it up or put it on a leash. I want it to come back and harass me. We have a weird relationship.

APRIL 13
10:00 P.M.
OLIVER TAMBO INTERNATIONAL AIRPORT
JOHANNESBURG, SOUTH AFRICA

The airport is cold. Winter should be winding down, but Joburg tends to be clingy when it comes to its seasons. I'm double-layered, jacket in carry-on just in case. I don't mind airports; they're like hospitals — you do your time and get out. Mostly. I do hate this particular red-eye, though. Departure: one-frickin'-thirty in the morning. The airline assured me the flight would leave an hour earlier than usual, but it seems they didn't take into account that the plane needed things like cleaning and refuelling before they made their wayward promises, so it looks like we're taking off the same time. I can't wait to leave. Airports get seriously wrong, creepy, after all the shops close. Like abandoned warehouses. Unlucky stragglers huddle by the gates, bleary-eyed, giving each other grim stares. And there are always a few gratingly cheerful chipmunks who want to story-of-my-life you until the boarding call sounds. I walk around to avoid them, Viber-flirting with Contender as I pace.

APRIL 14
12:00 A.M.
OLIVER TAMBO INTERNATIONAL AIRPORT:
LAST ROUND OF IMMIGRATION

The official asks me why I don't have a national ID book since I'm a permanent resident. I explain: I applied, and it took over a year for it to be processed, by which time when I went to collect it Home Affairs told me the ID had been misplaced and I needed to reapply. They assured me it would be no problem, and in the three years I've travelled on my permit stamp it's never been one. The official and I snicker over a Home Affairs joke. He raises his hand to stamp the exit permit, pauses for too long. (*Stamp it!*) He doesn't. He calls over a colleague; they confer at length out of earshot.

"Are you from Zimbabwe?" Official Two asks.

"No!" Immediately I twinge at my vehemence. I had good times in Zim. Jacaranda days.

They take my passport and other papers and disappear. On the other side of the glass partition passengers get to their feet, many throwing me worried glances. Boarding has begun. My skin prickles and my temper blooms; I suck the storm back in. I'm going home, dammit. They can throw me out if I want to stay; they can't hold me if I'm trying to leave. I'm going home.

The two officials in grey return and escort me upstairs, neither of them answering my questions. They leave me in an office with a new lot in navy uniforms. Ambient IQ drops fifty points. Office navies look more jaded, less equable. No, actually they just look shittier. Their job is to clear out the filth, and once you're dragged upstairs you've qualified, no negotiation. They begin filling out forms and throwing instructions at each other in Zulu, or Sotho, or Xhosa. Shaking, I remind them they're supposed to speak in a language I understand and explain what's going on. They shout that this doesn't concern me (*How the hell do you figure that?!*); what's concerning is a passport stating I'm Nigerian (*Liberian! Oh my God, can you read?!*), yet their system has me down as Zimbabwean. I shout back. Behind the desk, Navy Bitch, the most abusive and least helpful, decides to settle it. After a short phone call to their boss, who's clearly too big of a shot to be here fielding crises of this kind, she informs me at her leisure, "We're arresting you." (Later I realize they meant "detaining," but at that point, nuance.)

"For what?!"

Impersonating a resident. Carrying fake documents. Maybe they'll think of more infractions, but that's enough to be getting on with for now. One of the flight attendants, who followed me upstairs and is miraculously still outside, is deeply apologetic as she says my baggage will be loaded off the plane and put in hold-ing. They have to go.

"I get to make calls," I quail, already dialling. I wake Contender in Monrovia. He's a lawyer; he'll know what to do. He immediately realizes this is not a practical joke and switches to disaster response mode. He'll call my mother and the ambassador in Pretoria. I hang up, thinking if ever I've owed a man my firstborn, this is it. Drinks. We'll start with drinks.

Nothing else can be done. It's well past one in the morning. I didn't even hear the plane take off.

APRIL 14
2:00 A.M.–3:00 A.M.
JOHANNESBURG, SOUTH AFRICA: THE STATIONS

At the first station they put me in a cell alone, the sole insurgent of the evening. It's unbelievably cold. I'm totally blank as to how so many greats have produced great pieces of literature from lock-up. The place is a buzzkill, even for a crime writer. I wait for stirrings of productive angst and all I get are claws of hunger raking up and down my stomach; I haven't eaten in about five hours.

The next station is Kempton Park. This is lock-up, proper. The cops fill out paperwork, not asking for my story. I don't bother giving it to them. I expect monstrously vile mistreatment, shouts in my face, and the contents of my carry-on emptied onto the floor and lit into a pyre to warm their hands. They all look bored; this isn't Robben Island. This time round the cells are appalling, and I've seen a lot. Filthy, freezing, and cramped, the walls practically marinated in human effluent. I perch on an outcrop of the wall and try to sleep.

APRIL 14
5:00 A.M.–7:00 P.M.
JOHANNESBURG, SOUTH AFRICA:
KEMPTON PARK STATION ... STILL

The situation moves, in the wrong direction at first. I wake up in a cloud of my own stench. The officer in charge has updates: I'm to be deported, my permit revoked. For the first time I feel real fear, and rage. I earned that permit through hard work, mounds of application documents, and countless, bile-inducing visits to Home Affairs. Now I am to be hustled onto a flight, a disgraced imposter.

The threats fizzle to nothing at dusk. An official from Airport Immigration swoops in, barks orders at the cops, who gather me and my belongings together, and drives me to the airport. He tells me he assisted the Liberian ambassador in proving my permit's validity. In the head office I receive profuse apologies and pleas for forgiveness, from none other than the dickhead boss who couldn't be bothered to leave his bed to put a stop to my arrest. In the interest of security, they have to make certain assumptions, and sometimes innocent people get caught in the crossfire. They are incredibly sorry ... oh, and by the way, they cannot foot the cost of the forfeited air ticket. Collateral damage, unfortunately ... again, so sorry. I shout and cuss and deflate, tearful and exhausted. The ambassador squeezes my hand — let it go, the embassy will carry the cost.

APRIL 15
10:30 P.M.
OLIVER TAMBO INTERNATIONAL AIRPORT
JOHANNESBURG, SOUTH AFRICA

I'm finally going home.

MID-MAY TO MID-JUNE
MONROVIA, LIBERIA

Ebola is here. It's been at our back door since March, waiting like a wolf, the big bad wolf. The atmosphere I met when I touched down in April didn't indicate that there was a huge threat looming, which is reckless for a country that can't withstand its straw house being blown down. I wanted to look around the airport and be pleasantly surprised, see some handwashing stations and men in protective gear checking for ailing passengers, see signs screaming about what to look for, see something. I was disappointed at my disappointment; I know better. Monrovia is the Liberia that matters most, and this has always been so, shamefully elitist as that is, and until something unsettles our tiny capital it will never cause a stir.

Now Ebola has crept out of the deeply forested villages and truly permeated the psyche of Monrovia. "Real" is the buzzword for its takeover — *the huge reality, the horrifying realness!* — as if when it was across the border it was an underfed, coquettish slip of a thing, and now it's gorging itself to a respectable maturity within our borders. Hipco songs on the radio make light fun of it; others tell the populace to pull up their socks or die. For every believer that the threat is real, there's a naysayer guffawing at a mystery virus that skulks out of the jungle, riding bush meat as a host. Officials argue on the radio: the offensive strikers want the borders closed immediately; the more mercenary counter that it's already through the gates, what would isolation solve? Debate rages about "the responsibility of the international community" — how many aid agencies have come to our aid, will there be more, what measures would they advise us to put in place in the meantime? It's the usual distress code of all African countries to the West to bring the fury, the Bat-Signal in the sky to summon the superhero, the underhanded "we're not asking but ... okay, we're asking for your help." Things have gotten out of hand. In truth, there was never really a hand for it to be in in the first place.

"We've never had a health crisis like this before," shrills every radio and TV announcer.

LATE JUNE

News comes thick and fast from different communities about the steadily climbing death toll. It sounds movie script–bizarre and melodramatic — *bodies piling up!* — but unless there's an under-cover and seriously twisted Hollywood crew micromanaging the debacle for ratings, it really is happening. Facebook is electric with commentary. Liberians in the diaspora flare up, playing crisis man-agers: corruption has once again let us down in the worst way, how could the citizenry allow this to happen? Liberians at home fire back with righteous outrage: people are dying! We on ground and y'all don't know what's going on, step up or shut up! My own posts start off level-headed and descend into flatulent rants. Everyone on the outside feels they know what those of us in the mix should be doing, and it enrages me. Friends on social media aim and fire only two questions at me now: *Are you okay?* and *Are you doing something to help?* I lash out, but underneath the anger, my guilt creature taunts me. I'm trained to handle every substance that can ooze or squirt out of a human being, and in doing so have rarely felt afraid. Now fear taints everything. Ebola kills heroes, too. Helplessness is unfamiliar, and in typical me style, that which I can't solve or soothe makes me livid.

We are all on edge. Our tiny country has been through enough.

Every day, every newspaper, every body adds a new tale to the fray. There's the one about the household that lost both parents (or the aunt, or uncle, or grandparents) and the kids were left to fend for themselves. There's the household where everyone died save one, and the neighbourhood barricaded the lone survivor inside to stop the spread to other homes. There's the pregnant woman who ruptures like an overripe mango at a community clinic, her dead body dragged into a corner of the ward for the emergency response team to pick up because the nurses were too afraid to treat her.

Driving alone, I often stop to give lifts to hopefuls by the road-side, waiting for public transport. We drive to town in silence, everyone but me drenched, thanks to rainy season. I put the radio on — prevention ads and songs abound now, warning us that the crisis is no joke, listing symptoms to watch out for. A young nurse breaks the lull at last. She intimates in a leaden voice that she's stopped going to work and found a desk job doing data entry with an NGO (non-governmental organization). She's trained to help the sick, but this isn't what she signed up for, the possibility of bleed-ing out and liquefying to death. She looks like she'll never forgive herself. I want to tell her how much I get it, feeling like a coward, a deserter. I want to, but I don't. Something about this particular emotional tumult feels as if it should be borne alone, unalleviated by sharing and understanding. When the car empties out I drive on, realizing I ought to stop giving rides to strangers, because you never know. Another dick move added to my list.

EARLY TO LATE JULY

The life we know is fractured. By month-end the border will be closed, for God knows how long. We are advised of our civic duty to report via hotline anyone who looks vaguely zombie-like, or neigh-bours who are harbouring Anne Frankensteins in the back room. Physical friendliness is over. All unnecessary touching must stop: handshaking, kissing, hugging, humping, all of it. The embargo on frivolous sex seems to hit the hardest. Men across the spectrum of virility laugh uproariously: "Dah whetin you say — no eatin' sum-tin' because of Ebola?!" Women crow and flash superior smirks. Mother Nature is a girl after their own heart, cracking the whip so they don't have to. Now their significant others are forced, in theory at least, to come home to them and only them. Significantly othered myself, I am unfussed — Contender and I are now in a relationship, though it's more a polite passing of time, the only cool, composed thing going on in a frenzied hot zone.

Buckets filled with bleach water for sanitizing hands and in-ear thermometers have become *du jour* outside places of business. Conspiracy theories flow thick and fast. The United States designed Ebola and released it on us as a form of population control. Pharmaceutical companies wanted to run a massive trial of a new vaccine, but they needed to create an epidemic to test its legs. The cure-all remedies are not far behind. Bathing in hot water mixed with raw pepper or bouillon cubes will stop the virus from infecting you. Churches hold prayer vigils for the infected and pronounce them cured after all-night hallelujahs. Calamity breeds a tragic form of hilarity.

The three little ruffians from the house next door no longer run to anyone for hugs. They scamper away and peep from behind the mango tree in their yard, giggling and slow-waving at me whenever I pass. Their mother's face is grave as she shoots me an apologetic smile, *Don't take it personally.* They've been warned. We all have.

The inevitable media pile-on is in full swing. The worst has happened, in the worst way possible. After a sluggish debut, the outbreak is now headlining internationally. It has also acquired its first poster boy in the form of Patrick Sawyer. The government official travelled on business and singlehandedly turned Lagos International Airport into a biohazardous area, becoming the patient that drew Nigeria into the epidemic. In total, his case leaves nineteen infected and eight dead. Online, the Naijas spew pure vitriol: how could the Liberian government allow their people to travel willy-nilly, without getting tested for exposure? Where was the regard for protocol, for citizens of other nations, for international security?! All flights from affected countries must be monitored or stopped!

Clubbing and partying has petered out. Gatherings are furtive and sombre, and we can't help but pontificate and piss-contest.

Everyone is an expert now; the situation demands it. It makes us feel useful somehow, especially since the international health agencies have taken over, rendering the natives superfluous. We smelt questions into fiery debates: Was it ever a serious consideration to ground flights to and from affected countries when SARS broke out, or was the medical community simply put on high alert? In fact, didn't SARS spread even faster because air traffic to Asia was so busy? Come to think of it, this virus has never been known to spread this fast over so short a period — what's changed all of a sudden?

A friend drops by one afternoon. My father has banned all casual visitors, so she drops in for only a couple of hours while he's at work. Patrick Sawyer was employed at the Finance Ministry where she works, she says, partly horrified, partly amused, partly thrilled. Of course she only had dealings with him in a very peripheral way, and only saw him once from afar before he travelled (oh, he really didn't look sick ... you're only infectious when you look sick) but still. My sister and I are wild-eyed, practically levitating in disbelief. A possible contact of a celebrity index case is in our house. We all make light of it, scooching away and forcing her to sit at the far end of the living room and not touch anything, *ha ha ha this is so hilarious, right!* But she stays long enough for....

Three days later I have a headache that morphs into a mild fever. Our jolliness rises to screeching hysterics. "HA HA HA, SLEEP IN THE OTHER ROOM!!" my sister says, face clenched in a rictus smile that she thinks is reassuring. I know it's malaria. My pulse has always been a siren song to mosquitoes, my blood their elixir. Of course it's malaria. No one goes full-blown in thirty-six hours. I start the three-day treatment course.

At night, insomniac with fever, I strip down to nothing and examine my entire body for sores, lesions, any signs of bleeding or necrosis. None ... but my eyes look like marinara meatballs. (*This is how I go ... this is how I end ... and I won't be a hero, I'll be that fucking moron who should've known better, the infectious disease scientist that blundered into the worst infectious disease ever ... I didn't finish writing my book, my latest draft is tripe, no publisher will care to publish it posthumously ...)*

In two days, the malaria's melted off.

EARLY AUGUST

My neighbourhood, Duport Road, is now steadily reporting cases. We're not as badly hit as other high densities like New Kru Town, for instance; so far we tiptoe rather than sprint. Our watchman revels in regaling us with new developments. One morning he has an alarming update: at the marketplace up the road there's an uproar over a man's body. Nearly two days dead; the cleanup ambulances have been alerted, but none have shown up. Enraged, the market women have dragged the body from the vendors' compound and dumped it in the middle of the road.

Out loud I say it's rubbish, but make a mental note to keep an eye out on my way to the supermarket. I board a pehn-pehn motor-bike. As we zip down the road, I see nothing. Just before the super-market, we pass a blockade of sorts in the middle of the street. As the pehn-pehn driver slows and manoeuvres around it, I catch a glimpse of a human face. Or what looks like a human face, had it been whizzed in a blender. I tap the driver's shoulder till he stops, and I jump down. The misshapen heap of debris is indeed mostly human, the body of a man surrounded and partly covered by rocks and wooden planks. I tell the pehn-pehn guy to wait because I want to take a picture. He laughs and tells me kindly, matter-of-factly, to go fuck myself. He's not taking me anywhere after I've gone within selfie distance of an Ebola corpse. Chewing my lip at the side of the road, I think long and hard. I hear my parents' roars in my head, think of the household of trusting individuals that swarm around me day in and out. Think of what I'm contemplating, and the reason behind my compulsion to make up for one thing by doing an even stupider one. I trudge back and climb onto the bike. Pehn-pehn guy nods sagely before pushing off, as if proud of my sound decision. This time, regret boxes with my conscience. I feel horrible, but I wanted to take that photo.

He could have died of anything, I keep telling myself. Any old thing. (*But you've never seen someone's eyes caked with blood like that, their flesh turned to mush so quickly ...*)

My household is abuzz again less than a week later. There's an Ebola ambulance parked outside our gate, across the road. I slip outside to observe, the cook hissing and trying to pull me back inside. I try to sound brave as I tell her I won't get too close, but my heart is a fist in the back of my throat, trying to punch through. We've never had a van this close. All the nearby houses empty as the neighbours congregate to gawk. I creep close enough to get snaps of the white PPE-suited guys bringing the stretcher out. On it is the Old Ma from the brown house opposite ours. Some of the women start wailing, hands on their heads.

Later we get the news that she died. Some say she was just sick and the clinics and treatment units were too crowded to provide her care. Others say it was indeed EVD. The wildest theory is she was poisoned by a rival in the church, a schemer with the foresight to use the epidemic as a cover for darker deeds.

Monrovia's quickly emptying out, becoming a ghost town. Everyone is leaving, and by that I mean the privileged ones who can afford to. We who have stayed are often teased, "Yor dey kwii [civilised] pipo dem. The first to leave when there's trouble, like when the war happened ... how come yor still here?"

In that this epidemic is vividly reminiscent of the civil war, dey no lie. I feel ten years old all over again. Monrovia's aura even tastes like 1990, dense and indigo and hot-wired, like it did just before Charles Taylor marched into town and hell broke loose. I didn't get it back then. I remember being told that our family was taking "a lil' vacation" and doing twirls of rabid glee round the lounge, excited because I'd never travelled before. That vacation lasted two-thirds of my life and left behind a fragile ache where a solid sense of home should be. I've been moving, running, balancing on a razor's edge for too long. Damaged I may be, but grown and stubborn I have also become. I'm not going anywhere unless I bloody well must. My father pleads with me daily to reconsider, but I refuse — how can I leave the rest of my family behind? Besides, go where? South Africa has closed its borders to affected nationalities. Although I'm still furious over the detention, it's my first choice of refuge, and now that option is dead.

I walk. I don't know what else to do, and cabin fever from being cooped up all day is shredding my nerves. My route is Duport Road, Paynesville, and the neighbourhoods around Samuel K. Doe Stadium and Airfield Highway. Before the outbreak, walking was more to air my thoughts than for fitness, but in my current state I find I'm not untangling the gnarls in my brain as effectively, whether I'm mobile or stationary. So I just trudge, and look at people, and they look back at me. We all wear "coping" expressions. On the surface, life carries on as normally and best it can, but if you're local you can't miss the undercurrent of surrealism. The usual throngs on the streets have thinned and don't look as vibrant as they did before. Hardly surprising: the death toll has reportedly reached more than a dozen a day, the infection rate over a hundred per week. For the living, fear has driven us inside our homes or outside the borders. We've changed our habits, and I compulsively take snaps of the new normal with my phone: no more mystery meat — people buy only cuts they can recognize from market stalls and barbeque vendors; pickup trucks on cleanup duty zoom down the highway to burial sites, corpses in the back covered with tarp; shoppers leave stores with arms overloaded with provisions; the new game of tag children play is "don't touch me, you got Ebola!"

Walking on Airfield Highway one day, I see high walls and a metal gate, outside of which a line has formed. In a moment of total confusion, I think it's an awareness concert of some kind and people are queuing for tickets to get in. I tiptoe to peep over the fence. At the sight of tents, a concentration camp sprawl of white, it dawns in slow-mo horror: this is a treatment centre, and that's a line of sick or suspected patients hoping to get a bed inside. My heart aches imagining all those full beds; my brain hurts trying not to imagine the hole in which all those bodies will end up.

MID TO LATE AUGUST

My birthday comes — with relief I declare myself single again — and goes. I haven't heard from Contender in almost a month; I gather he's left without a word. I tried to end it before his departure (*This really isn't working, we're too different*) and he appealed for more time, a break (*We'll work on it once your book is out of the way*). Now we've fizzled into a ridiculous unsaid, a flaccid tale of love, or lack thereof, in the time of Ebola. This was quite literally not the time or the place — there are far greater worries.

The week after my birthday the residents of West Point, a slum settlement, mob and loot an Ebola clinic in protest, stealing supplies that may be tainted with the virus. Within days, West Point is quarantined. Riots erupt and spill into central town. Two days later, I take a taxi into town and walk around aimlessly. Never have I seen Broad Street look this dead. It's humbling and frightening at the same time, witnessing how the might of man can cower when challenged by an organism only an electron microscope can see. I wander down a street opening onto Waterside Market, close to the blockades that keep the West Point residents in. Camera ready, I try to bribe two of the riot cops loafing around to let me go closer, but I'm half-hearted about it. One wants the cash; the other tells me with lazy surliness to leave or he'll take my phone and break it. In that moment, photo-diarying becomes pointless. I take one snap before my phone dies, then I go home.

My hand is forced. The Port Harcourt Book Festival is hosting the Africa39 nominees at their annual book fair, an event I've been excited about since I was selected as one of the thirty-nine laureates. Now it's all gone sour in my mouth. The organizers have been pressing for my confirmation of attendance since June. It's far from simple: if I leave I cannot return, not for several weeks, perhaps months. Against the WHO's advice against strangling the virus-stricken countries by closing them off from routes of assistance, not only is the border still closed, but all major airlines save one have stopped flying to Liberia.

I confirm that I'm in. A leaden sense of déjà vu sits on me as I pack. Yet again I'm a clueless child about to be cast adrift, only this time there's no crackle of exhilaration for the adventure ahead.

I leave on the second-to-last Arik Air flight out of Monrovia. The airport is jam-packed but creepily silent. There's an international news channel filming the mass exodus; they ask a few of us for a quick interview, to share our harrowing tale with a world that wants to share our pain. I put my hoodie up and walk past them.

SEPTEMBER TO DECEMBER
THE OUTSIDE

It is the best of times as much as it is the worst.

Some weeks after I land in Ghana, it happens: my cousin dies of Ebola. He contracts it from his fiancée, and three months before their wedding the happy couple and three others close to them are gone. Everybody knew somebody who died, thousands of families were affected, yet you never conceive of a direct hit until it occurs. My family isn't big on emotional expressiveness, we cover grief with gruffness, but this numbs us all. I recall refusing to visualize where the bodies go for burial … now I have to. My cousin will not be returned to us, a family with Muslim roots, for final rites before sunset. We can't visit his grave with flowers on Decoration Day. His three-year-old daughter, my namesake, is fatherless.

I flit and day-trip — Accra–Kasua–Port Harcourt–Lagos–Kasua–Accra — like a nouveau brand of refugee, a fugitive of biological war, which sounds ludicrous even to me. I'm a hologram of myself most of the time, my emotions submerged, oddly calm and grateful some days, unable to get out of bed on others. People head-tilt and shoulder-squeeze me a lot, *Are you okay; We understand* ...

Life trudges on ...

... I embrace my first trip to Nigeria, although I maintain an internal chant to remind myself I deserve this, I worked for this. I am amongst my tribe of writers and it feels glorious. I am Liberian, I am not a virus ...

... Until I confide in a fellow scribe about my loss and am told, "Oh, wow. Well, at least it was only a cousin" ...

... At a literary fair, a journalist sits me down for an interview and asks nothing about my book and everything about Ebola, and how contrite Liberians should feel for killing Nigerian citizens ...

... Everyone seems to have money to burn while I pinch pennies, my face hot as I turn down every deal. I "party" but never really party. Guys grin and flirt, then flinch; one actually wipes the hand that brushed my shoulder on his jeans as he walks away. No hard feelings. I never want to stay out long ...

... I get robbed at Accra Mall, my passport graciously left behind. I want to leave, why can't I leave? I'm stuck. No flights. The body count back home is now in the thousands. I wait. Read, write, sleep two-thirds of the day. And wait.

DECEMBER 24

I've managed to wrangle a flight via Casablanca. I'm going home.

MAY 9, 2015
MONROVIA, LIBERIA

"But the whole country is rejoicing. We've been declared Ebola-free. It's gone, for, like, *ever*. Why can't you be happy like everybody else?" My friend looks disappointed in me.

I sip my beer and say nothing.

MADE IN NIMA
Kofi Akpabli

I sense awurey, a marriage ceremony, in the making. There is that smell in the air of sheepskin being burnt off the carcass. Women dressed in white lace are fanning freshly lit fire; the blue smoke rises gently to kiss white balloons festooned along a street light. Squatting over logs, young men are chopping bloodied meat. *Ta! Ta! Ta!* In a couple of hours this rhythm will be replaced by the happy sounds of the dondo, celebrating another union to increase the population of this community.

Even if you live in the capital, Nima provokes you with its exotic difference. Situated a few miles northeast of central Accra, this town represents a rainbow of Ghana's ethnic groups. Beyond that, Nima is what you get when Nigerians, Ivoirians, Malians, and Burkinabes reside together within a small space for four generations. Some call it a republic with its own lingua franca — Hausa. No matter where their parents come from, children here grow up spitting the language.

It is a Wednesday and market day. From Ring Road Central, trucks and vans haul in goods as well as traders, the vehicles circling the main roundabout and redistributing themselves in all directions.

Ghana's first president, Kwame Nkrumah, once nicknamed Nima "a city within a city." From a high point, the slumscape shows tiny boxes under tin roofs, with islands of alleys known locally as lungu-lungu. Housing sucks, drainage stinks, and lanes are screwed up.

Poverty lives here. But there is wealth too. Residing in some of these homes are the richest men and women on the land. Hummers and Jeeps frequent the back streets. These SUVs rub shoulders with donkeys, pushcarts, and the odd cow that has broken rank from the Fulani cattle herd. The paradox confronts you, and lingers. Nima may have some poor accommodation, but the residents seem not to lack good taste. Otherwise, what kind of place has visibly decaying houses with rooms that have air conditioning, plasma screens, and state-of-the-art ghetto blasters?

As I approach the Goil filling station on the Nima Highway, a salon car speeds up to my side and turns into the yard, manoeuvring to a screeching halt. A woman, cast in the frame of Queen Latifah, squeezes out. She is well built and looks tough. A colourful joromi shirt hugs her body. The fuel attendants seem to know her, and as they exchange pleasantries I cannot miss the acquired American accent. In a minute she crosses the street and is lost in the goings-on ahead. Today being a market day, Queen Latifah is probably here to shop.

The type is well known. There is this syndrome known as Nima-love. Some call it a disease. Those who show symptoms grew up here, travelled abroad, came back wealthy, and bought homes in the rich suburbs of the city. Nevertheless, every day they drive to Nima to have breakfast, lunch, dinner, or more.

One of my enduring memories is when at age five I was placed in the back seat of a Peugeot for a journey that changed my address. Having spent his teenage years living with craft masters and relatives, my father found real independence in Nima — his first rented room as a man. He hadn't been schooled much, his childhood and adolescence plagued by constant relocation with his itinerant father, a tailor, moving from station to station in pursuit of various other vocations.

With bushy grey hair that pointed everywhere and a stern gaze, Grandfather Christian of blessed memory was every bit the town champion. Wherever he found himself, he became an influential part of community life. He acted as the church choirmaster, town football team coach, and community letter writer. By 1948, he had moved with my father from Agbozume to Leklebi in the cocoa-rich middle belt of the Volta Region, separating my father from his mother forever, as it turned out. From Leklebi he settled at Bator, where he had secured employment as housekeeper at the Government Rest House. At Bator, in 1951, he married a princess from the royal palace. Around this time news had come to them of the death of my grandmother. As my father was now orphaned maternally, he became the first "child" to this new wife, with whom my grandfather would eventually have eleven children. In 1952, he was transferred to a bigger rest house at Adidome, 130 kilometres east of Accra.

Ghana's independence struggle was at fever pitch, and the nationalist leaders were criss-crossing the country for meetings. A 1956 plebiscite in the Volta Region made the area a hotbed of national politics. As a young child helping his father, my dad saw at close quarters personalities such as Ako Adjei, Asafoah Adjei, Arden Clark, and Kwame Nkrumah. By a twist of fate, my dad and Nkrumah's paths would cross again.

In 1957, my grandfather moved to Tadzewu to learn how to drive and to get his licence. In a newly independent Ghana, he had decided that government service ultimately provided more security. His son followed. School attendance for my father was erratic until 1958, when he decided to learn carpentry at Akatsi. His own boss moved with him to Teshie in Accra. After passing out of apprenticeship in 1961, he found his own space at Nima where jobs were easy to get and the cost of living low.

Somehow, my father realized that there was no harm in learning more than just a single trade. His own father was his example. Grandfather Christian eventually rose to become chief driver at the Ketu District Council while still keeping up his tailoring business; his clients included the very council he worked for and the Paramount Chief, Torgbi Hor II of the Some Traditional Area. But for my father, the hustles of Accra heightened the lesson not to focus on one vocation. So he picked up masonry and actually started taking building contracts.

"Why did you leave Nima?" I recently asked my old man.

Though a small-time builder, my father had been blessed with some good clients, including medical doctors, lawyers, and traditional chiefs. Another personality he built a house for was Alhaji Mumuni Bawumia, who later became chairman of Ghana's Council of State. At one point, he counted a governor of the Bank of Ghana, J.H. Frimpong-Ansah, among his clients. My father's proudest days were when he had to cash the governor's cheque. Bank cashiers couldn't hide their awareness of the fact that the signature on the cheque was the same as that on the currency to be paid the grinning young man.

The continuous mention of Nima as his address did not sit well with my father's clients. But that was not the only reason he felt he had to move. By this time he had married my mother, and they had had three of us children. Our house was made up of single rooms built around a courtyard. It was practically an open-air box, with the space in the middle serving as a common compound. Such a house didn't require a wall. A little gate was the only entrance. It was all facing all. Seventeen rooms occupied by seventeen families.

The landlord was Baba Nangali Alawusa, a Lagosian, originally from Abeokuta. A trader, he sold everything from nails to fermented fish, a delicacy. It was said that the landlord complained constantly that he himself had no room of his own. He had two wives, Yaami and Amina, each of whom shared their room with their children. So each night, Baba would decide which room to sleep in.

If my mother speaks a word or two of Yoruba, it was within these walls that she was schooled. Baba had many kinsmen from Nigeria, also renting. At evening mealtimes, while the preparation of palm nut soup and pounding of fufu was occurring there, eba and gbegiri sauce was being cooked in the corner. The mixture of the flavours of various dishes made the house a melting pot, literally. It was a truly multicultural space until a harsh political decision curtailed the harmonious existence. In November 1969, the government instituted the Aliens Compliance Order. In the face of a growing immigrant population in Ghana, the Busia administration aimed to combat crime, ensure national security, and achieve cultural homogeneity — all in one fell swoop. It was a chaotic evacuation of West African nationals. Across the country, farmlands, factories, and trading posts were all emptied of "aliens."

Baba and all his kinsmen had no choice but to pack for their home country. To move family and belongings back to Nigeria, the desperate landlord had to borrow money from his Ghanaian tenants, against future rents. For those tenants who remained, a minor, innocent incident drove home one effect of the policy. It was evening, and the unusual quietness was broken by the shrill voice of a toddler. My big sister, Edith, only a year old, had strayed into one of the several vacated rooms, probably looking for her playmates. "Sikiru ... Babatunde ... Titilayo ... Tofiki ...!" she kept screaming without an answer. The poor lass was rescued and put back in the arms of our mother. She had become the only child remaining in the house, and had no one to play with.

In my memory of the trip from Nima to Kotobabi, I am sitting between my two sisters. A third, also made in Nima, is in my mother's womb. It is a rainy night, and we are in the Peugeot 204 heading to the unknown. Kotobabi is some fifteen kilometres west of Nima. It is the final departure, as all our household items have already been sent on ahead. As Daddy drives, I cannot take my eyes off the dance of the windshield: it is brushing off rainwater, left right shwoosh, left right shwoosh, left right shwoosh. This goes on and on, becoming a long song in my head. Occasionally the headlights of oncoming cars brighten the spectacle.

As the journey proceeds, I become aware of something. I am not too sure; maybe my eyes are set for too long on water streaming down glass, maybe it is my childish mind. But each time Mummy turns from the front to be sure we are fine, I see water trickling down her eyes.

For my mother, Nima had been home in the warmest sense. When she had been betrothed to my father eight years earlier, her parents had not been in a hurry to let her join the eager young man in Accra. Being the eldest daughter of a farming family settled in Ghana's Eastern Region, her help was always needed at the home-stead. While my mother was waiting for permission to join her new husband, her own mother fell pregnant. It was considered best for the eldest daughter to be around to assist her mother when the new baby came.

When my grandmother eventually delivered, it turned out to be twins. "New birth; workload has doubled. The help of your wife will be needed for much longer than we thought," my father was told.

As the two families renegotiated the start of the marriage, my mother could only cherish a certain promised land in her mind — Nima, the escape she had long hoped for. She also held onto a small piece of paper that held my father's address.

The name of the town itself has two interpretations, at least. The first is that *Nima* is an Arabic word that means "blessing." The second possible meaning derives from the Ga phrase *Nii Maang*, meaning "Chief's Town." The area was first settled in 1931 by Alhaji Amadu Futa, a prominent cattle dealer and Muslim teacher who originally made his home at Cow Lane in Old Accra. Gradually cattle fields lost ground to human settlements. As Hausa was the language of the founders, those who joined the community picked it up. It was a way of conducting business and of belonging. The town expanded with many new arrivals to the capital from rural Ghana and from neighbouring countries.

Nima is not the only zongo (strangers' quarters) in Greater Accra with a dominant Muslim population from Ghana's north. The city is also home to similar areas such as Sukura, Fadama, and Zongo Lane. But go to Maamobi, Ashiaman, and Madina and they will all tell you that Nima is their headquarters. The powerful Council of Muslim Chiefs, which is the seat of Islam in Ghana, is found here. At the eastern end of town, near Kanda, is Rugga, an enclave of people from northern Ghana, while the western section of Nima is structured into lanes and lungulungu along which West African communities settled.

In a more informal structure, Nima society is organized along neighbourhood bases, each appropriating for itself an unwritten set of identities — a vision, a slogan, and an ideology. Effectively, each becomes a rival to other camps. One thing they are not is a rally around ethnic or religious causes. These are purely geographical demarcations and thus comprise elements with diverse persuasions.

Los Angeles, Hollandais, Michigan, Chicago, and Bronx. The choice of name goes with stories, stories that are grounded in the aspirations of the young men of each neighbourhood. Take Benghazi. This stomping ground was given its name because one or two local guys had once trekked from Nima across the Sahara to Libya by road.

Base allegiance aside, there is competition among sporting teams and fans of pop artists (the hip hop group VIP is based here). But while the bases are rival camps, they have much in common. In 2001, when Ghana recorded Africa's saddest sporting tragedy, 126 young men were stampeded to death during a match between Accra Hearts of Oak and Kumasi Asante Kotoko. No single community in Ghana was as affected as Nima, which is within walking distance of the National Sports Stadium. That day the town lost forty souls, and the tragedy saw all the neighbourhoods of Nima coming together to support one another.

Another landmark, built two years before the end of the Second World War, is St. Kizito Roman Catholic Church, the very first Christian structure in Nima. The magnificent tall, semi-circular structure seats a congregation of about fifteen hundred, and with its rich array of religious paintings and statues it is as much a museum as it is a place of worship.

At age thirteen, Kizito was the youngest among twenty-four Ugandan converts who were ordered by King Mwanga to choose to remain Christians and face death or to denounce Christ and live. "Until death," the young men all said. On June 3, 1886, after seven days of being held hostage, they were burnt to death. St. Kizito was the last to be martyred. By adopting this saint, the founding fathers of the Nima parish seemed to wish to remain forever young and brave. They were also wise — the domes that form the architecture of the church building blend well with the mosques that surround it. And, like the mosques, the church faces the east.

The very first converts the church baptized in 1949 were five Nigerians, three Ghanaians, three Togolese, two Beninois, and one Cameroonian. The local language and native dance of these people have, over the years, been incorporated into the church service. The parish also made history in Ghana by holding the first mass wedding for twenty couples in 1985. I was at the event as an usher, along with a couple of my teenage friends. At dance time, we gleefully abandoned our duties and danced as much as the newlyweds. Although we had left Nima, my family still attended St. Kizito on grand occasions, after which my parents and their friends would reunite over a Sunday drink at the Pan African Hotel, which was next to the church.

Originally opened by a Nigerian in the 1960s, with a name that echoed the euphoria of Ghana's independence and Africa's liberation struggle, the Pan African Hotel is an example of Nima's eroding landmarks. For some local old-timers, this was where they encountered fine dining and learned ballroom dancing. Presently, the glory of the Pan African Hotel has been reduced to concrete debris, as the hotel was recently pulled down.

Another post of past glory is Dunia Cinema. Up to the 1980s, cinema culture in Ghana was lively. Nima was not left out, and watching a movie among a Hausa-speaking audience at the Dunia Cinema was a treat on its own. In Hausa, *Dunia* means "the world." When Rambo shelled down an installation with firearm power, the audience would go, "Shejeya!" When Chuck Norris outwitted a bad guy with a double-leg jump hit, the chorus was "Walaahi." Did Wesley Snipes eventually catch up with a villain? "Baraawo, maarey shi!"

Today, Dunia is a desolate open warehouse. Maize, groundnuts, and millet arrive here from the country's hinterland before being taken to the market across the street. On the very top, the five metal letters spelling out the building's name have all rusted away, save the *U*, which contorts towards the heavens. In the very large hall itself, bags of cereals have colonized the space. Like the remains of an ancient civilization, only a few legs of the concrete seats are left, jutting out of the concrete floor.

It is nearly midday, and I hop into the back of a taxi. I can make out a lane that opens to a yard bustling with traders and goods. In the midst of the melee is a bus that is being loaded with bags of plasticware by two men in jalabya. Right from this lane the bus will take off, ending up in the Republic of Niger. In another three days the bus will leave Niger and come back to this yard.

A whiff of spices hits my nostrils, and I know I'm getting closer to the main market. Nima market spills over to the street, particularly on Wednesdays. Street hawkers and side stalls are in a frenzy. The windows of the taxi are open, allowing a potpourri of fragrance to reach me. I inhale ginger, rosemary, curry, nutmeg, cumin, coriander, thyme, onions …

Ahead of me in the slow-moving traffic, I notice a beat-up Jeep with "The Last Don" written behind it. The inscription is framed by a ring of fire. Now and again, market women stop by the window to talk to the driver. It takes a while for me to realize that the driver ahead is actually shopping. At every little advance the Last Don signals, and traders come by his car with their wares. He pays, items are dropped in the passenger seat, and he moves on, calling out to the next item, without ever pulling over.

The traffic moves up a bit, and we are flanked by food vendors. Cowpeas, rice, soya beans, maize, and wheat have been displayed in open sacks and giant bowls. Black plastic carrier bags are ready to fill up for customers. Another inch forward. More delay tactics by the Jeep in front. My taxi driver is patient. For an Accra driver, that is unusual. But I am not in a hurry either. To kill time, I play a game of "guess what the Last Don is buying this time."

Now it is a bowl of beans. The window is rolled down. The Last Don says a few things to the vendor, and the item is dropped on the seat. Don't blame him; there is hardly parking space along the Nima highway. With a go-slow, and hawkers on the hound, one might as well shop on wheels.

Jeep driver turns to the other side and signals a hawker carrying a tray of garlic. Same routine. Now it looks like hibiscus leaves. But just before he concludes business there is a big inch forward. The traffic has eased, and he must move up. But the Last Don doesn't. The truck behind us sees this and honks impatiently. Our shopper-on-wheels deliberately slows down, the hibiscus seller runs to catch up to seal the deal. Oh, no. There is awkwardness over change … *Paarrh!* The horn blowing behind us persists. I feel the honking is actually at me and the taxi driver for *not* honking at the errant driver.

I look out my window. "Ooh, are those dates?" The exotic fruits are displayed all over town. Imported from the Middle East, they are eaten to break the Muslim fast during the Ramadan season. The young girl brings her fruits closer.

"How much?' I ask.

There is space, but my taxi driver waits for me to finish business. *Paaarrrh!!* Make no mistake; that horn blast is now directed against yours truly.

The heat is sweltering. I turn to the other side more out of desperation than relief. There is a fresh guest by my window. It is a blind beggar. I notice a girl of about nine years old who accompanies him with a begging bowl. "Fisibis-ilahi!" Before I can decide to drop a coin or not, my driver dashes forward fast enough to leave them behind.

I get out of the taxi as a young man on roller skates nearly bumps into me. Before I can say, "Watch out," his friend, also on skates, appears from behind, and they high-five and speed into the crowd ahead together. I enter the market proper, sidestepping tubers of yam and cassava on the ground. Some stalls are stocked with fresh tomatoes, cabbages, and garden eggs. Smoked fish and bush meat are also on display. Now I smell groundnut paste, then it's the sting of powdered pepper and dawadawa. I plod on, manoeuvring my body around the crowd within small spaces. Eventually, at the back, I arrive at an interesting section — the juju market.

Nima is one of the very few places in the capital that has an open market of items for spiritual warfare. People come to buy the bizarre prescriptions that Christian and traditional priests task their followers to bring. I bump into a customer or two. The trick is to look away. This is no place to flaunt your identity. People come here because they are desperate. They have to buy odd items for sacrifice to save a sick person, reverse a curse, or seal a spiritual claim. Others have come for assistance to cause spiritual injury to someone they do not particularly love.

On display are snake and chameleon skins, crocodile hides. There are eagle feathers, elephant shit, and lion fat captured in tiny bottles. Also for sale are charms: for good luck, protection, wealth, travel visas, and "for girls." One medicine in a small box claims it can cure "ninety-nine diseases."

I am on my way to a makaranta, a Koranic school. But before I get there I see, far off, in all its majesty, the Flagstaff House, Ghana's presidential palace. In 2007, the original structure received a high-rise facelift courtesy of an Indian government grant. From the east, only one street divides Nima from the presidency — and because Ghana's first president used the Flagstaff House, he shared an affinity with this community. "We walked from here to Kwame Nkrumah's office to present his Party membership card," an octo-genarian at Nima told me during my visit.

I find myself wondering just how the people in this slum con-nect to that view. For one thing, folk here are busy with their day-to-day existence, just as my father was as a young man making his way here in Nima.

After toiling at A-Lang Limited for two years early in his working life, my father was lucky to land a job as a carpenter-cum-mason at the Flagstaff House in 1963. More than that, he was privileged to be assigned to the highest workplace in the land, the president's office. His anecdotes about his limited observations and inter-actions with the first president and the first family could brighten the pages of any official memoir. In our family, however, we all have one favourite episode. It took place in 1965.

"One afternoon, a special gift arrived for the Head of State," my father would begin each time he told the story. It was the biggest television set he had ever seen. What made it even bigger was that it came encased in a wooden frame.

"The TV arrived from Russia or Bonn ... one of the two," he would always add. Everyone at the Flagstaff House was delighted, but there was a problem. The TV was too big to go through the door of the president's office. Quickly, my father and his small band of workmen were summoned to prevent a national incident. Gingerly, they removed the door and frame, sent the giant TV in, and then fixed the door back in position. All this happened within a couple of hours. "And Osagyefo told us, 'Ayeeko,'" my father concluded each time.

But my old man's experience with the seat of government wasn't always pleasant. On February 24, 1966, the military teamed up with "foreign elements" to topple Africa's foremost liberation leader while he was away in Hanoi, Vietnam.

For my father, then a twenty-three-year-old, and other unsuspecting citizens, it was just another day in Accra. But it turned out to be a day that would force him to hide in the gutters in front of Broadcasting House for hours to escape gunshots. As he walked to work from his single room at Nima, the streets were eerily quiet, but he didn't notice anything untoward. He heard gunshots, but, as he tells it, he never thought the *ra-ta-ta* had anything to do with his place of work. At a barricade that led to the Flagstaff House, soldiers asked him to go back. He tried to explain, to show his security pass, but no one was interested.

He was told there'd been a takeover and he couldn't go in. Coup? Well, he still had to go in. Could he be allowed to pick up the one item that guaranteed his daily bread — his toolbox? My father didn't need a second warning shot to flee. He never got the chance to go back.

"Alif-bau-taun-saun ..." The rhythmic recital of the Arabic alphabet serenades me as I go past the school. My walk brings me to an area known locally as Filli Dokyi, "Horses' Yard" in Hausa. Time was when horse racing was a great pastime in Ghana. Because of the Hausa and Moshi heritage, Nima was, for decades, home to a vibrant equine husbandry enterprise. With the closing of the racecourse, the area has now become a slaughterhouse for sheep, goats, and cows.

I jump into another taxi going in my direction. At the post office I roll out of the car and take the right turn. This lane and those parallel are as lively as a community can be. Through a lungu, I arrive at another lane where I settle in a café-cum-food joint. The set-up here is like you would find in the *quartiers* of Dakar, Bobo Diaolosou, or Timbuktu.

"Allahu Akbar!"

From afar, I hear the azarn announcing the Assr, the third Muslim prayer of the day. I sit on the stool and order water, jollof, and coffee in that order. Baba Amadou, the Senegalese owner, has operated the café for decades. His specialties are macaroni, spaghetti, sandwiches, and rice dishes.

Other customers are having ataya, tea served in very small glasses. When boiled it is poured from cup to cup, creating a heavy foam. "Make sure you have food before you take that," someone advises amidst loud laughter.

Amadou opens at 5:00 a.m., closing well after midnight each day. His clients include Guineans, Togolese, Burkinabes, and Malians. As the ataya goes round it fuels a lively discussion, but after finishing my food I leave them to it.

This lane has African antiques of all kinds. I see a shop with Ibo beads of varied shapes and colours. A masalachi (mosque) connects to another street with "Belgium City" boldly written on the wall. Just one step from the area and I am ambushed by a double whammy. I cannot tell which hits me first: the whiff of marijuana in the air or the raspy voice of Bob Marley singing "Sun is Shining."

I descend further to a neighbourhood base called Down Side. It is close to an open drain that is as big as a sea bed. On my right I see two men weaving a traditional Burkina textile. Three women are frying maasa, a rice cake snack. I watch the little white round maasas sizzling in oil. There is a rich variety of delicious meals available, more than one can get anywhere in Accra: nakiri, wagashi, Brukina, waachey, touzaafi, chinchinga, koosey, hausa kooko ...

Eventually, I am at The Bronx. Both sides of this street are packed with kiosks, some of which are actually homes. One hardly sees spaces in between. Here, as elsewhere in Nima, sanitation could be better. And yet this very neighbourhood has produced a

World Boxing featherweight champion. In September 1975, David Kotey, known as D.K. Poison, beat Rubén Olivares in a split-points decision in California. When he returned, D.K. Poison was carried shoulder high on this very street in Nima. Also from this corner is Eklu Johnson, a football great who played for the Ghana national team in the early 2000s.

The grounds may be littered, but every kilometre of Nima soil is soaked with cultural and historical significance. Through Alhaji Road I continue towards the imposing Nima Islamic Research Institute. I take a lungu and walk towards the back of another Islamic monument — actually, the biggest mosque in Nima. The loudspeaker is deafening with the recital of holy scripture. The Koran, the Hadith, Tasbir, and men's small caps are displayed for sale on tabletops.

Folks are fetching water for ablution, while on the loudspeaker the muezzin keeps chanting and chanting. Men hurry on. Still more men carry water on their shoulders. The Kardo Mosque fronts the Nima Highway. Though uncompleted, it is serving its purpose, as hundreds worship here every day. With its twin towers, Masalachi Buba looks commanding. Squash back two hundred metres and St. Kizito Catholic church will be directly facing the Kardo Mosque, counterbalancing the power of the church.

Finally I arrive at this place in Nima that I call the Dream District. All day and all night gambling and gaming takes place, with bets on horse racing, English Premier League, and local football matches. This area is also the base of the Sakawa boys. It is claimed that these young ones use all sorts of means, not least impersonation and tech savvy, to defraud unsuspecting people they meet online. Victims include citizens of the First World. Amounts involved run into thousands of dollars. There are other such joints across the city. I hold my breath for a minute and step into a world filled with a long line of computers, dozens of young men sitting busily typing away. *I'm very happy to see you guys*, I say to them in my mind.

But no one seems to notice me. With no signal of welcome from the attendant, I back out.

I cross the street to the other cyber café, and here too there are youths with eyes glued to computer screens. The whole room feels like a recruit data unit, with every young fellow typing in high-security inputs. The intensity of their concentration is almost intimidating. In a society where the youth can hardly afford higher education or find jobs, it is hard to blame them for deploying what skills they possess to survive. In today's world, it is their social media skills.

The sun is almost down and the Nima rush hour has started, although it seems it has been rush hour all day. I come out of the Internet café and walk in the direction of the market. Today, again, I have come back to this place where it all started for me.

But one encounter does not leave me alone. At the start of my tour, I was at Big Dreams to send a few emails. Next to where I sat was one of the Sakawa boys. Spying from the corner of my eyes, I couldn't help but notice golden rings and golden chains. Bling-bling man was, however, not my focus. What attracted me was the person he was with — a skinny boy of not more than nine years.

The lad was almost on the older boy's lap as they worked the computer together. Because it was school hours, I was curious. And in my friendliest whisper, I asked the child why he was not in class.

In Hausa, he muttered, "Naa zo nkoyo wani." I have come here to learn some.

EATING BITTER

Kevin Eze

I stand in a queue in front of the Hotel de la Ville in central Dakar. The Lions of Teranga, Senegal's national football team, will be hosting their Ivoirian counterparts, the Elephants, and I am waiting, along with hundreds of fellow fans, for a ticket to the match on October 13, 2012. In front of me is a man with a head shaped like a football. I see the sweat on his neck, the 3:30 p.m. July sunburn. I see the long-range Galaxy cellphone and the missed calls log on a dim red mark arcing towards the edge. My own cellphone rings, and I speak in English with a caller from Lagos. The moment the man hears me, he sees an opportunity to practise his English, turns to greet me and introduces himself as Yun.

When I arrived in Dakar in 2009, as a researcher charged with studying Senegal's model for interfaith peace, the likes of Yun, second-generation Chinese immigrants ("the businesspeople" — the first generation, Henan Construction — having arrived in the 1980s), were the most successful entrepreneurs in the city. Many of the merchants ran shops only to mark time until they secured a building contract. Registering a business was expensive, and the rigid labour code confined many of the locals to informal employment. The Senegalese government's hunt for diversified investment opportunities and trade partners favoured the more experienced Chinese immigrants.

The Chinese led construction work at the Leopold Senghor Stadium, working for six months, exclusively at nighttime, with a team of prisoners, convict labourers, and free citizens. The locals watched the Chinese at work with earthmoving equipment, excavators, skid steer loaders, graders, and tractors. With a force that made spectators both fear and respect them, they built the stadium. The result was a circular open-air structure with a grass surface bordered by an athletics track, sixty thousand all-seater capacity, and VIP and hospitality facilities.

The stadium now serves as the home ground of ASC Jeanne d'Arc, a Senegalese Premier League football club based in Dakar, and the Lions of Teranga.

Yet despite the acknowledged success of the project, the Chinese immigrants who followed in the wake of this first wave existed without firm roots, like pale, windblown trees in a barren landscape — always yearning for China.

The day we first met, Yun told me he owned some shops and asked if I had ever been to Dakar Chinatown. I shook my head. He invited me to visit his shops for a drink after we purchased our tickets for the match. I was already intrigued by the growing number of Chinese businesses in Dakar. Chinese companies have been winning construction tenders over European companies and exporting labour and commodities in the process, with Chinese newcomers taking over an entire city district. It seemed an opportunity to interrogate the trend, so I accepted the invitation. After collecting our tickets, we boarded a taxi to Boulevard Charles de Gaulle — commonly known as Allées du Centenaire. Yun led the conversation in bumpy English, sometimes switching to heavily accented French.

We reached Boulevard Charles de Gaulle and made our way to Yun's shop. Senegalese vendors who saw us shouted, "*Nǐ hǎo, nǐ hǎo*" ("Hello, hello"), instead of the regular "*Toubab, ça va*" or even "Hello, my friend" — greetings one heard elsewhere in the city. There were no pagoda roofs or Chinese characters or red lanterns. There were no signs of Chinese restaurants. Yet we were in Chinatown.

The shops owned by the Chinese are small, nearly half the size of a modest car garage, their walls lined with wooden shelves stuffed with Chinese goods in demand: carvings and lacquerware, a large variety of silks, women's sandals, framed photos, umbrellas, purses, bags, slippers, office supplies, mirrors, and electronic toys. The day of my first visit, the Chinese traders went about their business with alacrity. One trader climbed a small ladder in his shop, took down some goods from the counter, and handed a package to the buyer while extending his other hand for the money before counting up the total and nodding. They spoke quickly, gesticulated and carried out their business transactions with speed and precision. All this frenetic activity was contrary to the usual slow pace of life in Senegal.

Yun's family is relatively low down the socioeconomic ladder in the Chinese community. They are merchants and not contractors. But this does not hinder his ambitions. The merchants follow the builders; the builders call on the merchants for day jobs when they win a contract. Some builders even double up as merchants themselves as they wait for the next construction job. The connection between the two activities tightens the bond among the Chinese community and enables them to make money at both ends. Such a bond favours their principle of using equipment and labour imported from home. Skills are not transferred to local communities.

All the shops were numbered serially in ascending order at Allées du Centenaire. We entered Yun's first shop, Number 10, after walking through the crowd of buyers moving in opposite directions, happy to have made it to Dakar's Chinatown with its wide range of products and low prices. Watching Yun and his Senegalese employees attend to their customers, I had a small glimpse of the tenacious dream he had of making money in Africa as a shopkeeper, returning to China to get married, with some money left to acquire a small piece of land in a remote area, some bicycles, and maybe even some wheelbarrows. Watching him work, it was entirely possible to believe that he could achieve all this in the end.

I gradually pulled out a pen and paper from my bag. Yun noted my writing materials and nodded his permission, smiling; he then promised to take me on a walk through the lineup of shops, as I had requested, but not that same day. He attended to four more customers before waving me on for the day's excursion through the informal market set up on the pavement by Senegalese traders in an attempt to draw customers away from the Chinese shops.

"The Chinese must go!" a loudspeaker blared. "Enough of cheap goods."

"Many, many Senegalese buy from you. Business was better before you," a protester said, pointing at Yun.

"You see," Yun said to me in riposte. "They do not talk about their government allowing us in, they don't consent that they benefit from house rents, and they're not grateful for the millions of dollars they receive yearly in Chinese development aid." Yun concluded that the protestors were mere noisemakers, and that if they had any real grievance they should report it to the government.

We said our goodbyes and agreed to meet in Shop 22 the following week.

On a Monday, nine days after the football match, I join Yun in Shop 22. We talk about the match, the rioting at the stadium, and Senegal's disqualification from the tournament as a result. Walking along the cycling lane in front of the Senegalese-owned stands, sipping a soft drink from a small can as if at a picnic, Yun enthusiastically explains the process of building small connecting shops, and points out the urban transformation visible to the eye. Pointing forward and sideways, the gestures needed to support his struggling English, he tells me that initially, Allées du Centenaire was predominantly residential, with only a few grocery stores concentrated around the two roundabouts along the road. He tells me that the Chinese sell affordable products to the local population and gain popularity doing so. The Senegalese like beautiful things, and so the Chinese were moved to expand and open new shops. He goes on to confide that the more money and success stories went home, the more fellow citizens came to settle, rented the front yards, built stalls, or transformed the existing garages into small shops.

Listening to Yun it becomes clear to me that "need" and "means" came together in this story. The locals needed what was an unexpected but welcome source of income; the Chinese needed space to sell their products. The locals were ready to give up some space, and the Chinese made a big offer through local real estate brokers.

"We charmed the locals by paying the rent a year in advance, and in cash," Yun says, "and they became tantalized." His face creases up with laughter.

We arrive at Shop 25, and Yun introduces me to the first member of his large colony, one of the seventeen members of his family now residing in Dakar. "We need to band together," Yun says. "No one is going to do it for us. Whenever you see a Chinese harassed by a group of local hooligans, go up and give that Chinese love. Tell him as we say, 'Good job. Keep it up, brother. We're in this together.' We provide newcomers with safety nets. We tell them to learn Wolof as quickly as possible, especially commercial terms; to indulge in the greetings custom to avoid annoyances from the locals like petty thefts and muggings and the local 'bumsters' or 'beach boys' who loiter the beach side of the Corniche; and to avoid conflict among Chinese nationals, becoming good ambassadors of the Chinese nation." The sum of Yun's impassioned speech is that the Chinese are friendly to each other; newcomers are seen not as rivals but as a means of increasing the community's numerical strength.

From Shop 25 we stroll to Shop 34, also belonging to Yun's family. I meet Li, his twenty-seven-year-old son. As he searches for an article for a customer, Li complains of sometimes missing home, Kaifeng Town, wishing that he could bring it here now, that he could bring Xuande Palace, Gate Tower, Millennium City Park, or Henan University (which he was not able to attend), communicating all that in "Frannois," a blend of French and Chinese.

As we leave the shop, Li calls Vanessa, his charming girlfriend, a Senegalese-born girl of Cabo-Verdean parentage. Yun tells me that Li was prohibited from marrying her, impeded by cultural barriers.

The Chinese either marry in China before coming to Senegal or return to marry in their home region after they make some money. Distrust of the locals and a fierce desire to preserve their communal bond away from home informs this choice. Trade is what they're about. They avoid mixed marriages because Senegal is not the final destination for most of them. Their aim is to return home, but in better financial circumstances than when they left. Because Li's family seemed established in Senegal, the couple hoped sentiments had risen above these barriers. Vanessa worked at a restaurant in central Dakar, where they met. The third time Li came to her restaurant, he told her he loved her. Vanessa was attracted to him too, and love blossomed. Eventually Li presented her to his parents as his girlfriend, and she began to frequent the family home in the Chinese quarter, the couple unaware that Li's father and uncles interpreted their relationship as being only temporary.

Yun does not know Li has told me all this. It wasn't only the menfolk who were of this opinion. The women in the family shared it too. Eventually Li acquiesced to family pressure and married a girl from home. Vanessa feels disappointed being relegated to mistress status, but she keeps seeing Li because he agreed to support her financially. This type of accommodation is not uncommon.

Later that same week, Yun and I continue our promenade, advancing to Shop 58, which specializes in women's sandals, and we go in to greet Yun's wife, Chun, and a Senegalese former employee of Shop 22 who is assisting her. She is learning the trade before she joins her husband's main shop. Welcoming us, Chun pulls out two stools and orders some drinks. The moment she discovers I am taking notes, she becomes chatty, speaking in Chinese, with Yun providing a French translation.

She is a recent immigrant and met and married Yun in China. The deciding factor for her leaving home was China's one child policy. "'One child is too *small*,' we say, but they don't listen. Outside China, here in Africa, in addition to business, couples have another chance, to *make* another one or two more children, aided by dual nationality for these children born in Africa. Our children will wrap both nationalities, so their breakthrough stands unhindered." On this hopeful note Chun smiles with pleasure at her family's future prospects.

As we speak, Chun's son runs in, dropped off by the Chinese school bus. Chun hugs him and lifts him up and asks him in Chinese if he learned a new French song. Within two years the Chinese nursery school in Dakar filled up, and Yun's friends and doctor convinced him and his wife to give the child a good basic education so he could aspire to schools in Europe and North America.

High school educated, Chun left Henan province at the age of twenty-five, when she was sure Yun was well established in Senegal, and with his help she secured herself the passport of a female relative already resident in Dakar. This kind of illegal immigration is not unusual — the "they all look alike" prejudice many Chinese face here also makes it possible to beat immigration officers.

Since arriving at the Cap Vert Peninsula, Chun has been learning French and Wolof at the same time. This determination to learn the language is something that other Chinese immigrants share, acknowledging that they need to communicate with the locals to remain in business. This is their home away from home, a place where they can influence things, do business, have cooks and house girls. This wave of migration bears the allure of settlement, but where previous settlements in Africa colonized "from above" (to govern), Chinese migration colonizes "from below" (to sweat it out).

Africa's Chinese immigrants are setting up homes. They suffer with the local population, unafraid of loneliness, boredom, power blackouts, and other inconveniences as they make their fortunes — and with an encouraging push from the home government, happy to help with financing. It is an approach driven by chi ku, a Cultural Revolution–era expression that translates as "eat bitter," or endure hardship. All of those hardships are more bearable, Yun and his fellow immigrants say, than the stiff competition, rigidity, and corruption back home.

I return a week later to visit Yun, sitting and reading newspapers while he and Chun attend to a group of Ivoirian customers. The headline is bleak: a Chinese woman and her son have been killed.

Sun Fengzhi and seventeen-year-old son, dead: murder, local police believe.

"Again?" Yun asks. "Again?" An instant feeling of anxiety and sadness clouds his and Chun's faces. It becomes apparent that Chun knew the dead woman. Amid tears, she recalls how Sun Fengzhi welcomed her when she first arrived in Dakar as the newest immigrant from their home region. Chun remembers her face, her hair like a cap, silvery laughter ever present in her smile.

As I listen in, the family begins to piece the story together from the newspaper report. The third Chinese to be murdered in Senegal, Sun Fengzhi, in her fifties, and her son, Wang Kun, were found dead on a Tuesday night at their home in Dakar. There were signs of an altercation, and there was blood on the floor and wall. The apartment was ransacked. Police had yet to determine the exact time of the crime and what kinds of weapons were used.

The mother and son were people everybody loved. Sun was three-time secretary-general of the Chinese Association of Senegal. She gave birth to her son in China and left him there under her sister's care until he was old enough to make the journey to join her. Seventeen-year-old Wang Kun was already working with his mother in Senegal when he was murdered.

Although the Senegalese pride themselves on their cultural tradition of teranga, or hospitality and openness to outsiders, many of them resent foreigners making money in their country. As we walk back to Yun's first shop, he tells me that there are currently 214 Chinese shops in Allées du Centenaire. In ten years of migration, he and his compatriots number roughly ten thousand residents in Senegal alone. Often, police response to violence against the Chinese community is slow. "Investigation of the first two murder incidents followed the same sluggish pattern," he laments.

We are interrupted when Yun receives a call on his cellphone. The leader of the Chinese Association of Senegal has convened an urgent gathering. Yun asks me to wait inside his shop, Number 10, while he and the other Chinese merchants at Allées du Centenaire gather in front of a nearby CAS leader's shop, Number 7. I stretch my neck to watch. They didn't expect moments like these in Senegal, moments like finding Sun and Wang Kun dead in their home.

During the meeting, a faint breeze of the spirit of teranga returns. A few Senegalese merchants join the circle in support of their Chinese counterparts.

The heat finally departs, the sky turns off-white, and a ceiling of cloud lightens with the sudden change in temperature. Yun puts prayer beads, framed pictures of marabouts, and other items linked to Muslim beliefs at the front of the shop. Korité, the end of Ramadan, will be celebrated in a few weeks. The pictures are strategically displayed with imported frames. A passerby observes the rims while I admire the artwork. She walks in, touches the frames, the line of the pictures, the line of the frames. Yun removes one picture from the shelf and throws it out on the counter before the woman. I think the glass will break, but it does not. The woman asks for the price, debates, and buys the photo.

Oceans away from home, Yun makes a profit selling not pictures of Chinese deities but those of mythical Senegalese marabouts.

Shortly after, another female customer enters and looks at a piece of cloth in the far northwest corner of the shop, tucked against two shelves. She reaches for the cloth, touches it, and asks Yun if a better quality is available. Yun says it *is* the better quality. The woman inspects the cloth again, hisses in doubt. She reminds Yun that the quality of the products the Chinese sell is often criticized, and that most people, even those who buy goods from them, agree on this. Then she really upsets Yun when she says that the Chinese commodities are not only of low quality but can sometimes even be harmful to human health (she points to plastic toys for children by the corner as an example), and that the Chinese consider Africa merely an outlet for "rubbish" goods.

Vexed, Yun retorts that for a slightly higher price he could immediately provide better quality. But most African customers prefer to purchase the cheaper versions, even though they know that the quality is lower and that the products will not last very long. Yun says the Chinese could immediately raise the quality of the goods if Africans would agree to pay more.

In the end the woman buys the cloth and receives from Yun the gift of a small framed picture from China. She opens her eyes wide in surprise, possibly thinking it is a way of enticing her to come back. Yun touches my arm and smiles.

"Not a bribe, woman," he says.

One evening toward the end of the month, Yun and I go on the last lap of our promenade. Li rushes in, whispering into his father's ear. Henan Construction has won a new contract, and all the Chinese builders working as part-time merchants are invited to the site.

"Are you going right away?" Li asks his father.

"Immediately," Yun says, leaping up and signalling that we leave.

Not long after, we arrive at La Noix d'Or restaurant. The menu at La Noix d'Or states that the hotel is situated at Fann

Résidence, the diplomatic heart of Dakar, and serves several hundred Chinese immigrants in a week. A step away from the Chinese embassy, La Noix d'Or is acclaimed as one of the best places to savour Chinese food in Dakar. The colour red is every-where in various combinations: on the double table cover, the cushions, the candles, the bulbs, the pavilion. Even the plates and cups. My eyes retreat from the red dominance when the pre-prandial aperitif arrives. On the plate are a map of honey, small and medium-size closed shrimp, and a few more unusual things than the standard entree.

Yun and I eat the dish as we wait for "Chairman," the name they call the man in charge of the registration. When he arrives, min-utes later, Chairman sits in an old metal chair with vinyl backing. Dim red-tinged light filters in from the window. His legs crossed, a lit rolled cigarette in his left hand, he runs his right hand through a list beside his ashtray.

"Have you registered?" he says to Yun, squinting towards the paper.

"Register me and my son," Yun says.

Yun orders three plates of *nems au poulet*, which arrive nes-tled on a huge lettuce leaf. We throw ourselves on the *nems*, the Chinese delicacy producing a crackly sound when chewed.

"The *nems* are delicious and crispy," Yun says. "Dissolves well in the mouth."

As we eat, Chairman receives still more calls for registration. His phone rings ceaselessly with calls from fellow Chinese immi-grants wanting to enlist as labourers with Henan Construction. Chairman avoids the calls for a while to attend to his food. In the end, he begins to calculate figures on his smart phone.

Then Yun's own cellphone rings. Chun is on the line.

After listening to the complaint Yun promises to call her back, still engrossed in the food.

As we wait for the rest of the next course to be served, Yun tells us about his wife's phone call. Coumba, the beautiful young woman shopkeeper we met at Chun's shop, has asked for seven days off to observe the Magal, an annual religious festival of an indigenous Senegalese brotherhood, the Mourides.

She wants four days off to travel to her village for Korité and an additional six days to celebrate the holiday. She routinely asks for both Christian and Muslim holidays on the annual calendar.

Chun warned her that she would be fired (like eight others before her) if she continued with the absenteeism, but Coumba remains adamant. Her aunt, Yun's customer, has come to explain to the Chinese couple that days off for Muslim feasts are imperative. But Chun will not swallow it. "*On ne peut avoir le beurre et l'argent du beurre*" ("You can't have your cake and eat it too") Chun keeps repeating, practising her newly acquired French proverb.

I ask Yun if he thinks that Chinese immigration comes like a fresh wind to change the climate from downtrodden to celebratory for both China and Africa. He nods swiftly, and goes on to elucidate this thought. The Chinese modernized Touba, the holy city of Senegal; they built the Leopold Senghor Stadium and increased their foreign direct investment. Their state-owned enterprise, the China National Fisheries Association (CNFA), invested in two Senegalese subsidiaries, Senegal Pêche and Senegal Armement, and now with deep fingers they're diving into joint ventures in the areas of transport and telecommunication.

"Does that benefit Senegal?" I ask him boldly.

He pauses. "It should," he says. "We play our card. Senegal should play its card."

Chairman's smart phone nearly slips off the table, and he rescues it. He looks at his watch and gets up, yelling to all those waiting outside to hop into the buses lined up.

The band of Chinese immigrants rushes into the buses, chanting their celebration of the victory of Henan Construction in winning the bid to build the new international conference centre at Diamniadio, the new face of Dakar, thirty kilometres south of the city. They carry boots, hard hats, and other construction accessories and head out to Diamniadio, the new emblem of Chinese presence in Senegal.

Yun says he feels he has to leave with his compatriots in order not to lose the opportunity. They've found a good job. Their eyes are on the final reward. The way Yun's eyes light up when he speaks of the benefits is a clear reflection of a man willing to sacrifice to reach his goals. His face is full of hope, and thinking of the future he smiles. "Africa loves China," he says, and it becomes apparent to me that the happiness he feels is greater than all the criticism and violence that he and his compatriots may face. In the heat of the departure I thank Yun for his time and tell him I have to go. Before I depart, he makes me a gift of a Chinese desk flag he brought along, and we agree to keep in touch.

Back in my apartment, I place the Chinese flag northwest on my writing desk. I approach the window, and I notice the new Chinese baby boutique across the street.

A text message from Yun informs me that because the municipal government had driven out illegal traders squatting downtown, unknown persons went to set fire to ten Chinese shops on Allées du Centenaire.

I slowly drop the cellphone and raise my head, turning back into my apartment.

I recall my first encounter with Yun on the queue — the sweat on his neck, the sunburn. I tell myself that despite the ache of living in a hot climate and other challenges clouding their journeys, Yun and other Chinese immigrants are forging their lives here, thousands of miles away from their home. Chinese migration falls within a wider gamble of foreign powers pitching their tents of influence in Africa. From all that I've seen, Yun and his compatriots are not so much enriching Africa as they are attempting to build a future in their own homeland. Despite Yun's "China loves Africa" claims, it's clear that as China's influence rises, its political demands on Africa will not shrink.

In the end, though, it's up to us. If Africans fail to capitalize on the wealth beneath their soil and on their young population, it won't be Yun and his compatriots' fault.

SAFE HOUSE

Isaac Otidi Amuke

SATURDAY, SEPTEMBER 18, 2010
NAIROBI, KENYA

That Saturday morning I wore faded blue jeans, a pair of well-worn but still in vogue brown suede loafers I'd bought from the flea market outside City Stadium on Jogoo Road, and a black long-sleeved shirt tucked into my pants. The thing about the City Stadium loafers was that as much as they were pre-owned by someone in either Europe or America, they were still in pristine condition, and whenever I wore this particular pair, which I had owned for over a year, I got the same feeling of comfort and self-assuredness I'd felt the first time I put them on.

I had obsessed about owning a solid black shirt for a long time, and when I bought this particular one I'd spent more time admiring it in my wardrobe than daring to put it on, fearing it would wear out. But that morning I didn't worry about any of this. All I wanted was that fitted-shirt-fitted-jeans-leather-lined-loafers feeling, one that made me feel ready for the weekend. That's what I went for.

It was that rare time of the month when I had money on me. I had received my $300 stipend from the Kenya National Commission on Human Rights a few days earlier, which was supposed to cater for my monthly groceries. The commission was housing me in a $1,200 furnished and serviced one-bedroom unit at Ler Apartments on Chania Road in Kilimani, where I had now lived for over five months, starting in April 2010. I had struck a deal in which they had offered to house me on condition that I didn't let anyone know about the arrangement. If anyone got to learn of it, I was told, the deal would be off, immediately, with no room for renegotiation.

Technically this was supposed to be a safe house, for which the commission was willing to pay an arm and a leg, since one had to pay "neighbourhood tax" in Kilimani — the go-to neighbourhood for young Kenyans who wanted to show social arrival, some announcing their new middle-class status, real or perceived, and others working to maintain whatever status had been handed down to them by their parents. The price of this middle-classness was paying exorbitant rents for apartments with wooden floors and sliding French windows leading to balconies with ashtrays placed on garden tables, where they'd come out to have a smoke after a long day of chasing money to keep themselves living in the neighbourhood.

I lived in apartment B2, which was the door on the right as one came up the stairs on the first floor of the block of one-bedroom apartments. The sliding door leading to the balcony gave a view of the other apartment block within the property, with its office, kitchen, and gym on the ground floor.

A huge abstract painting and a mirror mounted in wrought iron were all there was to the walls of the small lounge area of my apartment, where a 45-inch flat screen TV set sat in the corner next to the balcony. Two couches covered in orange linen seat covers formed a 90-degree angle facing the TV set, with one of the seats leaning against a wall. A stout, brown, square wooden table placed on a beige rug sat at the centre of the lounge, with a round four-seater dining table adjacent to a fully equipped open-plan kitchen. The bedroom had a huge bed — which I'd comfortably share with my three cousins whenever they visited — and on the side was a floor-to-ceiling mirror mounted on a wooden frame made of driftwood.

To some, this would be the life. To me, life was in limbo.

THURSDAY, MARCH 5, 2009
NAIROBI, KENYA

My journey to the safe house began on the slow-moving Thursday evening of March 5, 2009.

I was standing outside the Yaya Centre, the imposing shopping mall and high-end apartment tower block at the junction of Argwings Kodhek Road and Ring Road in Kilimani, waiting for my friend Zoe, with whom I was to watch *Notorious*, the newly released biopic on the life of American rapper Notorious B.I.G. We had both watched *Redemption*, the life story of B.I.G.'s main rival, Tupac Shakur, and we'd spent many evenings talking about it over coffee. When I got tickets for *Notorious*, Zoe was my natural choice for company.

She was taking too long to get from Westlands to the Yaya Centre, where we were to proceed to the movie theatre at Prestige Plaza, Ngong Road. She called and said she was running late. There was no public transport and so she'd had to take a cab. Between wondering how Zoe would be dressed and speculating over how the evening would unfold, whether we'd enjoy the movie as I hoped and possibly grab a meal thereafter and wander into deeper conversation about anything and everything — as we always did — my thoughts were interrupted by a phone call from our friend Wachira.

"Amuke, GPO amepigwa risasi," Wachira said.

Our friend George Paul Oulu, known as Oulu GPO, had been shot.

Wachira sounded out of breath, panting on the other end of the line as if he was being chased. We had always felt invincible as student activists, imagining that the worst that could happen to us would be getting kicked out of school. GPO had been suspended from the university by the time Zoe, Wachira, and I were freshmen. He had led a student protest against fees increments, and the university had slapped him with a three-year suspension. He had been barred from student politics upon readmission and used us as proxies in fighting the repressive administration.

GPO had been shot on State House Road, next to the University of Nairobi, alongside Oscar Kamau Kingara, a civil society benefactor we had befriended. Wachira had been having a beer at Senses, the pub at the student centre a few metres away, when he had heard the gunshots. It was 6:00 p.m.

GPO was dead.

I called Zoe and told her the news, which I still hoped wasn't true. I knew GPO had been stepping on powerful toes lately, but I also knew that only the state had the means to execute someone in the manner Wachira had described to me, and I didn't see how the state would come for GPO with such brutal force as if he was a direct threat to its very existence. Not wanting to believe Wachira, I chose to remain ambivalent, but the apprehension of confirming my worst fears once I got to the scene remained real.

"Are you sure?" Zoe asked.

"Yes. Wachira has just called me," I told her, asking her to meet me on State House Road.

I crossed the road and took a bus from the stop opposite Yaya Centre. By now it was starting to feel real, because I was moving physically to the scene where GPO was supposed to have been killed. The fact that I had made Zoe take a detour to State House Road made me start believing Wachira's words. I felt a need to keep my composure, fearing that once I lost it I wouldn't regain it.

As the bus rode down Argwings Kodhek Road and into Valley Road, I kept wondering whether any of my fellow passengers were weighed down by emotions too, even if not as heavy as my own. I got off the bus at the Serena Hotel stop and started running along Nyerere Road.

I wanted to get to the scene and prove Wachira wrong.

At St. Paul's Chapel I saw a crowd gathered on State House Road, next to the gate leading to Hall 11 on the Lower State House Unit of the student hostels. I arrived at the scene and pushed through the crowd, spotting Oscar seated upright on the driver's seat of his white Mercedes-Benz, his entire upper body covered in a thick layer of now clotting blood. He had been shot in the head a number of times. I reached out to touch his body but was held back. I was shaking, and the sight of Oscar's bloodied body made me start crying. I looked around and saw Wachira, who was also weeping. It was true. GPO too must be dead. We embraced, both trembling.

Wachira took my hand and led me through the growing crowd gathered around the scene. We found GPO lying on the tarmac facing up, because, apparently, he hadn't died on the spot. University students had tried to save his life by dragging him out of the vehicle to rush him to the students' clinic, but he had stopped breathing only a few yards from the vehicle. I knelt down and held GPO's body. I shook him, but he wouldn't respond. He wore an African-print shirt, black jeans, and black sports shoes — one of the rare days he hadn't worn a suit. I wept, calling out his name, but he wouldn't respond.

Zoe arrived at the scene, her hands held tightly against her chest, her eyes looking teary as she looked down at me, shaken and confused.

I saw a bullet wound through GPO's right arm, as if he had tried blocking a bullet using his hand. This was typical of GPO — not going down without a fight.

We knew the police would eventually come to take the bodies away, and with everything pointing to the likelihood that these executions were the work of the state, I wanted to be gone by the time they got there. I had a growing fear that there were state security agents already at the scene, monitoring who came and how they reacted on seeing the bodies. I knew I had probably been spotted and marked. Wachira was the only member of The Liberators who had not graduated. He was now a fourth-year student, and he agreed to stay behind at the university to watch as events unfolded that evening, after the rest of us left the scene.

The Liberators was a clandestine group we had formed as university students and hoped to transform into a national movement, emboldened by Oscar's offer to finance our activities, allowing us to expand on the back of some of the political work he had already done, including offering free legal aid to the downtrodden. The other members of the group, aside from GPO, Oscar, Wachira, and me, were Booker, Pascal, and Frank — all former student activists.

I wiped my tears and told Wachira I had to leave.

As I walked off, navigating through the now noisy crowd, I felt strangely invincible, as if I'd sneaked away without leaving behind any trace of my presence at the scene. Zoe and I held hands, as if to reassure ourselves that we still had each other. She asked me whether I was still going for the movie. I didn't know where else to go or what to do at that moment, and going home wasn't an option. I feared I'd be followed. The fear bordered on paranoia, and much as I knew I would be helpless if the state chose to come after me that night, I decided that I would play a game of hide and seek, that they wouldn't get me at the gate to the flat I shared with my brother. They'd have to follow me around a little harder.

Zoe stayed calm, maybe shocked, maybe trying to process what had just happened. She told me she had called her mother, who was coming to pick her up. She was worried for me, but I kept reassuring her that I would be fine. I didn't want to burden her with my fears.

We got to the Nairobi Java House on Koinange Street, where she was to be picked up by her mother. She told me she would be okay inside the coffee shop, and that it would be fine if I went ahead to the movie. She looked concerned for me, but there wasn't anything I could ask of her at the time. She gave me a hug before I left.

I walked onto Loita Street and crossed Kenyatta Avenue at the end of the street, taking a night bus at the General Post Office bus stop to Prestige Plaza. Once again riding a bus that evening felt surreal, with everyone minding their own business, the same way I was minding mine.

By the time I got to Prestige Plaza the movie had already started. I showed my ticket to the stewardesses, who smiled back and did the whole "Welcome, sir" routine. I thanked them and moved to the next booth, where I was offered popcorn and soda.

There's something the big screen does to you, instantly transporting you to a faraway place. I was soon in Brooklyn, where Biggie, as he was known, was starting out as a rapper. As I kept watching, Biggie became GPO, because like everyone else, I knew the movie's ending — he would be assassinated, just like GPO earlier that evening. When the movie ended, I told myself that if someone appeared in the night and shot me, I would die with pride like Biggie or GPO. In hip hop speak, I had heart. I checked my phone and saw I had twenty-six missed calls. Although I had not noticed at the time, it turned out that there had been a news crew filming at the scene of GPO's murder. My movements had been captured, my friends told me when I called back, and the footage had appeared on the nine o'clock news. Now everyone wanted to know if it was true. Was GPO really dead?

I was home alone that night in the fourth-floor two-bedroom flat I shared with my elder brother in Nairobi's Donholm neighbourhood. My brother was away for work. I had left the movie theatre close to 11:00 p.m. and moved through Nairobi's deserted streets as if I were being pursued by my own shadow. I got into the main gate of the six-floor block of flats and ran up the stairs, quickly let myself in and locked the door, sat on the couch, and started crying. Things would have been different had my brother been home. I'd have shut myself in the bedroom, as I always did. I later walked to the kitchen and warmed some leftovers, but the moment I put food in my mouth I spat it all out. I locked myself in the house for the next two days, oscillating between fear of being killed and sadness at the deaths of my friends.

SATURDAY, MARCH 7, 2009
NAIROBI, KENYA

On March 7, two days after the killings, Booker sent me a message saying that Pascal had gone missing. Two days later, a leading human rights activist, Okiya Okoiti Omtatah, called asking whether I knew who Pascal was. He asked whether I knew who Wachira, Booker, and Frank were. I told him I knew them all, explaining our association with Oscar and GPO. He told me he had received an email from Pascal — who was in hiding — informing him that the lives of those he had listed in the email — Frank, Booker, Wachira, and I — were in danger. Omtatah had made calls to contacts within the country's security agencies and had been informed that our names were on a list associated with Oscar and GPO, seeming to suggest that, like Pascal, we were in danger.

Omtatah assured me that the threats were real in his view, and that he was going to try to reach the Minister for Internal Security, George Saitoti, to request a guarantee of our safety. He would also reach out to Prime Minister Raila Odinga, who was seen as progressive enough to come to our aid. The prime minister's own political history was full of stories of detention without trial and exile, a fact we hoped would make him readily sympathetic. This notwithstanding, Omtatah suggested that Booker, Frank, Wachira, and I should report to his office first thing the following morning. He had a plan, he said, and we needed to bring along our passports.

I refused to get out of bed the following morning, on March 10. My phone started ringing at around 8:00 a.m. Booker, Frank, and Wachira were already at Omtatah's office.

Omtatah was one of Kenya's most recognizable activists. Following the post-election violence in 2007–8, he had gone as far as staging a one-man protest armed with nothing but his rosary, chaining himself to the metal grill fence outside police headquarters at Vigilance House, asking that the police give Kenyans back their country. We had no reason to doubt him. If he meant well for Kenya, then he meant well for us.

My friends' persistence eventually got me out of bed at around 10:00 a.m. The relief in Booker's, Frank's, and Wachira's eyes was evident when they saw me.

Once we had settled in his office, Omtatah gave us a briefing on our safety. He'd learned that we were suspected of being associates of Mungiki, a proscribed group whose members were victims of the extrajudicial killings Oscar and GPO had been investigating at the time of their death. We had to be careful, he said, because there was no guarantee that once the security services caught up with us, they would give us the opportunity to defend ourselves or tell our side of the story. He told us we better leave the country immediately.

In the late 1990s to the early 2000s, Mungiki emerged as a cultural and spiritual uprising by youths from central Kenya, before it had morphed into a political pressure group that shifted allegiances from one politician to another at different times. In the end the group had turned itself into an enforcer of a parallel tax–collecting regime, stationing its members at busy bus terminals where passengers were dropped off and new ones picked up, demanding a daily fee from all public service vehicles in Nairobi. The group was also associated with the beheading of their suspected critics in central Kenya, and it was believed that when the state couldn't find a way of dealing with their growing lawlessness, it resorted to enforced disappearance of its members. This included extrajudicial killings. It was in documenting these killings and disappearances that Oscar and GPO became enemies of the state.

Omtatah had exhausted his contacts in trying to ensure that word of our plight reached the highest echelons of the country's security apparatus. But there were no guarantees regarding our safety. After the briefing, which left us all feeling cornered and afraid, he asked us to follow him out of his office, taking us through the back gate of the National Social Security Fund building in which it was located. We went down a slope leading to the Shell gas station on Valley Road — sandwiched between the NSSF building and the Sarova Panafric Hotel. He then gave me a small, folded piece of paper with the address of a house in Muthaiga, a leafy suburb that was home to a number of official diplomatic residencies. He told Booker, Frank, Wachira, and me that we would be dropped off at the gate at the address, and that once there we should use whatever means possible to gain entry into the compound, after which we would announce that we were there to seek asylum.

The plan sounded sketchy, with no assurances of a ride to safety. But the fact that Omtatah had thought it through and gone out of his way to be of such immense support to us was enough to make us loath to second-guess him. If it was a risk he was asking us to take, then it must have been a calculated one. Omtatah led us to one corner of the gas station, where we found two identical cabs waiting. He told the drivers where he wanted them to drop us off in Muthaiga, asking the four of us to split into groups of two so that we could go in separate cabs. Booker and Frank teamed up, leaving Wachira and me to form the other pair. Omtatah paid the cab drivers before we said our goodbyes. As we drove off he had one last instruction. He gave me a secret phone number and asked me to send him a text message with the word "DONE" once we managed to enter the compound. With that we were off to the unknown.

The compound Omtatah had sent us to was the residence of the Botswana High Commissioner to Kenya. We arrived just before noon. At around 5:00 p.m., a call came in, possibly after the verification of our claims, and one of the stewards in the compound came and asked us to follow her into the high commissioner's house, as if we had become proper guests all of a sudden. We were led into a porch at the back of the house, facing a well-maintained lawn on the left and a swimming pool on the right, before being offered tea and coffee. With this simple gesture of hospitality, we knew we were on our way to safety. The high commissioner eventually showed up and informed us that Botswana had no capacity to handle our case. Upon learning of our presence at his residence, he told us, he had met up with fellow diplomats to discuss the situation. He didn't tell us who those other diplomats were, but the end result was that it had been agreed that the Americans and Europeans would take over our case. In time we would learn that the group of diplomats had been in touch with a secret civil society group. It was this group that had provided verification of our plight. As we spoke, two vehicles drove into the compound. The high commissioner went outside, returning with a man and woman who we later learned worked for a human rights defenders protection agency, a near-clandestine organization.

The duo asked us to take our SIM cards out of our mobile phones and keep the phones off, then to split into two groups of two. Again Booker paired up with Frank, Wachira with me.

We drove into the night, and this is how I ended up living underground in Nairobi for a month and a half. I eventually fled to seek asylum in Uganda following a meeting with the American ambassador in Nairobi, who pledged to get us to the United States once we had refugee status. The ambassador facilitated the receipt of $4,500 for each of us for our upkeep in Uganda, promising that the paperwork for our eventual acceptance as refugees in Uganda before being resettled in America would take a maximum of three months.

It would end up taking almost a year.

JUNE 2009–JANUARY 2010
KAMPALA, UGANDA

I arrived in Kampala in early June 2009, thinking I would be there for three months at the most. After the meeting my friends and I had had with the American ambassador in Nairobi, we had been assured that we would be off to the United States as soon as we had been granted refugee status from a third country. In our case this country would be Uganda. After meeting the American ambassador, Booker and Wachira had decided against leaving the country, for personal reasons. Frank and I had left for Kampala and gotten an apartment together. Pascal was already settled into life in Kampala by this time, choosing to stay away from Frank and me.

This separation was also the beginning of the end of our operating as a group. We'd all end up choosing different paths, politically and otherwise.

I had budgeted for three months, and my time in Kampala was frenetic. I spent most nights in nightclubs, reminiscing about what I had left behind in Kenya and trying to imagine a new life in Los Angeles, New York, or Washington, DC. But getting refugee status was taking longer than the promised three months. It became four, five, then six months. We ran out of cash, and now the Americans said the $4,500 stipend given to us initially was a one-off payment. Our apartment lease was running out. We had to cut down to a meal a day. Broke, and with no clear completion of the process in sight, I started spending all my days and nights in bed, only waking up to fix the one meal a day.

This was when I realized that if I didn't return to Kenya I was in real danger of slipping into depression or something worse. Up until this point in my life, I had always had the basic support of my family. Never before had I been in a situation like this, alone and having to fend for myself.

Now here I was, twenty-six years old, broke and anxious, cut off from family and friends, wondering whether being stuck in a foreign capital was all that my life would amount to. I had not even wanted to leave Kenya to begin with.

Reasoning that anything would be better than this unhappy enforced exile, I used my scant resources to make my way back home, arriving in Nairobi in December 2009. I had only been back at my brother's flat in Donholm a short time when I received a call from the American embassy informing me that I had been granted refugee status in Uganda and that I needed to pick up my status letter. The embassy wasn't aware of my exact whereabouts, whether I was in Nairobi or Kampala. I immediately started raising money from friends to make the trip back to Uganda. It was at this point that I came across Onyango Oloo, a friend and activist who had been jailed for five years in the 1980s as a student at the

University of Nairobi for being in possession of an essay that the state considered seditious.

Oloo told me there were some Kenyan friends hiding in Uganda. One of them was O.J., whom I knew from my student activism days. I got in touch, and O.J. told me he was hiding in Uganda with a gentleman called Eddy, sharing a two-bedroom house in Muyenga, one of Kampala's high-end suburbs. The place was secure because the property opposite belonged to a senior Ugandan government official. He invited me to join them.

I arrived in Muyenga around the second week of January 2010 and was picked up by Eddy, who took me to the house. I had on one set of clothes, thinking I'd be in Uganda for merely a day or two. Shuttling between Nairobi and Kampala would violate the terms of my refugee status, but even with the change in circumstances I did not feel I could risk being destitute in Kampala. So I would take what then seemed the lesser risk: I planned to go home once I had my papers.

I picked up my refugee status, but the same day I received a call from the United Nations High Commissioner for Refugees (UNHCR), inviting me for an interview the following week. I would have to stay.

One morning that week I woke up, put on my pants, and went outside bare-chested. I had been washing my single shirt and T-shirt every evening and would wear only one of the two the following morning. As I stood in the compound, one of the guys living next door was leaving his house. I waved at him.

"Ssebo, ogamba chi?" I said. How do you do, sir?

"Sili na lugambo mukwano," he replied. I am well, my friend.

He took a few more steps before he stopped abruptly, asking me whether I was Ugandan. I told him I wasn't. He asked whether I spoke the language. I told him, "Katono," just a little. He asked me to follow him into his house. He wanted to have a quick chat.

Salim, as he'd introduced himself to me, worked for the Ugandan intelligence services as part of the security detail of the senior government official who lived across the road. He told me that he had chosen to speak to me because I was a nice person — I had said hello to him. I panicked a little but knew I had refugee status, which was my only shield. He asked me who my friends and I were. What we were doing in Uganda.

Once I had told him the particulars of our story, Salim confided that his bosses had a problem with my two friends, O.J. and Eddy. They were arrogant, he said, and never spoke to anyone. The first problem, he told me, was that one of them always smoked marijuana late at night outside the house. That was Eddy. The other problem was that someone's girlfriend always came to the house as late as 2:00 a.m. That was O.J.

The big man across the road had instructed his security detail to take us in for questioning. He wanted to know who we were and whether we posed any risk to him. Salim had asked his bosses to give him time to observe us, he told me, to collect more intelligence before taking things further. He had been given a week to complete his report.

Now all this had changed because I had said hello to him. He was going to report that we were Kenyan refugees. He also asked me to have my documents and those of my friends ready, since his bosses would pass by sometime during the week to verify the information he gave them. I told him there was no problem.

But there was a problem. O.J. and Eddy didn't have refugee status or asylum-seeking documents. All they had were their passports. When they got back home that night I told them what had happened. They panicked. The following Saturday I was making lunch when I heard a knock on the door. Salim came in accompanied by four men who drove into the compound in two cars with Ugandan government registration plates. They were his bosses, there to see my documents.

I went inside and brought out my papers. When the men asked me about the whereabouts of my two friends, I told them that O.J. and Eddy had gone to Kampala city centre and would be back later in the day. They told me I should ask them to photocopy their documents and hand them over to Salim. Confirming that my own documents were in order, and advising that as long as we observed Ugandan laws there would be no problem, they returned my papers and left.

After this, O.J. and Eddy decided I had to leave the house, and they were not subtle about it. By this time I had completed one UNHCR interview and was waiting for the follow-up. But now I had no place to stay. It was February and I had been back in Kampala for three weeks.

When I had first arrived, I had asked my brother to send me money so that I could pay my share of the rent for at least two months. The money arrived on the day O.J. and Eddy kicked me out, but I decided I wouldn't leave Kampala just yet. That Saturday evening R. Kelly was performing at Lugogo Oval, and, determined to forget my troubles, even if only for a short while, I made my way to Kabalagala, a famous Kampala stretch with nightclubs on both sides of the street, and partied until daybreak, choosing to keep to myself the whole time, buried in my own thoughts. I didn't have anywhere to sleep that night, and so I went to Al's bar, which was where people went to drink from the early hours. By midday I was exhausted. I crossed Ggaba Road, which passed right in front of Al's bar, and walked into an open field on the other side of the road, where I passed out.

Later that evening, I went to one of the lodges in Kabalagala and paid UGX5,000 for a shower, then had a meal for UGX1,500. When I was done I strolled down the road into Capital Pub, and the first girl I saw looked like an identical twin to Hazel, the first girl I ever had a crush on as a first year wearing dirty jeans and Converse Chuck Taylors at the University of Nairobi.

"Excuse me. Can I buy you a drink?" I offered.

"I don't mind," she replied. I still had some charm left in me — even if I was down and out. I made her laugh, and by midnight we were both ready to turn in. We left the nightclub together. I booked a room behind Capital Pub. I was too tired, and so we only kissed and touched before I passed out.

I woke up alone the following morning.

The girl had left. I cursed, convinced that she had made away with my money, phone, and passport. I looked under the pillow, where I had stashed them before passing out. Everything was still there, but when I looked inside the wallet I saw that more than half the currency notes were missing. She had taken a good chunk of the money my brother had sent me, but not all of it. More importantly, she hadn't taken my phone or passport.

I counted the money, realizing that it would be just enough to take me to the Kenya-Uganda border. I was willing to risk cancellation of my status, but I wasn't willing to risk getting stuck in a foreign capital without means to support myself. That afternoon I travelled from Kampala to Malaba, the border point less than an hour from my home village. I spent the night in the village and immediately began making plans for Nairobi.

SATURDAY, SEPTEMBER 18, 2010
NAIROBI, KENYA

Extrajudicial killings in Kenya remained a mirage to many, because the police would always deny any such things happened, and those killed would be labelled criminals who had been killed in an exchange of fire. But I had seen the evidence Oscar and GPO had gathered on the suspected state-sponsored executions of members of Mungiki, of bullet-ridden bodies dumped in forests, some already decomposing, just as I had witnessed that evening when I saw the bullet-ridden bodies of my murdered friends.

Then, that Saturday morning, seven months after returning home, I bore witness to the state's excesses once again.

Wearing my pristine City Stadium loafers, I left my flat at Ler Apartments, heading to the Nakumatt department store at Prestige Plaza on Ngong Road, where I usually replenished my groceries. It was a five- to ten-minute walk, and I always went to shop on foot and only took a cab on my way back. The walk gave me a sense of Kilimani — clean, serene, and well guarded with electric fences and private security alarm response trucks parked in strategic locations, ready to pounce on anyone disturbing the peace of the hardworking new Nairobi middle class.

I said hello to the day guard, a tall, slender man who I assumed was from the Kenyan coast, going by his uncorrupted Kiswahili. As I opened the pedestrian gate, a white Toyota double cabin pickup truck pulled up directly opposite. The passenger door behind the driver's seat opened. A burly man wearing an oversized jacket and carrying an AK-47 rifle stepped out.

I made brief eye contact with him, but he didn't seem bothered. He pulled out a passenger seated in the backseat and took him behind the truck, asking him to sit on the ground.

Two other men, also carrying AK-47s, appeared from the other side of the vehicle. They assembled at the truck's rear, where the unarmed passenger was now sitting on the tarmac.

The burly gunman ordered him to lie on the ground.

"Lala chini," he said in Kiswahili.

"Tafadhali msiniuwe," the man pleaded. Please don't kill me.

I didn't have a sense of where this was going until the man on the ground began to plead for his life.

The set-up looked ideal. Plainclothes policemen luring their victim into a trap before executing him in cold blood. Sometimes a toy gun, nicknamed bonoko in Nairobi street parlance, would be placed next to the victim. The police would almost always claim the victim was a dangerous armed gangster.

My body felt numb. The gunmen acted as if I was invisible, but I knew they had seen me. By this time, the guard was asking me what I was looking at. I was standing still at the gate, neither going out nor coming back in. I couldn't answer him. He peeped outside through the small opening in the gate, where he caught the unfolding drama.

The moment the burly gunman cocked his gun, I shut the gate and rushed back inside.

By the time I got to my apartment's balcony on the first floor, shots had already been fired.

The loud AK-47 bangs sent everyone in the apartment complex out onto their balconies. A housekeeper standing outside the gym on the opposite block kept gesturing at me, asking me what had happened outside the gate. She had seen me rush back in before the shots were fired. I gestured back at her, fingers modelled into a pistol, telling her someone had been shot outside the gate. For the first time in my life I had heard gunshots at close range, and the feeling of the ground shaking and my eardrums almost bursting did not seem exaggerated.

A few minutes later all was silent, and we all came down from our balconies and went to the gate. The man outside the gate now lay on his back, lifeless. I kept replaying the scene of the burly gunman asking him to sit down, then to lie down, before cocking his gun and sending me running back inside the apartment block.

Now he was dead, his blood turning black on the tarmac.

WALKING GIRLY IN NAIROBI

Mark Gevisser

1.

After my meeting with Peter,* I dropped him on the Ngong Road to get a matatu (minibus) back to where he lived, outside of the city, in a communal house with twenty other refugees. I watched him tuck his long braids back into his red beanie and martial his slight frame, rendered even skinnier by his tight green jeans, into the step of the street. He arranged his eloquent features into a blank rictus of masculinity and disappeared into the rush hour throng.

If asked a question by someone else in the matatu he would try to mutter something in Swahili, he told me, even though this was a language he still barely spoke. If he answered in English, he would be identified as a foreigner. If there were a policeman, he might be asked to show his papers. And that is "when the trouble will begin," he said. "There's no war in Uganda, so when someone sees that I am asylum-seeker here, they know there can only be one reason."

A few hours earlier, I had watched Peter pull the beanie off and shake out his braids, parted in a line along the top of his crown so

---

* Peter is a pseudonym, as are the names of all the other Ugandan refugees referred to in this story. This is to ensure their safety while they undergo the resettlement process.

that they fell down the sides of his head to make a heart of his fine-boned face. I had not seen him in a year, and I noted immediately how he was both more feminine and more assertive than the shy and composed boy I had met in Kampala. There was something in his manner, even in the way he threw his tote bag down in rage and frustration, that told me he had stepped into himself since I had seen him last.

Just nineteen, he had been in Nairobi for six months, seeking asylum on the basis of his sexual orientation. He had come to meet me straight from the United Nations High Commissioner for Refugees, where he had been to get new documentation. This was because his papers had been torn up by Kenyan policemen when he had refused to pay a bribe. At first, he told me, the guards at UNHCR had mocked him and denied him entry: "You Ugandans are bringing sin to Kenya!" Finally he had been granted access. But when his new papers had been issued he had been told he would have to repeat the refugee eligibility interview he had done a few weeks previously.

This had thrown him into a panic. "They don't believe me, that I'm a real LGBTI. *I know it.* They must think I'm one of the fraudsters."*

Initially, Peter had been told to come back for his Refugee Status Determination in November: if found to be eligible, he would receive an Alien Card from the Kenyan authorities, which would give him more protection and enable him to work and to begin the process of applying for resettlement to a gay-friendly country like the United States, his preferred choice. Now this path seemed unclear. He was consumed with anxiety: "I don't think I can make it here. Let me go back to Uganda to die." It was a teenager's plea, a threat, a cry for help. "It's better than staying here. Nobody cares for me here."

---

* LGBTI: Lesbian, Gay, Bisexual, Transgender, and Intersex. From "LGBTI Rights," which is how the struggle for the rights of gender and sexual minorities was conventionally known at the time of writing. I have used "LGBTI" in this piece to mirror the way Peter and his friends talk about themselves.

I had first met Peter a year previously, in June 2014, when he was still in Kampala, the day before he was to go to court to testify against a man who had entrapped him via Facebook, extorted him, beaten him up, and tortured him sexually. The attack had happened just after Uganda's president, Yoweri Museveni, had signed the country's Anti-Homosexuality Act into law. Two years before that, while the campaign to get the law passed was in full throttle, Peter had been thrown out of his home, aged fifteen. I had been struck immediately by how carefully and thoughtfully he spoke. He told his story dispassionately, the way traumatized people often do, as if he were looking at his violated self from far away.

There was no doubt that Peter's life had been extremely tough in Uganda. But he had been drawn to Kenya by what the UNHCR itself has admitted was a "pull factor for young Ugandans." In December 2013, the first twenty-three LGBTI refugees presented themselves at the Kakuma refugee camp, in the arid north of the country, after the Ugandan parliament passed the Anti-Homosexuality Act. Usually refugee resettlement to a third country takes between three and five years, but the UNHCR saw immediately how vulnerable this population was, particularly in an environment such as the vast Kakuma camp, filled with Somali and Sudanese refugees. And so it streamlined the process to an unprecedented six months: by mid-2014 the twenty-three were in the West, mainly in the United States. When a second group of Ugandan refugees protested the conditions at Kakuma, the UNHCR decided to allow them to live in Nairobi and to give them financial assistance of Ksh6,000 ($60) a month, in lieu of the shelter and food they would have received at Kakuma.

These, then, were the pull factors: the promise of rapid resettlement and a monthly stipend in the interim. The agency was quickly overwhelmed with applicants, even after the Ugandan Constitutional Court nullified the Anti-Homosexuality Act on procedural grounds in August 2014. A year later, there were five hundred Ugandan LGBTI asylum-seekers registered in Kenya, but the

UNHCR and its service partners estimated that at least a hundred of these were fraudulent: the agency had been alerted that a busload of new applicants had been told by their traffickers to play the gay card. Other applicants were still living in Uganda, popping over at the beginning of each month to receive their assistance.

The UNHCR put the brakes on and reverted to its standard procedures. Now hundreds of refugees expecting quick resettlement found themselves stuck in Nairobi, a place where things are often as tough for LGBTI people — in terms of the prevailing social attitudes — as they were back home in Uganda. To complicate matters further, the Ugandan LGBTI refugees did not have intergenerational refugee communities to slot into, to provide them shelter and even employment, the way, for example, Somali or Eritrean refugees do. And the reason for their having been persecuted in Uganda in the first place was linked, in many cases, to their very inability to fit in, because of their gender nonconformity.

And they were young, urban, educated, and fully aware of their rights. Unlike Somali or Congolese villagers fleeing war, they had left their home country with the clear understanding that these rights had been violated and with the expectation that they would be respected elsewhere. But here they were in a society at least as intolerant as the one they had fled.

When I came to Nairobi in July 2015 to meet Peter and his fellow refugees, I found aggrieved and dissatisfied young men (there were a handful of women too), seemingly unable and unwilling to integrate into Kenyan society. Even Nairobi's own LGBTI community viewed them with suspicion: one Kenyan friend referred to them contemptuously as "professional gayfugees." Word was out: they were hustlers, and trouble.

Peter lived in a communal house run by a Ugandan LGBTI refugee group called Ark Communes, in a peri-urban area about thirty kilometres outside of Nairobi. To get there, you had to turn off the main road at the local bar and general store and bump down a steep dirt track to a steel gate in a high cinder-block wall. When I visited in July 2015, the house was aging and somewhat decrepit. There was a netball pitch cleared in the dust and a big old couch on the verandah, leaking its upholstery. The house had no running water or oven — cooking was done on an open fire in the kitchen — and a few pieces of mismatched furniture were scattered about. At the entrance, a list of house "officials" was neatly tacked up: the Ugandan cleric who had founded the project, Father Anthony Musaala, was the "President," and Peter was the "Deputy Minister for Education." Also posted was a daily schedule and a list of rules and regulations, alongside the punishments for infringing them: a fine of KSh500 for not maintaining "self-discipline and present-ability at all times"; a fine of having to fetch five jerry cans of water for spending the night in someone else's bed without permission.

At the time I visited there were twenty residents in the house, some sharing bedrooms, some in the double garage or in outdoor storerooms. A few rooms had signs of settlement — carefully made curtain-dividers, photos on a mantelpiece, neat racks of clothing — but most reflected the transience of their inhabitants. Peter's room, a pantry off the kitchen, was dark and sparse: there was a mattress on the floor and a padlocked duffle bag beside it. I had brought provisions, and as Peter's boyfriend, George, supervised a lunch team, the other residents gathered in the communal area to tell me about their lives.

Frank, the laconic matinee-idol director of Ark's dance troupe, had collapsed recently due to the high blood pressure condition he could not afford to treat, but he had had to flee a hospital when the attending doctor realized he was gay and threatened to call the police. Mo, an articulate professional, was one of the more recent arrivals at the Ark house: he had been forced to leave his place of residence a week previously, when it had been surrounded by a mob that had discovered the residents were homosexuals.

Here, too, the Ark residence had begun to arouse the suspicions of the neighbours. In response to the terrorist attacks of 2014 and the influx of Somali refugees from the north, the new president, Uhuru Kenyatta, had initiated a program called Usalama Watch: all Kenyans were to get to know their neighbours ten-deep on either side and to report anyone they did not know to the authorities. Inevitably this triggered xenophobia and made life even more difficult for the Ugandans. A complaint was lodged about them, and the police came to investigate. The residents had insisted they were political refugees, as they had been coached to do by the UNHCR, but both neighbours and authorities were unconvinced.

This dissembling created an almost impossible dilemma for the refugees. "On the one hand, we are told to keep a low profile, and even lie about why we are here," Peter said. "But on the other hand we're told we need to integrate into Kenyan society. How is it possible to do both?"

The group was still smarting from a message that they had been given in a UNHCR communication a few weeks previously: "It is essential for LGBTI persons in Kenya to act in an inconspicuous and discreet manner for their own security ... It is therefore of utmost importance that applicants keep a low profile." Peter was trying hard to "go on the down-low" and to check his instincts to "gay it up," he told me. "But nature obeys no law."

Peter's mentor at the communal house was a man in his early forties, a primary school teacher named Joseph who had been fired from his job when his sexuality was revealed. "Peter is my daughter," Joseph told me. "Since he has come to Nairobi, he is so much more comfortable with himself. He is realizing that he is not gay, but actually transgender. That is why he gets slapped so often in the streets, for walking girly."

Peter agreed with this assessment, and had even chosen a female name for himself. But this would have to wait until he was resettled in the West, he told me. For now, he needed to hold his femininity in check if he was going to survive.

Why, then, did he get the braids?

"I did it because, huh! I just felt I needed to be myself. In Uganda there were rules, but here I'm independent. No one can tell me, 'Don't do this, don't dress like that, Peter don't braid your hair.'"

Peter needed the braids and he needed the beanie, the former as part of his process of self-actualization and the latter to keep that very process in check, given where he found himself. It would be a difficult balancing act for anyone to maintain, let alone an impetuous nineteen-year-old just discovering his agency in the world. He had left Uganda on a journey towards being himself, after a violent and oppressive adolescence where his very survival was at risk because of who he was. His crossing the border to Kenya was the first step towards this imagined freedom, to the life that he believed awaited him in his preferred destination, the United States. And he was living with a group of other people with exactly the same expectations. How, in such a context, do you temper such expectation? How do you gather up your hope, particularly after such abjection, and pile it back into the beanie?

2.

"I will tell you, Mark, my problems began with love." This is how Peter began his story when we first met in Kampala. I was not the first person to whom he had recounted it, and he understood how to craft it. A *GQ* journalist had interviewed him the previous day, and he had featured prominently in a Human Rights Watch/ Amnesty International report, which is how I found him.

His lover — a classmate — had drunkenly revealed their relationship in early 2012, at the height of the government's campaign to outlaw homosexuality, aided and abetted by the tabloid press and the church. Peter's father was a soldier, his mother an evangelical pastor. They banished him from church, and his father sent the military police over to rough his son up. He was forbidden to be in the presence of his siblings in case he "infected" them. When he asked for school fees, his father sneered, "Go and ask those people who taught you homosexuality to pay your tuition."

His family stopped feeding him, and so he left, making his way to Kampala. A stranger found him weeping at the bus station and gave him a live-in job, but he was let go after a month. On the streets again, he fell into step with a Christian crusade that took him in and put him up at their church's school, the Destiny Boarding Primary School. At the end of the year, the pastors took Peter home, and his drunk father confronted them with a panga (machete) and the words: "Are you the ones who are teaching my son homosexuality?"

Discovering the reason why Peter was on the streets in the first place, the Destiny Boarding School decided to put him back there. When my Ugandan researcher, posing as a concerned fellow Christian, contacted the school's head pastor, Evah Murgerwa, over Facebook, the pastor explained, "We could not be with someone who was a gay person; there was fear that he will spread it among other students." When my researcher gently reproached her, the pastor shot back, "Why would a born-again Christian even think that we did something wrong to let a homosexual go?"

Through his first job, Peter had saved enough to buy a smart phone, and this keyed him into the Ugandan capital's gay community. "It was Facebook that saved me, and Facebook that hurt me," he told me. He hooked up with a series of dodgy benefactors, including one man who pimped him. Eventually he was taken in by a gay student activist named Apollo, who would follow him into exile in Nairobi.

In early March 2014, Peter received a friend request on Facebook from a man who said he had been moved by the story posted on his wall and wanted to help him get back to school. Peter agreed to meet the man and, because he "was talking like he was gay," decided to trust him: the man asked him to come to his home, where he said he would document Peter's story.

Peter was led into a bedroom where, he told me, he was confronted by "a gay guy, stripped naked on the floor, being kicked and beaten by two other men." Peter was held there for about eight hours: during this time he was told to masturbate with cooking fat mixed with red pepper, he was urinated on, he was burnt with hot water, he was tied up, he was kicked and beaten to the point of coughing blood, and he was coerced into sex with a third hostage. "All the time they were asking me, 'Who made you gay?,' 'Why are you gay?,' 'Who paid for you to be gay?'"

The assailants took Peter's wallet and his phone. He told them he could get them more money, and they released him. He found Apollo, who took him to a clinic for treatment and then — with the help of an LGBTI organization — to the police station to lay charges. Here he encountered one of his assailants, who had been identified by one of the other victims.

The process of reporting his attack traumatized Peter further, from the way the police officers shouted at his lawyer, "You human rights organizations are helping gays," to the fear of reprisal once his assailant was released on bail. Indeed, about a week later, a group did arrive at Apollo's door. "We will deal with you, we know what you do, we'll hunt you down," they said. Peter became paranoid on the street, worrying that someone was following him.

With the help of Apollo and others, he enrolled at a boarding school and got out of Kampala, coming back whenever he needed to testify in court. His assailant was found guilty of assault and extortion, and sentenced. According to Peter, he was released in December 2014.

That month, too, Peter left for Nairobi. He was one of about seventy Ugandans claiming asylum on the basis of sexual orientation or gender identity that month, an all-time high. He was registered, taken to a transit centre for a few days, and then collected by HIAS, the American-Jewish refugee agency that UNHCR has subcontracted to look after LGBTI refugees in Kenya.

Peter was given the initial financial assistance of KSh12,000 ($120), and he shacked up with another Ugandan refugee. But a week later, while shopping at a nearby market, Peter was shoved by three men: "Why you acting like a girl?" They threw him to the ground and kicked him. He returned home with bruises and a swollen eye, horrified that no one had intervened to protect him. The words of his assailants haunted him, in the way they sliced through his fantasies of asylum: "Museveni chased you from your country, and now you've come here, also to spoil it."

In January he moved to a more central district, in a building identified by HIAS, where many refugees lived. But a few weeks later he was arrested in a police raid on the building after neighbours lodged a complaint about a raucous party. The party was to bid farewell to a refugee who was being resettled, and Peter insists it was over by 8:30 p.m. He was awakened after midnight in his room, he told me, and taken to the holding cells at the local police station along with thirty-four others, all Ugandans.

Peter had been having panic symptoms since his entrapment in Uganda, and now, when the detainees seemed set to spend a second night in jail, he had an attack so severe that he fell unconscious. He was taken to a hospital, and when he was discharged he learned that the refugees could not return to their lodgings: they had been exposed, and a mob was allegedly waiting for them.

With not enough funds in the middle of the month to find a new place to live, the released refugees gathered at the UNHCR's offices in the upmarket suburb of Westlands, but were denied entry to the building. With nowhere else to go, they staged what became a protest at the compound gates, sleeping there over three nights. In a remarkably eloquent appeal — drafted in part by Peter's former benefactor Apollo, now also in Nairobi — the refugees demanded not only accountability from the UNHCR but also to be consulted on all decisions involving them. They also wanted increased financial assistance and the reintroduction of an expedited resettlement process, given how vulnerable they were "to abusive acts by both security forces and the general public."

But things turned nasty. The Kenyan police were called in to disperse the protestors, because, the UNHCR says, they had become violent. Peter and his friends allege that they were com-pelled to sign a document stating that if they came to the UNHCR again without an appointment, their process would be stalled: this has proven to be a major inhibitor to their approaching the agency when there is a problem. The UNHCR insists that the document merely committed the Ugandans to refrain from violent protest; I have not been able to see a copy of it.

Out of this crisis emerged a more consultative system, with a group of leaders elected by the Ugandan refugee community to rep-resent them. Peter and the others were given a few nights in a hotel while alternate plans were made. Meanwhile, Father Anthony Masaala — the gay Ugandan cleric living in Nairobi — came up with a solution: he formed the Ark Communes and signed the leases on two properties. Here the refugees would be safer, outside of town, in big old houses on walled properties. They would also live com-munally, pooling their scant resources.

Peter moved into one of these residences to await the results of his eligibility interview. He enrolled in a computer course, but dropped out because he could not afford the transport fees. He tried to go to a driving school, but no one would take him because he did not yet have his papers. He wanted to go back to high school, but he could not be admitted because he'd failed to bring his records with him from Uganda.

3.

I was one of those who had helped Peter stay in school in Kampala in late 2014, after his attack. I had met him as part of the research I was doing into the new global debate on "LGBTI Rights" and the effect it was having on different parts of the world. I do not pay informants for their stories, but very occasionally, when they are clearly in need, and when they have taken time that might otherwise have been productive to talk to me, I try to find a way of assisting them in advancing their lives. In South Africa, for example, I pay a refugee rights organization a small monthly amount to employ a transgender refugee from Malawi once a week. Struck, here in Kampala, by Peter's unschooled intellect, I felt compelled to assist when I heard there was a plan by elders in the community to get him back into school. I could not but think back to my own coming-of-age difficulties as a gay man, living in financial comfort and not rejected by my family: how could Peter even begin to accept himself in his current situation? I was clear, though, that I would not advise or influence him: I was, indeed, deeply surprised — and dismayed — when he contacted me in early 2015 to tell me he had fled to Kenya.

In 2014, while he was still in Uganda, I paid $200 for him to complete Form 3. I did a go-around with friends and I gathered commitments from others for him to go further should he pass the year. Later, after he failed to return to the school and fled to Kenya, I told him that the offer still stood. To tide him over during a period when the UNHCR stopped paying its financial assistance to some refugees as it investigated fraud, I made another $250 available to him once he was in Nairobi. This was meant to be for food and shelter, but, having heard from his brother through Facebook that his mother had been in a road accident, he chose to send a large part of it to her.

Peter told me, when we met in Nairobi, that he had pretended to his mother that he was in Kenya for work.

"Why didn't you tell her the truth?" I asked.

"I didn't want her to know that the money I was giving her was gay money."

"What's gay money?"

It was a leading question, and he got it immediately. He shot his eyebrows up in a characteristic arch and nodded his head forward, in my direction, by the slightest of degrees.

I offered the help. Neither Peter nor anyone else had suggested it. But as my relationship with him developed, I came to realize that I had become part of a dynamic of solidarity and dependency that is intrinsic to global LGBTI politics in these times. It is a dynamic that fuels the "recruitment" narrative of homophobia, giving tinder to the prejudices of people like Peter's father, who shouted, "Go to those people who taught you to be a homosexual for your tuition!" or like Peter's assailants who demanded to know, "Who paid you to be gay?"

The Anglican archbishop of Uganda, Henry Orombi, told a researcher in 2009 that "promoting gay relationships have attracted people financially." If "a boy needs school fees and you offer him money," Orombi said, "the temptation is very strong." The Ugandan ethics minister, James Lokodo, said something similar to a British journalist in 2014: "I am worried about recruitment, about those gays who come to our country and turn our children into homos, pay them money to become homosexuals."

Perhaps it is easier for many traditional Christian Africans to understand homosexuality as a material relationship than to accept it as natural and perplexing human behaviour — or even as an offence against God. If my son is gay because of his desire or something innate, then the world is inexplicable. What becomes of all the Church's teachings about sin? And what will happen to the family's bloodlines and wealth? But if my son is gay because he is needy, or greedy, it makes more sense.

Peter's homosexuality is manifestly not a strategy for getting out of poverty. But perhaps it could be said that his identity as an "LGBTI" is connected to the capital this label carries in a new global economy where the wealthy West values such identities and understands them as vulnerable. Since 2008, the UNHCR has accepted "fear of persecution on the grounds of sexual orientation or gender identity" as a category to qualify a person as a refugee. And several developed countries — particularly the United States and the Nordic countries — have expressly committed themselves to taking in LGBTI refugees. Individuals in these countries, furthermore, have felt the solidarity-pull of conscience. As their own battles for equality have been won, they have cast their eyes elsewhere and noted, with heightened consciousness, the troubling new global equation that seems to have come into play: as these rights are confirmed in some parts of the world, they are denied, increasingly, in others.

When Peter found himself orphaned, the LGBTI ticket became his surest means of survival. But while the initial connections he made on Facebook may have been transactive — they may, even, have been sexual — they were also affective. Over time and over space, from the "Nellies" of late Victorian England to the voguing houses of Harlem or the third-gender hijra communities in India, there has been a constant to the gay, or queer, communities that develop among outcasts: alternate families form, intergenerationally, and bonds are cemented by the way people become "mothers" and "daughters" or "brothers" and "sisters."

When Joseph claims Peter as his daughter in Nairobi's refugee community, he is taking on a responsibility, but also laying claim to a relationship that he hopes will sustain him, emotionally and materially, in the absence of the family that rejected him: he will mentor Peter, and Peter no doubt will help him with the limited funds he has garnered due to the relative celebrity of his kidnapping and torture case. Likewise, when Peter calls Apollo "Big Bro," it might be the expedient expression of affection, but it is so much more, a hankering for the family that has been lost to him — along with, of course, this family's support, emotional as well as material.

In this digital era, where such families are virtual as well as physical, and where social media allows for a dizzy fast-tracking of intimacy, it was inevitable that Peter would acquire an American "father." His name is Shane Phillips, and he is a gay born-again Christian in his late forties. He is an itinerant construction worker who lives in Phoenix, Arizona.

Phillips told me his story through a Skype conversation in September 2015. He had been bothered by the evangelical right's role in Uganda since hearing about it in 2009, and had felt compelled, as a "loving conservative," to show Africans a different face of Christianity. He set up a philanthropic organization called One World Voice, the goal of which, he told me, was "to save more lives than anyone has on the planet, because nobody tries in the world anymore." He wanted to set up a safe space for resettled refugees in Phoenix: he offered himself as Peter's "anchor host" in the United States should he be resettled there, and his dream was for Peter to be this centre's first resident.

He became increasingly horrified by the stories he was hearing from Uganda, and the prospects of what he called, on his website, an imminent "genocide" against gays in the country. He raised $500 from a local pastor "to get a few people out" and began connecting with Ugandan networks on Facebook. "I was delivering pizzas for Papa Joe's at the time. Every bit of extra money I made went towards getting people out of Kampala."

Phillips is one of several U.S.-based activists who have become involved in this way: the most prominent, Melanie Nathan, set up a "Rescue Fund to Help LGBT People Escape Africa." Such initiatives have been slammed by the leaders of the Ugandan LGBTI movement, who feel they offer impossible promises to Ugandans who then find themselves stranded in Nairobi. But Phillips counters, with emotion, that every person he has helped personally — he estimates there are about forty — was in a life-and-death situation, and that many, like Peter, were suicidal.

Immediately after Museveni signed the anti-homosexuality bill into law in February 2014, Philips was online, looking for people to help. He found a man named C.K., whom Peter was staying with at the time. Phillips sent enough money to get both C.K. and Peter to Nairobi to apply for asylum, but when C.K. stole the money and left Peter in the lurch, Phillips and Peter began messaging each other. "When Peter told me his story," Phillips told me, "I said to him, 'I promise you I'll be a father to you for the rest of your life, no matter what it takes. I will never leave your side.'"

Phillips told me that Peter was one of three young men with whom he had developed such close bonds. And indeed, Peter — who is emotionally labile — does talk about Phillips as a lifesaver. Certainly, as one listened to both their accounts, one heard the strains of many father-son relationships in the guilt trips and manipulations, but Phillips was true to his word: they messaged almost daily, and had weekly scheduled audio conversations. They met, finally, when Philips visited Africa for the first time in February 2015 and spent a few days in Nairobi. Both men wept, and in the photographs posted online, Philips — bald and bulky and full of expansive American bonhomie — towers over his beaming ward.

Phillips's material contributions to Peter's welfare were small: he said he was overextended already with the support he gave to others. But when Peter began messaging him in early December 2014 with increasingly panicky messages, stories of nightmares, and threats of suicide, Phillips felt compelled to act. "It was clear that he had to get out," Phillips told me. "I sent him the funds for a bus fare and told him to go to Nairobi."

Richard Lusimbo, a leader of Sexual Minorities Uganda (SMUG), the main Ugandan LGBTI rights organization, had arranged a small relief grant for Peter after his ordeal. Lusimbo told me he was shocked when he heard about Peter's departure. "He had, of course, been thrown out of home, and he was the victim of this terrible assault, but everything had seemed to be working since then. The police had found his attacker, and the courts had ruled against him. The community had rallied around Peter, he was back in school. His story seemed to be moving towards a positive resolution, and we need those stories to balance out the 'Worst Country in the World for Gays' stereotype."

Why, I asked Peter, did he leave?

He confirmed that Shane Phillips had counselled him to do so, but he insisted that, at that point, he really did have no other option. He had received the grant from SMUG, but he had felt compelled to send some of it home to his family to buy cattle, and besides, he had nowhere safe to stay in Kampala until he went back to boarding school, as he had fallen out with Apollo over money.

His benefactor wanted a cut of the SMUG funding. To exacerbate Peter's insecurity, he heard that his assailant had been released from jail: "I felt it was only a matter of time before they would come and get me."

4.

On my last day in Nairobi, I went to watch the Ark dance troupe perform at a resort in the Ngong foothills; the kind of place city dwellers with a little money to spare might drive out to for a drink and a weekend nyama choma (barbecued meat) lunch or a swim. Brightly painted in blues and yellows with exclamatory Swahili slogans on the walls, it consisted of a series of open thatched pavilions set around a huge swimming pool. It was not far from one of the Ark Communes houses, and a group of the Ugandans had become friendly with the owner after patronizing it a couple of times. They had been rehearsing their troupe to participate in a dance competition on World Refugee Day (they would win), and they proposed to the club's owner that they provide entertainment on Sunday afternoons. The troupe raised funds for costumes and rehearsed diligently: they were a huge success, and the club paid them KSh15,000 ($150) a gig.

Peter was one of the dancers — in the contemporary rather than the traditional category, he told me. He, like all the others, was passionate about the project: "It gives us a chance to express ourselves, as Ugandans and as LGBTIs. To be proud of being Ugandans too!" It also created a space where they could connect with local Kenyans, rather than living in fear. The way they could express themselves "as LGBTIs," he elaborated, was by using the cover of dance to "gay it up a bit," and, in the traditional dances, to make space for those members who were "girly" to play the female roles, on the pretext that they were an all-male troupe.

I noticed, however, that as the Ugandans arrived at the club, there were several women too. The group's "PRO," Zacky, explained to me that the club owners had become solicitous and had not invited them for several weeks: in fact, they were performing for free this afternoon, just so they could show me what they did. Zacky worried that the owner — or the patrons — might have become uncomfortable with the "girly" factor and begun to suspect that they were gay: for this reason, they had decided to rope in a group of female Ugandan LGBTI refugees to join them, as cover.

Zacky was the compère. "Representing!" he shouted into a microphone from a DJ box, wraparound sunglasses glued to his face. "Rep-REEEE-SEN-TING!!!!" He pumped the beat, a Ugandan jive, and after shouting the gerund a few more times, he finally came to its object: "Rep-re-sen-ting UUUUUUUUUU-gan-da!" and the dancers emerged, in a line, led by James, the muscular lead dancer whose ability to transform the traditional Baganda hip-swing into a rapid-fire twerk stole the show. The men were bare-chested, with cinched traditional skirts hitched high up the thigh; the three women were decidedly more self-conscious.

The program ran through traditional dances from across Uganda, and threw in some stirring gospel numbers too. The crowd was thin that afternoon, just a handful of punters who giggled occasionally and applauded politely and seemed to be enjoying themselves. No matter. The Ugandans had brought their own home crowd, and each dance was enthusiastically documented by a battery of smart phones: clips would be all over social media that evening. The troupe was loving it, and I was too. The showstopper was a song from the north, called "Eteso Emali," in which a prospective groom bargains a bride price with his betrothed's family. The strapping James played the groom, mugging burlesque; Peter's boyfriend, George, was the bride's father, his lanky charm sheathed in a long white robe. Rabia, the only female resident at the Ark Communes, played the bride, and another woman her mother. Both women were exceptionally — and no doubt accurately — diffident in their roles, and I wondered, with a giggle, whether the guys had restrained themselves similarly when they played the female parts, before they felt compelled to bring these shy beards into the show.

In another song, "Okuzala Kujjagana," which means "the joy of having a child," a mother counsels her betrothed daughter about the pleasures of parenthood. There was something terribly poignant about the manifest satisfaction these queer outsiders took in performing such family-making rituals, given the way that most of them had been cast out of their own.

Peter had participated in these traditional dances, albeit with his braids held in check by the knitted red beanie. His expression was more earnest, more interior, than most of the others, and he chose to keep his T-shirt on. He re-emerged, during the costume change, in his skinny green jeans, the beanie still in place, to dance the "contemporary music" interludes, either alone or with one other guy. His moves seemed carefully planned at first, and were striking in the way they swirled a macho hip hop staccato style into something more feminine.

Peter would leave the Ark Communes house in October 2015, because it was beginning to seem unsafe; indeed, two weeks after his departure the remaining Ark residents would face off against a mob and would have to call the UNHCR to help evacuate them. The agency would put them up in a hotel for four days and then advise them to live in smaller, and less conspicuous, groups.

Four months later, on 1 February 2016, Peter would finally receive his "mandate" from the UNHCR and the Kenyan government: he would now have formal refugee status, and the right to work and study in Kenya. But he and the other LGBTI Ugandans would also be told that, due to the UNHCR's limited resources, financial assistance to them would be discontinued by the middle of the year. While there would be some aid available to those with viable business plans, and emergency funding to particularly vulnerable people in need, most would have to fend for themselves — or move up to the Kakuma refugee camp.

But all this was to come. Now, on a mild August afternoon, as the speakers pumped hectic bass into the Ngong foothills, Peter closed his eyes and allowed himself to be shaped by the beat. His movements became less structured and more fluid. The earnest expression he had worn in the traditional dances released itself into a beatific smile.

No one was watching him but me.

Part II

BEING AND BELONGING

THE KEEPERS OF SECRETS
Elnathan John

"This is the market," Michael* says as we drive slowly around pot-holes, past stalls made of wood and zinc, which lean against each other in ways that seem both steady and precarious. People weave their way through the slush of mud made by rain and cars, defiantly wading through dirt roads, leaping from one more-solid patch of ground to another. Bodies touch in the now reduced space, seeking access to stalls selling vegetables or meat or huge piles of crayfish. Motorcycles groan through the thick meal of mud, sliding some-times before regaining balance. By the roadside, women invite cus-tomers to haggle over piles of large, muddy, freshly harvested yams.

Cars parked along the single narrow road leading into this sub-urban district of Nigeria's Federal Capital Territory (FCT),** make traffic slower than usual, and Michael suggests that although Tukur, who we are here to see, is right here in the market, we would be better off driving to his house five minutes away to wait for him.

---

* Some names and identifying details in this essay have been changed to protect the privacy of individuals.
** The FCT, a federal territory located in the centre of Nigeria and created in 1976 out of three states in central Nigeria, houses Abuja, the city which replaced Lagos in 1991 as the capital of the country.

As we are approaching, Tukur walks toward us with two others, smiling and looking away when his eyes meet Michael, the social worker who provides health and social services to the small community of 'yan daudu that Tukur heads.

"Why have you kept us waiting?" an irritated Michael asks in Hausa.

"I was trying to get the others; they were all in their shops, tending to their wares."

Tukur struts confidently as he leads us through a shortcut in front of a mosque. We walk even further into the quiet, deserted area and stop at a painted room, the first in a row of uncompleted shops and buildings.

Following Tukur, the two lanky men file into the room behind us, removing their shoes at the door as he walks out again to get the others. They are not as coy or as playful as Tukur and seem so nervous that I start to feel nervous too. I tell them I am speaking to 'yan daudu in the area and would like to chat with them about their lives and challenges.

I speak for about ten minutes with Garba, originally from Jos — the darker and lankier of the two. He is pensive and mentions that he "like[s] the company of fellow men" and has no ma'amala or hulda (dealings) with women. Because he is not specifically identifying as 'dan daudu, I am a bit thrown off — all the questions I need to ask are premised on this self-identification.

I ask him why he came to the FCT from Jos.

"There is just one reason," he begins. "The death of my elder sister, who was everything and everyone to me. I never knew struggle or worry or want when she was alive. But then she died suddenly, and I was left with no one to care for me. And I can't burden my old parents. So I came to Abuja to look for money for myself and to help my parents."

"Do your parents know you have male friends?" I ask, referring to men he may be having sex with.

"Yes. They know."

"How do they react to it?"

"Well, they know I am a calm, peace-loving person who does not steal. They know I am not one who pays heed to women. Because women, they can lure one who spends a lot of time with them into having undesirable traits, traits unlike that of a man — they can make a man begin to act like a woman ..."

I am confused by his statement.

"How do you mean?"

"Okay. For example, I am a man, a young man, no? It can happen that constant mixing with women can change my orientation from the way God made me — a man — to become something else, to become something like a 'dan daudu, for example."

My eyes light up with this. Although a lot of his friends in the MSM (men who have sex with men) association Garba belongs to are 'yan daudu, and he admits to having sex with men, he refuses to be identified as a 'dan daudu.

"How can God make you a man and you decide to become a woman?" he says. His explanation betrays a slight irritation with effeminacy, with what he perceives as an unnatural gender non-conformism. He has no problem with same-sex relations.

Garba's attitude provides an important perspective into who a 'dan daudu is. For him, it is primarily a gender and occupational categorization; he sees them simply as men who do things that women ought to be doing or in the manner of women, whether it is cooking, referring to themselves with female pronouns or adjectives (or with feminine names), or walking and talking like women. I ask him how he views 'yan daudu.

"Well, I view them as people, friends, males. I do not see them as female in any way. I view them as persons created by Allah as males, as He also has created me a male. I disregard their effeminacy and see them as males, brothers of mine."

He pauses for a short while and adds, "Because everything the 'dan daudu has [in his body], I have. Why should I consider him female?"

I am a bit surprised that he is saying this sitting in the room of Tukur, a self-identified 'dan daudu. Shortly after, Tukur returns with five other young men.

FEMININE MEN

Although Tukur's small room is full of clutter — pots, pans, plates, bowls, clothes, bags — ten of us find a way to fit in. Before long, the restless young men give up trying to look dignified and well-behaved in the presence of their uwa (mother), as Michael playfully calls Tukur. Giggling, play fighting, and innuendoes ensue between four of the young men sitting on one of Tukur's thin mattresses.

I begin speaking to Mahmud, a handsome twenty-five-year-old whose texturized hair glistens even in the dimly lit room, a permanent grin on his face as he shares his stories with risqué humour.

He sells food, as do many of the 'yan daudu in the room, an occupation, at least in many parts of Muslim northern Nigeria, considered women's work.

There are various translations of the term 'dan daudu (singular, the plural being 'yan daudu) from the simplistic "male homosexual" to "transgendering men." The history of the term has been connected to the practice of Bori, a religion of possession by a pantheon of spirits. Fremont Besmer, in the book *Horses, Musicians and Gods*, writes that "daudu is a praise name for the Bori spirit 'dan Galadima."

'Yan daudu such as Tukur and his "children" belong to a close-knit socio-vocational network of men who are effeminate in manner and appearance and who engage in trades — such as cooking and selling food in the market — traditionally associated with women. Most, in addition to their given male names, have female names used by fellow 'yan daudu.

As I travel between Kano and the FCT, where I am connecting with and speaking to men like Tukur, I have in my bag the book

Allah Made Us: Sexual Outlaws in an Islamic African City, by the academic Rudolf Pell Gaudio, one of the most important contemporary texts dealing with 'yan daudu. Gaudio calls 'yan daudu "feminine men," a description I find apt, cleverly avoiding as it does the common oversexualization (and thus oversimplification) of the 'yan daudu as persons who are *merely* homosexuals. To be a 'dan daudu is certainly not simply to have sex with men, as I have noted in the case of Garba, who even finds the way 'yan daudu carry themselves undesirable, to the extent of calling it an unfortunate choice caused by bad influences. Garba also used the phrase "a glitch in God's creation, people made with a defect."

This is an entire subculture complete with codes, speech patterns, coquettish banter, songs and dances, and, sometimes, religious practices as conducted in the Hausa religious order of spirit possession, Bori (what Tukur calls "hawan iska," "the mounting of spirits").

This coquettish banter, complete with clever innuendoes and what is considered among the Hausa "al'ada na mata," or the habits and customs of women, is perhaps the primary distinguishing factor between other, masculine, men who have sex with men and 'yan daudu. The manner in which the 'yan daudu play and speak is also a feature that makes some heterosexual Hausa men consider them frivolous, as Hausa culture greatly values politeness, modesty, and formality.

"You know sometimes, when people see you speak and act like a woman, they want nothing to do with you, they withdraw from you," Tukur explains.

Mahmud is especially adept at clever flirtatious talk and often sends the room roaring in laughter with his retorts. When I ask him if he ever wants a wife, a woman, he responds, "Oh yes! As it is done to me, so also I will do to her."

Tukur has introduced me by phone to a man called Babajo who leads a state-wide association of 'yan daudu in Kano. Although

Babajo is happy to show me the ways of 'yan daudu and Bori when I arrive in Kano, he begins with a caveat.

"You know, we are Hausa people and this, our thing [daudu], is cultural and some traditions are not supposed to be told out in the open because we need to guard our dignity and that of our families. Some [NGO] people come with cameras and other recording equipment and that is why many of us shy away from speaking to [strangers]."

I assure him that I have no intention of using any cameras, and he promises to show me everything, even taking me to the home of a Bori priest if I feel so inclined, to see how spirit possession is practised.

While many of the activities that 'yan daudu are engaged in run contrary to orthodox Islam as practised in Nigeria — having sex with men and Bori dances and spirit possession — all the 'yan daudu I have spoken to in Kano, Kaduna, and the FCT profess Islam and try hard, at least in public, not to appear to go against the teachings of the religion.

In a restaurant I visited operated by a 'dan daudu and frequented by 'yan daudu in the FCT, one of the first conversations I overheard between the young men was an argument about Islamic theology, with at least one person quoting a Hadith, a tradition of the prophet, to prove his point.

DOING HARKA

"My name is Tukur and, honestly, I do harka."

This is the openness with which my relationship with Tukur begins. It is a refreshing start to our conversation, and I am relieved that I don't have to work my way to one of the questions to which I ultimately want an answer: whether or not, like most 'yan daudu I know, he offers sex to masculine men.

Mahmud also admits that one of the main reasons he moved from Kano to Abuja was to do harka, or have sex with men, for money. He goes on to regale me with tales of his escapades and the few times he almost got in trouble. There is no shyness as he tells his stories because he considers masculine men to be hypocrites who condemn homosexuality in the open but seek male lovers in private.

"There is an alhaji in my neighbourhood in Kano who has four wives and many children and wallahi, there is no day he does not do harka with many boys."

Homosexuality is spoken of in Hausa society in a way that does not make assumptions of identity based on sexuality. Homosexuality, especially among males, is seen as what men (even 'yan daudu) *do*, not something that they *are*.

I ask if there are any among the 'yan daudu who do not do harka.

"Of course," Mahmud replies.

Tukur has a son and tells me that if Allah wills it, he would love to remarry. His first marriage ended because people brought gossip to his wife that her husband did harka.

"When she confronted me," he says, "I told her: 'So will you believe what people say about me and doing harka instead of trusting me [when I say I don't]?'"

Ultimately, Tukur divorced her because she would not let go of her suspicions.

HIDING IN PLAIN SIGHT

Speaking of the importance of taking care of one's parents, Garba talks about young men who, in deference to their parents, do not identify as 'yan daudu in the towns in which their families live. Many have to move to bigger or different cities to live freely for fear that they would become to their parents "abun kunya" (an object of shame). Among those who choose to stay are 'yan daudun riga — closeted 'yan daudu assuming or discarding effeminacy depending on who they are with.

Since the adoption of the Sharia penal code (a strict version of Islamic law) in many states in northern Nigeria starting from the year 2000, many 'yan daudu have had to, at least temporarily, go underground. Certainly all have had to become more circumspect, especially in socializing with fellow 'yan daudu or meeting potential sex partners. For example, in Kano, the wealthiest and most populous state in northern Nigeria, a committee set up by then governor Rabiu Musa Kwankwaso to review the Sharia penal code that was about to be passed in November 2000 recommended that the government introduce measures for the "rehabilitation of the destitute as well as persons of easy virtue like karuwai [prostitutes], 'yan daudu [transvestites] and kawalai [pimps]."

One of the implications of this was that for the religious morality vigilantes — which became organized into hisba, unarmed paramilitary units backed by law, in states like Kano — the 'yan daudu suddenly became more visible. 'Yan daudu could no longer hold open parties or send out open invitations to their celebrations. Their "female" occupations were under threat, and many of them felt uncomfortable doing work that easily identified them. At least for the 'yan daudu I spoke to who came to the FCT from Kano, Kaduna, Jos, and Adamawa, business patronage in Sharia states began to drop, with a few finding themselves unable to survive.

One week has passed since I first met Tukur. In that time, he received a visitor, a 'dan daudu known to him in his community. The young man said he felt ill and needed assistance.

"I opened my bag, gave him some pills, and told him to rest a bit," Tukur later tells me.

Then Tukur, who had returned from receiving cash contributions for a party, dropped his bag containing his phone and a wad of naira notes and went to take a shower. When he returned, the bag, together with the money and phone, was gone. So, although we had arranged to meet the next weekend, I could not reach him on his number.

I decide to take a cab to his neighbourhood anyway since I know the general area where the 'yan daudu sell food. The driver drops me close to the market, and I make my way on foot to try to find Tukur. I do not want to attract attention with the cab, and, moreover, many of the roads are not navigable by car.

Inside the community market I take a wrong turn that leads me to the very end of the market, close to a swamp. Turning left and walking further to see if the road would lead me back, I find myself in what looks like a dead end. In the distance I see an open stall with tables. *That could be them*, I think. Moving closer, none of the men I see look familiar, and I take the next turn.

From behind me people begin to shout, asking me to come back.

"What for?" I yell to one of the young boys.

"They are calling you."

"Who is calling me?"

Then I see three large men begin to run toward me, one with his hand underneath his shirt. I immediately realize the danger I am in and walk calmly toward them. I am afraid that walking ahead might immediately lead to a chase. They might think I am a thief or something.

"Who are you and where are you going?" the biggest and oldest looking of the men demands.

"I am just looking for a thoroughfare. I think I may have lost my way."

"Where are you from? What are you doing here?"

By now the three men have become six, and some begin to draw out shiny daggers and knives.

"I am a journalist, looking for Tukur, slim like that, a bit light-skinned, who cooks somewhere around here."

"Do you not have his phone number?"

"I do, but it is switched off."

"Well, we do not know any Tukur."

One younger man is coming toward me, pulling his dagger from a sheath at his waist. I quickly show them my little notepad in an attempt to prove I am only a writer.

"It is that 'dan daudu he is looking for," a voice behind me says.

"How do you know?" the older man asks.

"Did you not see him flailing his hands when he was trying to describe the Tukur?"

The older man turns to me.

"Is the Tukur a 'dan daudu?"

"Yes," I say, trying to smile. The younger man who was coming toward me has completely unsheathed his dagger and wants to strike at me.

"Stop it," the older man orders. "We will not spill this one's blood." Then he continues, "If you are looking for 'yan daudu, go right ahead turn left and go straight down. Their stalls are all there. You can't miss it."

I thank him and began to walk away quickly.

"You know when we see a grown man like you snooping around here, we are bound to react," he says to me, explaining why I was almost attacked.

I follow his directions, and as soon as I reach the general area he described, I ask a young man selling provisions where the 'yan daudu are.

"Just right ahead," he says, pointing to the exact location where, it turns out, Bulus, who was in the room when I first came to see Tukur, is sitting. His eyes widen into a smile as I approach, and he quickly offers me a chair to sit. He asks me if I want some food, and I politely decline. I tell him of my encounter, and he explains to me that I walked into a drug den called Jungle, where marijuana and other drugs are being split up for retail.

Tukur eventually shows up, and I walk with him to a quiet single-room dwelling close to the stream where there are three older women.

"This is one of our rooms where community members hang out away from the public glare," he explains as we sit on mats. He motions with his head for the women to leave.

"Who are those women?" I ask as soon as they leave.

"Oh," he sighs and smiles. "They work with us."

"How do you mean?"

He hesitates. "The women, I brought them from a village far on the outskirts of town. They stay with us to give the illusion of men and women mixing. You know, if someone comes here to ask, 'Do these people do funny things?' those around will be doubtful and say, 'We see women with them all the time.'"

The 'yan daudu recognize that although many tolerate them, especially in the Hausa communities in the FCT and its environs, there is danger in taking this for granted.

After our chat, Tukur gets up to walk me to where my cab is parked. As he steps out, one of the 'yan daudu sitting in front of the room playfully calls him amarya, bride. I wonder if the party Tukur told me he had attended all weekend has anything to do with this. But I decide not to ask.

His red silk shirt shimmers in the sun as he sashays, smartly putting one foot in front of the other. He is catcalled by young men in the stalls we pass. While he does not respond to any of them, he smiles shyly each time.

UNFAVOURABLE TESTIMONY

Michael, who introduced me to Tukur and the FCT 'yan daudu, works for an Abuja-based NGO that provides free specialized health services to men who have sex with men, among others. His group organizes outreach programs (in which Tukur takes active part) for MSMs in and around Abuja, which include safe sex campaigns.

Ifeanyi, the director of the NGO, explained to me why it was important to have a separate, dedicated clinic that treats and cares for MSMs with HIV/AIDS and other sexually transmitted infections. Many doctors in government hospitals are unfamiliar with certain conditions peculiar to MSMs. Some patients have reported doctors being shocked at seeing anal warts, leading to intrusive questioning about sexual habits, mockery, and chastisement. Many who were receiving treatment in those hospitals stopped going because they were afraid of being outed. The NGO's clinic treats men (as well as female sex workers and female partners of MSMs) with dignity and discretion.

According to the director, officials of the Nigerian secret police, or DSS (Department of State Security), as well as the Abuja Environmental Protection Board (AEPB) — notorious for arresting, abducting, and manhandling women suspected of being sex workers in Abuja — have conducted searches and arrested and interrogated him, and on at least one occasion men working with the AEPB physically assaulted him.

In January 2014, the Same Sex Marriage (Prohibition) Act was signed into law by then president Goodluck Jonathan, adding to the existing body of laws criminalizing same-sex marriage, prescribing ten to fourteen years for offences such as public display of same-sex affection and operating gay societies. Shortly thereafter, officials of the DSS began snooping around in some communities in the FCT, looking for gays. Tukur was identified as the head of the association of MSMs in his community and interrogated.

"When they realized that no one in the area was [concerned with] outing us as homosexuals or complaining about our existence, they did not bother us so much," Tukur explains.

No one gave mummunan shaida, unfavourable testimony, about the 'yan daudu.

"You know the Hausa [MSM] community is not like the English [-speaking MSM] community. Here we don't have problems [of outing]."

Tukur's room was searched, and when the DSS officers found condoms and lube, his explanation, without giving away the fact that he had sex with men, was that he was trying to protect himself from STIs and HIV.

KUNYA

The difference in the general attitude toward 'yan daudu in Hausa communities beyond the reach of Sharia and the attitude toward MSMs or gay persons in non-Hausa communities is significant. 'Yan daudu have never taken the relative tolerance they have enjoyed over many decades for granted. Like most in Hausaland, they understand the concept of kunya.

Kunya, shamefacedness, is an essential part of daily life and interaction. Kunya makes it vulgar to be loud, lousy, or forward in public places, in the presence of one's superiors or elders, and, especially for women, in the presence of one's husband, parents, or other men. 'Yan daudu particularly assume the role of women here in public life, exhibiting shyness and being respectful.

Mahmud, the boldest in the room the first time I came to Tukur's house, had taken a few minutes before he admitted to me that he did harka in addition to his business of selling food. Tukur waded in to encourage him, saying, "This is not a discussion where you need kunya."

Mahmud also explained what prompted his move to the FCT from Kano in 2014.

"If you are in your neighbourhood, you will not feel free to do what you desire, because of your relatives and parents and especially because there are hypocrites who will out you to your family. So I advised myself, packed a bag, left Kano, and came to Abuja."

In explaining how he navigated the spaces between his male clients and the conservative Kano community he had lived in with his parents, Mahmud talked about protecting his dignity and the dignity of his clients, many of whom are respectable members of the community — masculine men with wives and children.

"I kneel to greet every older man in my community I pass on the road. You see those five daily prayers? None of them passes by without me in the mosque. So, you see, if anyone should publicly accuse me [of harka], there will be doubts in people's minds and they will say, it can't be that a respectable, religious young man like that will do [harka]."

Mahmud used the term "kare mutunci," or guarding one's dignity, several times. Kare mutunci often saved him from falling into the hands of zealots seeking to attack people doing harka. He related how at least one of his friends who did not know how to kare mutunci was attacked when he was entrapped by a young man who did not have ido,* or eyes. Against Mahmud's advice, his friend had propositioned the heterosexual or "blind" man, and when the man said yes they fixed an appointment. Mahmud's friend was lured to a remote place and thoroughly beaten by many "blind" men.

While the FCT is by far a safer place for 'yan daudu in particular, physical violence against MSMs does exist, albeit less so than in non-Hausa communities. Michael told me of a recent case where an MSM from southern Nigeria was found days after he had been stabbed to death in his room. Because the murderer had locked him in from the outside, no one realized he was lying in a pool of his own blood until the body began to smell.

I asked him what the police did about it.

"You know, once they know this person is [gay], they don't take the matter seriously."

I wake up to several of Tukur's phone calls on Monday morning, one week after our chat in the little room.

"Are you okay?" I ask when I call him back.

"There was a raid, and several of our people have been arrested."

"Where?"

"In Abuja city. Three of them are still locked up. They ransacked their houses and took them away."

---

* The term "mai ido" or "one who has eyes" is used by 'yan daudu to refer to men who have sex with men, while "makaho" or "blind person" is used to refer to men who do not have sex with men.

I ask him to call the human rights department of an NGO that helps members of the Nigerian LGBT community. He tells me that he has called a senior, influential politician who often discreetly supports 'yan daudu in times of crises. He fears that the matter will be unduly escalated if it is treated as a human rights issue.

"The man has sent his lawyer and is making some contacts," he says.

Later that night Tukur calls to say the three men have been released.

"We thank Allah," he says.

SURVIVING UNDERGROUND

By far the most important problem facing almost all the 'yan daudu I spoke to was economic. It is interesting that not a single one of them specifically mentioned the anti-gay law as an issue before I brought it up.

While those who had left Kano, Adamawa, and Bauchi and moved to the FCT did not necessarily do so because of any persecution based on their gender nonconformism, many found it increasingly difficult to make a living while freely doing "women's work." Before the adoption of Sharia, many 'yan daudu in places such as Kano, for example, once had thriving feminine businesses; some have had to either change their line of work or move because of the fear of the hisba paramilitary. The majority, however, simply carry on as discreetly as they can.

Tukur's position as leader of a community of 'yan daudu in the FCT gives him a clear picture of another very serious problem.

"The issue of illnesses, HIV/AIDS especially, seriously affects our community," he says.

In the first week that I spoke to Tukur, four men in his MSM community alone died. He often has to organize contributions to help send people to the hospital or, sometimes, for those who are too ill and probably dying, back home to their villages. He works very closely with the NGO that provides free health services and health awareness outreach in the Hausa MSM community in the FCT.

"Illiteracy complicates our problem in the Hausa community, and a lot of [sexual health] awareness brought by the NGOs reaches the English-speaking MSM community faster than it reaches us in the Hausa community. We have a peculiar problem."

Tukur speaks English and sometimes translates messages brought by NGOs to members of his community. He estimates that the Hausa-speaking MSM community far outnumbers the English-speaking one.

The public health implication of criminalizing the uninhibited delivery of sexual health services and education to MSMs is easily imagined. Driving people underground only complicates the fight against HIV/AIDS in a society that can be very sexually fluid. The morality argument presented by proponents of criminalization of same-sex relations falls flat in the face of reality: we are much more sexually connected to each other than we think.

NEW TOWN, OLD TOWN

The freshly painted bridges and bright street lights of Kano welcome me to the city as I arrive late at night. The car I was travelling in had to make a few stops on the way, and it is midnight by the time I check into my room at the hotel.

The receptionist makes sure I see the rules: No drinking alcohol. No prostitutes. No girlfriends. No gambling. The room has an ashtray, a prayer mat, and a clear bold sign showing the kibla, the direction of the Ka'aba, situated in Islam's most sacred mosque in the Saudi Arabian city of Mecca.

The following evening, I am finally able to meet with Magaji, designated to speak with me by Babajo, the head of one of the main associations of 'yan daudu in Kano.

Magaji decides that we should leave the area where my hotel is and find some other place to chat. We take the ubiquitous commercial tricycle — called A Daidaita Sahu in Kano — to Sabon Gari (literally New Town), a densely populated part of Kano where most of the "visitors," those who are not originally from Kano, or non-Muslims, live and where it is permitted to sell alcohol. He stops by the roadside, where there are tables of vendors selling provisions by lantern light and people cooking. He orders noodles and eggs.

There, by the side of the road, are five veiled women and twice as many young men, chatting and smoking. This part of town has a lot of 'yan daudu as well as women who live alone in rented houses or lodges, Magaji tells me.

Magaji is visibly uncomfortable and seems to be in a hurry to leave. He does not have any of the mannerisms of the 'yan daudu I have been speaking to. I wonder if he really is a 'dan daudu or just a masculine friend of Babajo who does harka — if perhaps that is why he is uncomfortable.

"Since the hisba came, it became harder to meet openly or hold parties," he says. "Sometimes, right there in the midst of the ['yan daudu] event, there will be a snitch who will tell the hisba the exact location and before long they show up."

A few metres away from us, one of the veiled women, with a gold tooth that usually marks out a person who has made the pilgrimage to Mecca, attracts the attention of many of the men who take turns to drag her away and whisper in her ear. She brushes each one aside after a few minutes, playfully telling one of them, "You have no dignity!"

Magaji does not sell food or do any "women's work." He is a student at a tertiary institution, studying for a combined law diploma that includes both Sharia and secular law. As part of his course he had been attached to a magistrate's court and had personally seen as many as four men convicted of offences related to homosexuality, mostly outed by "blind" men they had allegedly propositioned.

While he is not a Bori adherent or practitioner, he admits to attending a Bori dance or two when he has the time. He is too busy with his studies to keep track of 'yan daudu events.

I am confused because Magaji is referring to 'yan daudu and to masculine men who do harka in the third person — "them" and "those who do harka." I stop asking him about 'yan daudu and begin chatting about the city in general.

As I notice him loosening up a bit, I say to him, "Forgive me, but do you mind if I ask a potentially rude question?"

"Please ask," he says.

"You yourself do not do harka, do you?"

"Honestly, I do. But I keep a low profile. I don't like identifying with it."

"So you are not 'dan daudu, then?"

"Well ..."

He hesitates.

"Or are you perhaps a 'dan daudu mai riga?"

For the first time since we met this evening, Magaji's face widens into a smile, and he reflexively high-fives me after I suggest he might be a closeted (literally "shirted") 'dan daudu.

"Well, yes. You can say that. In fact, if I see a 'dan daudu in public, or someone shows me that he has eyes, I avoid the person. I have to safeguard myself. When I go to a safe place in the midst of 'yan daudu then I can relax and do my thing. But once I leave such a place, I begin to act normal."

I ask him if he knew when the Same Sex Marriage (Prohibition) Act was passed in 2014.

"Oh, the fourteen years' law? Yes."

"Do you think it affected people here in Kano?" I ask.

"It did. Everyone became more cautious."

He pays for his food as soon as he finishes eating.

As we walk to the road he explains to me how some 'yan daudu would become sexually involved with each other, a phenomenon called kifi (literally to flip or turn upside down), a word also used to refer to lesbians.

"It is just like two women," he says. "In fact, it is exactly like two women because you know the 'dan daudu is not just like a woman but like the most girlish woman. Who will [penetrate] whom? They are not compatible, just like two women are not. It becomes laughable."

We walk to the main road, and he asks me if I have any more questions before we get an A Daidaita Sahu out of Sabon Gari. He does not want anyone overhearing our conversation.

KEEPERS OF SECRETS

Magaji alights a few junctions before my stop and bids me farewell. I am thinking of all that I have learned about the guardians of a culture that is threatened by contemporary incarnations of religion. I worry that someday, as Nigerian society becomes increasingly conservative, the spaces currently occupied by the 'yan daudu might disappear altogether. However, it is not lost on me that they owe their protection in part to the fact that they are discreet — keepers of secrets. Secrets of civilians; secrets of some highly placed politicians and individuals who would never risk being exposed; secrets of society.

When I get back to Abuja, Tukur calls to inform me that the lively Mahmud is ill and bedridden. I tell him to send my wishes of a quick recovery to Mahmud, and he promises to do so.

"I would have come to see him, but I am travelling for a bit tomorrow. Maybe when I return. Also my number will be unavailable for a short while."

He prays excitedly: "May Allah let you conclude [your dealings] well. May Allah protect you from mishaps on the way. May Allah bring you back safely."

A MURDER IN CLOVELLY*

Bongani Kona

There are things photographs of missing persons can't tell you. The proportions of their bodies for one, or how they walk, whether or not they have a limp — the details people remember. They belong to that genre of official photographs — the headshot used for an ID, say, or a driver's licence — which privilege function over form. But the information they convey is almost always incomplete.

For months I've carried a manila folder with a photograph of Rosemary Theron, a thirty-nine-year-old clown and stilt walker who went missing in early March 2013. In the black-and-white headshot, which circulated in a few of the local papers during the seven months of her disappearance, she's wearing an Eskimo hat and a tight smile. You get no sense of how small she was, yet it is the thing everyone close to her remembers. "She was tiny, man, like this," one policeman said to me. It was a description I heard many times. Standing at 1.45 metres tall, Rosemary Theron was, as one friend said, "a pretty little pixie woman."

Rosemary, or Rosie to her wide circle of friends and acquaintances, vanished on March 7, 2013. It was a Thursday, late summer

---

* Some names and identifying details in this essay have been changed to protect the privacy of individuals.

in Cape Town, and she was last seen getting into a silver Mercedes driven by an unidentified white male with long blond hair. She wore blue jeans, brown boots, and a brown synthetic leather waistcoat lined with fur. According to the missing person's report filed at Fish Hoek police station a few days later, she went out to meet friends for drinks at around seven o'clock that evening and never returned.

"I think she's left us," her eldest daughter, Phoenix Racing Cloud, is said to have told the police during the early days of the investigation into her disappearance. Phoenix said her mother had done that sort of thing before. When Phoenix was five years old, Rosemary had left her with her father — the couple had split up by this point — and went to live in Chile. When Rosemary came back months later, she was pregnant with her second child.

In the months before her disappearance, Rosemary and Phoenix weren't on good terms. The tension in their relationship had been caused by the arrival of Phoenix's boyfriend, Kyle Maspero, a lanky seventeen-year-old high school dropout with short-cropped brown hair and tattoos running down the length of his left arm.

Something about him didn't seem right. He'd been in and out of different schools, and each time he was forced to leave because of some disciplinary violation, usually drug related. Once, when he was in Grade 8 at Knysna High School, he was expelled after he tested positive for *dagga* (marijuana) and *tik* (crystal methamphetamine). Another time, while attending Weltevreeden Park Primary School in Johannesburg — he'd been sent there as punishment for his part in starting a fire at a neighbour's house — he was served with eleven formal disciplinary charge sheets. The school sent him to a child psychiatrist and a family therapist, to no avail.

By all accounts Rosemary didn't get on with Kyle. She had asked Phoenix many times to break off the relationship, but she refused. Phoenix would later say it was because she was "deeply in love with him." She and Kyle had met in 2010 in Knysna, a sparsely populated town approximately five hundred kilometres from Cape Town, where she lived with her father, Ivan, during the school term. Phoenix and Kyle started seeing each other in 2012, and as with many intense teenage romances, it seemed like some cosmic force had pulled them together.

They had both come from troubled childhoods. Kyle, the last of three children, had been virtually abandoned by his father since birth. His father was a violent alcoholic, and he was physically and emotionally abusive towards Kyle's mother and his older siblings. After Kyle was born the relationship between his parents deteriorated even further. Twice his mother tried to commit suicide. His father accused her of lying about Kyle's paternity. He didn't believe the boy was his son and remained cold and emotionally distant towards him. After his parents' divorce — which came within a year of his birth — Kyle maintained minimal contact with his father. His mother died suddenly when he was seven years old, and by the time things were getting serious with Phoenix he had already been through a couple of foster homes and was displaying obvious behavioural problems.

Phoenix similarly felt neglected as a child. She was born at the back of a caravan, and for the first three years of her life the family travelled across the country in a horse-drawn cart. This was in the mid to late nineties, a time of relative optimism and ease in South Africa. Her parents identified themselves as hippies and made a living selling puppets. They took psychedelic drugs and went to trance parties. When Rosemary came back from Chile, she took Phoenix to go and live with her at Transformation Farm, a hippie colony in Knysna. And like Phoenix, Rosemary's second child, a boy, was also born at the back of a caravan.

Early in 2013 Phoenix found out she was pregnant, but she decided not to have the baby. By this time she and Kyle were living together in Rosemary's rented house in Clovelly — a seaside suburb overlooking the Atlantic Ocean, roughly an hour's train ride from Cape Town. This new domestic arrangement, however, didn't sit well with any of them. Fights with Rosemary were constant. Kyle would later claim that it was because Rosemary objected that he took to cleaning her house. The relationship soon reached its lowest when Rosemary kicked them out of the house days before she vanished. Stranded with no place to go, Phoenix and Kyle decided to camp out on the mountains that rim the Cape Peninsula. Rosemary only allowed them back in after they were robbed on their way to work one morning.

Phoenix and Kyle worked as surfing instructors for a middle-aged white couple who run one of the surfing schools by the beachfront. Edward and Liz had known Phoenix since she was "about fifteen or sixteen years old." They called her by her second name, Jess, and they remember her as "sweet," "lovable," and "a compassionate little girl." She worked with them during the school holidays when she came down from Knysna. "She helped give lessons, and she enjoyed it. She was good with people," Edward said.

Sometime in 2012, after Phoenix had matriculated from high school, Edward and Liz got a phone call from her inquiring about job prospects. "She said she wants to move to Cape Town, but will only be allowed to do so if she has work for her and her boyfriend," Liz said. "And that's when we were told about Kyle."

Though they had never met Kyle, Edward and Liz agreed to give him a job. But when Phoenix showed up with Kyle she wasn't the same person they had known. She had always been reserved, but this time she appeared "submissive and quiet." Liz also had her reservations about Kyle. "There was just … a feeling. He didn't do anything to trigger it; there was just something about him."

"Prior to knowing Kyle," Edward said, "she was super friendly and open, happy. It was obvious she had issues, but it didn't appear to be worse than any other teenager's." Despite their reservations, Edward and Liz resolved not to intervene and were content to let the young couple be. "At work, they didn't really do much, if we had a customer they would take them out [to the water]. But otherwise they would just hang out at the beach. They were always together, you'd see them there on the beach, looking a little lonely," Liz said.

The exact chronology of what happened on the morning of Rosemary's disappearance is still in dispute. In Kyle's version of events, he and Phoenix got up at nine o'clock that morning and smoked dagga in bed. He then smoked tik in the bathroom before making coffee for the two of them. Rosemary stayed in bed until midmorning when she was awakened by the clatter of plates as Kyle was cleaning the kitchen. She scolded him for making noise, and the two got into an argument when he told her she should not sleep so late.

But according to Phoenix they left for work that morning and then walked back home at around noon to make lunch. They found Rosemary sitting with Julan, an old friend of hers from Kommertjie, a neighbourhood close by. Rosemary and Julan had met at a trance festival in Rustler's Valley in the Free State in 1997, and both of them had lived at Transformation Farm in 2000.

Rosemary's second child had, a few years earlier, been sent to live with his father in Chile, and she'd since had a baby girl, Willow. That afternoon another argument ensued after she asked Phoenix to look after her baby sister because she had to get to a casting. Phoenix resented her mother for having neglected her as a child and harboured some painful memories. She had been sexually abused by a family friend when she was six, and again a few years later when they were living in the garage of someone's house in Muizenberg.

Phoenix had accused Rosemary many times of displaying the same level of neglect with her baby sister. The girl was eight years old and she still hadn't been to school. Her cognitive development lagged behind girls her age, and she had hardly any social skills. "She growled and acted like a monkey," Phoenix would later say.

Rosemary said she couldn't afford to send Willow to school. Phoenix was familiar with her mother's excuses and her recurring troubles with money. In the early 2000s, when the family was down and out, living in an abandoned school bus, she kept having to change schools. In Grade 3 she attended Observatory Primary

School, but Rosemary pulled her out because she was behind on payments. Later that year Phoenix completed her Grade 3 at a school in Tyger Valley, but again she had to stop going because Rosemary couldn't afford the fees.

It was about this time that Rosemary fell pregnant with Willow. The day she came back from the hospital, Phoenix said, Rosemary handed her the baby and went straight to sleep. The following year Phoenix started using the Clonrad home schooling system to teach herself, and in between she managed babysitting duties, washing and changing Willow's nappies and giving her her bottles at night.

All that accumulation of emotion boiled over that afternoon. It was only after Julan intervened that peace was restored. Phoenix and Kyle agreed to babysit, and Julan drove Rosemary to the Fish Hoek train station down the road. That would be the last time Julan ever saw Rosemary alive. Seven months later, on October 3, when Kyle and Phoenix appeared at Simon's Town Magistrates Court as accused number two and three respectively in the murder of Rosemary Theron, Julan would play back the events of that afternoon. In a letter she addressed to Rosemary before her funeral she wrote: "Over and over in my mind I think of ways I could have stopped that happening. So you would be alive and my friend Racy [Phoenix] would be free to surf and lead her life, saving up for college."

Late in March 2013, Chris Clark, a British freelance travel journalist living in Cape Town, received a knock on his front door. Standing at the other side was Detective Chris Cloete, a heavyset man with fleshy cheeks and a thin moustache.

As a junior in the South African Police Service (SAPS), back in the early nineties, Detective Cloete had been part of the task force assembled to apprehend the "Station Strangler," Norman Azval Simons, the rapist and serial killer who murdered young boys and buried them in shallow, sandy graves. He had been pulled into the search for Rosemary after the initial investigation had failed to yield any concrete leads. The story the police had to go on was that she was last seen getting into a silver Mercedes driven by an unidentified white male. Hours of scouring CCTV footage of cars that matched that description had led Detective Cloete to Chris's front door.

Detective Cloete showed him a black-and-white photograph of Rosemary with the words, "missing March 7, 2013" scrawled underneath with a blue ballpoint pen, and he asked if Chris knew her. "Yes," Chris said, though he had met her only once before, in December 2012. Someone had talked him and his girlfriend into giving Rosemary a ride back home after a performing job in Claremont. With her small frame perched in the backseat, Rosemary had cut a forlorn figure that night. She looked out of the side window and in between long silences talked about her passion for being a clown.

"But how do I come into all of this?" Chris asked. At this point Detective Cloete pulled out a photograph of him driving a Mercedes with a Rosemary lookalike sitting in the passenger's seat. The car was a rental, and Detective Cloete had traced it to Chris's address in Lakeside. The grainy photograph had been captured on CCTV, minutes after Rosemary was said to have been last seen leaving her house.

In the following days, though, the cloud of suspicion around Chris lifted after statements accounting for his whereabouts were supplied by his father, his girlfriend, and a mutual friend of Rosemary's. It was, however, one of several dead ends the investigation into Rosemary's disappearance would come up against before any kind of breakthrough.

The investigation itself had gotten off to a slow start. Phoenix and Kyle had hesitated about going to the police. "It was me who took the kids to the police station originally," Julan said. "They wanted to put it off." She had come looking for Rosemary two days later, on Saturday, March 9. She was leaving soon for AfrikaBurn, and Rosemary had promised to paint a banner for her, but Julan hadn't heard from her. None of her other friends had seen or heard from Rosemary either, and her phone went straight to voice mail. Phoenix and Kyle told Julan that they had last seen Rosemary on Thursday.

Edward and Liz said they didn't know Rosemary was missing until much later. Even though Phoenix didn't say anything to them, they do remember getting a feeling that something was wrong when she and Kyle "absolutely devoured a piece of bread" in the shop. "There was only about half a loaf, and we saw the way they ate, and that's when we realized there's definitely a problem," Liz said. Phoenix later told them that Rosemary had vanished.

"Mom does this to me," Phoenix had said.

"And we said, 'Look, she left you with no money, she's not answering her cellphone. This is not a common scenario.'"

Despite the pressure from Edward and Liz to report the matter to the police, Phoenix remained obstinate about her decision. "I don't want any trouble for my mom," she said.

As the days wore on, Julan eventually succeeded in getting Phoenix and Kyle to file a missing person's report at Fish Hoek police station. The details contained in that report — the story about the silver Mercedes and the man with long blond hair — would lay the groundwork for count two in the matter between the State and Phoenix Racing Cloud Theron: attempting to defeat the course of justice.

Clovelly has a population of less than six hundred inhabitants, and it falls under the jurisdiction of Fish Hoek Police Station, the large suburb next to it. In the language of the former apartheid times, both are white areas — affluent and with spacious housing. According to census data from 2011, 88 percent of Clovelly's residents are white, and the majority of households have an average monthly income falling between a low of R12,800 ($777) and a high of R25,600 ($1,547).

Bordering Fish Hoek and Clovelly is Ocean View, a Coloured (mixed-race) township where four out of five residents have not finished high school and nearly a third of the population is unemployed. To complete the picture, also close by is Masiphumelele, a black township with approximately eight thousand residents housed in shacks. In an article published in *Business Day*, writer and academic Jonny Steinberg writes, "an astounding three-quarters of those aged between twenty and twenty-four are unemployed. Of those who do work, most earn between R400 ($25) and R800 ($50) a month. One in two will still not have work at the age of thirty."

The problem with reading statistics is that sometimes they can cloud situations instead of shedding light. Disembarking from train number 0131 at Fish Hoek station one cold morning in June 2015, I got an inkling of what it might mean for such disparate communities to live side by side. Fish Hoek has the subdued, lethargic feel of a holiday town, the kind of place where no one is in any great hurry. The business owners and the pensioners who fill the coffee shops and restaurants dotted along the beachfront and the main road are white, and the labour force — the shop attendants, waiters, cleaners, et cetera — is made up almost exclusively of people who are not.

South Africa's apartheid past is not only written into its geography but also embedded in the distribution of life chances — how one lives and how one dies. It's true to say that the distribution of violence remains split along racial lines. In 2012, for instance, SAPS recorded a total of 15,609 murders across the country, which evens out to forty-three a day. In the same period, 607,877 other cases of violent crime — assault, rape, robbery, and attempted murder — were reported to the SAPS. Those numbers are high by any measure. But a closer inspection of the homicide statistics tells you more about where violence is clustered. Half of the murders in 2012 occurred in only 13 percent of the police precincts located in under-resourced and overcrowded urban neighbourhoods. An overwhelming number of the casualties are young black men under the age of thirty, and most have not finished secondary school.

This explains the disturbing undercurrent that coursed through the media coverage of the murder of Rosemary Theron. The intense media interest was in part because all the protagonists were white. The question that went undeclared, but could nonetheless be discerned by reading between the lines, was how could these things happen to white people? The reams of press coverage that followed after Phoenix and Kyle were arrested and charged with Rosemary's murder were devoted to answering that question, and it seemed as if it was Rosemary's unorthodox lifestyle that was on trial.

Even though I caught the case after the wave of media interest had subsided, the people closest to Rosemary, neighbours and friends, still felt aggrieved at how she had been portrayed. They felt Rosemary — and by extension, they themselves — had been harshly judged. Consequently, they erected a wall of silence and barricaded themselves in. As one member of the Clovelly community phrased it, they "wouldn't agree to be part of anything sensationalist." To find my way around the silence, I talked to a number of officials who were involved in the case — police officers, attorneys, court clerks, etc. — and consulted a considerable trail of paperwork.

That morning I had come to visit Detective Cloete at the Fish Hoek police station, a rambling brick building along the main road. He wore a short-sleeved shirt and black trousers. We sat in his second-floor office, furnished with just the basics — a desk, telephone, chairs, and metal cupboards housing several case files. By leaning across from Detective Cloete's window, you can see the outer edge of the house Rosemary rented in Clovelly. He had kept an eye on Phoenix and Kyle during the seven months of Rosemary's disappearance.

Detective Cloete believed the story about the man in the silver Mercedes, and he had followed up a dozen leads, all of which led to a dead end. From the background check he had run on Rosemary, he could tell that her life had been unstable. Rosemary had been in a few abusive relationships in the past, and on more than one occasion had ended at the police station, filing a charge. "She was one of those people, you know, a hippie," he said.

It's a description I heard many times in news reports and from those close to her who were willing to talk. "Rosemary, she seemed like ... a free spirit. I don't want to be rude, but like a hippie, an out there kind of person," one hairdresser said. Janine, a shop assistant with short blond hair and square-rimmed glasses, said the same thing. "My impression was, oh no this poor girl, her mom's gone missing, who's probably into drugs. That was my impression. Her mom was eccentric — barefoot, dreadlocks, so when she went missing people didn't think too much of it."

Detective Cloete said he empathized with Phoenix. Once, when they were going over the facts of the case in his office, she broke down and cried. At the time he thought it was because she was taking considerable strain, with her mom gone and having to look after her baby sister. Despite everything, however, she was diligent in her duties. She met with welfare officials and took Willow to school every day and washed her clothes. She also helped with her homework. "It was like they [Phoenix and Kyle] were the parents to that little girl. Even the way they spoke to her. I remember I was in Shoprite and I heard her saying to her, 'You can pick whatever you want for supper this evening,'" Janine said. "The mother seemed like the flaky one."

Parallel to the police investigation, the search for Rosemary galvanized a large number of her friends and acquaintances. They also raised money for the upkeep of her children. "When we heard she had gone missing, we were a bit unsure," said Felicity, a shop manager in Fish Hoek who was close to Rosemary. "We were almost suspicious to see why or what had happened. We tried to get some psychics in to see where she was, and they couldn't give us answers, although two said she was no longer with us."

They considered all the possible leads, no matter how outlandish. That maybe she'd had a serious head injury and she was checked into a hospital anonymously. Or maybe that she'd had a nervous breakdown and was locked in an institution somewhere. Or that maybe she had been kidnapped and was being held against her will. All these avenues of inquiry led nowhere. Rosemary had taken none of her belongings, and the evidence at hand, such as her bank account remaining idle since the time of her disappearance, pointed to one logical conclusion: that she was no longer alive.

Out of all of Rosemary's friends committed to finding her, Richard Kraak appears to have been the most devoted. He and Rosemary had met each other in the early nineties, and they had remained close friends for more than twenty years. Detective Cloete said if it wasn't for Kraak's persistence — he phoned constantly to check up on the progress of the investigation — the mystery of Rosemary's disappearance might not have been solved.

I spoke to Richard three times over the phone, and each time he rebuffed my request for an interview. During the seven months of Rosemary's disappearance, and for a brief while after Phoenix and Kyle were arrested, Richard was generous with the press. Naively so, perhaps.

In her controversial book, *The Journalist and the Murderer*, Janet Malcolm says there is something "morally indefensible" at the heart of journalism. The journalist, Malcolm says, is a "kind of confidence man, preying on people's vanity, ignorance, or loneliness, gaining their trust and betraying them without remorse." Richard would not be so quick to disagree. He felt betrayed by most journalists and how they gleefully portrayed Rosemary's life as rudderless and self-destructive.

There is, however, something heartbreakingly sad about reading his extensive Facebook updates from that year.

Initially, there was optimism, a belief that Rosemary will soon be found.

Rosemary's friends are the most wonderful people in the world and launched an extensive search for her that covered the southern peninsula. Several private cars full of her friends and family went out and physically searched the southern peninsula and spread posters of her and visited old haunts like Redhill, Scarborough, Glencairne, Clovelly, Fish Hoek. Kommetje Cape Town. People on horseback were organized to specially look for her. Bike riders were asked what they saw around Silvermine dam and other remote places where they go every day, people walking their dogs were asked etc. etc.

Later that month, as the investigation kept turning up blind alleys, optimism gave way to anger.

ROSEMARY THERON UPDATE: the friends and family of Rosie are still making an effort to get more info about how Rosie could just vanish. THE MOST IMPORTANT LEAD WE HAVE HAS NOT BEEN EXPLAINED. ROSIE WAS PICKED UP ON THURS EVE/night BY A BLONDE MAN IN A FANCY SILVERISH CAR. IT COULD BE A MERC. FANCY MIGHT MEAN SPORTY. THE CAR COULD BE MOST LIKELY A MERC NO OLDER THAN 10yrs. AFTER 20000 plus shares of rosemary missing person information AND HUNDREDS OF THOUSANDS OF THEIR FRIENDS SEEING IT ON THEIR NEWS FEEDS HOW IS IT THAT NO ONE HAS COME FORWARD WITH INFORMATION CONCERNING THAT OCCASION/PERSON.

Then in August, after five months of desperately searching for Rosemary, despair set in.

I am still tired so this will be brief. A trail of leads is still being followed by the police and privately. In other words every effort is still being made to find her. Leads have not run dry. I thank everyone that has generously helped to find rosemary. I would like to remind you here that I have played a central role because I was thrust into it, and duty bound as a friend to make an effort to find rosemary. A circle of hearts needs to be defined so that I can take my place in the circle and not be close to the centre anymore.

Despite the intense activity swirling around them, Phoenix and Kyle maintained a veneer of calm. Four months after Rosemary's disappearance, they moved from Clovelly to Gordon's Bay, a harbour town nearly sixty kilometres away. They rented a small flat on the same property where Godfrey Scheepers, a friend of theirs, lived. Shortly after completing the move Phoenix posted the following message:

> Hey mom! We have moved to a beautiful new home that is so fancy Willow is blown away everyday! She has her own swimming pool and her school is epic. We talk about you every day and pray for you wherever you are, don't worry about us we are happy and strong. You'll be happy to know that [Willow] cleans her room everyday on her own accord (she even says please and thank you) and her teachers think she is the loveliest girl in the world. We love you.

In September 2013, seven months after Rosemary went missing, when it seemed as if the mystery of her disappearance would never be solved, twenty-year-old Godfrey Scheepers, accused number one, walked into a police station and said she had been murdered and he knew where to find the body.

In the sworn statement he gave to the police, Godfrey said Phoenix and Kyle had murdered Rosemary and buried the body in the backyard of the house in Clovelly. Then, when they moved to Gordon's Bay, he had helped Kyle to dig up Rosemary's decomposed body, which they dumped in an open veld near the intersection of Baden Powell Drive and Strandfontein Road. Rosemary's body lay there for another two months before Godfrey came forward after falling out with Kyle.

The next day, one of the newspaper headlines read: "Missing Woman Found: Murder."

As writers — to quote Joan Didion — we're inclined to "look for the sermon in the suicide, for the social or moral lesson in the murder of five." We turn over the details of a murder, searching for hidden clues and the wider meanings it might yield about the society we live in. But browsing through the *Cape Argus* the day after Phoenix had been sentenced to twenty years in jail, somehow the sermon — the social or moral lesson — seemed to elude me.

Judge Robert Henney, who presided over the case at the Western Cape High Court, said, "this is a very serious offence — the planned and premeditated murder of her mother. The sentence agreed upon is, in my view, just. This case is where she killed someone ... her mother, and it will haunt her for the rest of her life."

Murder arouses incomprehension. The first question everyone asks is why? As an explanation, Phoenix's attorneys told the Cape High Court that "the accused was neglected by the deceased virtually since birth."

After Rosemary had come back from Chile she met and married a man named Darren, and they moved into a house in Knysna. But the relationship was turbulent from the start and fights were constant. Once Rosemary called the police on Darren and had him arrested because he was physically abusive. They separated for a short while but got back together again, this time in Cape Town.

Phoenix said they drifted from place to place, and Rosemary's on-and-off relationship with Darren finally disintegrated after he developed a tik habit. The fighting and arguing got so bad that one time they got thrown out of the cramped flat they were renting in Table View. It was around this time that Phoenix says she was sexually abused a second time by her grandmother's boyfriend. She was nine years old when it happened.

When she was twelve, Rosemary sent Phoenix to live with her father. She commuted between Knysna — where she was being home-schooled by her father — and Cape Town. She re-entered formal schooling again when she was sixteen. Her father sent her to Knysna High School, where, according to various reports, she excelled at art and English. She also became the editor of the school newspaper.

She'd also started drinking and experimenting with dagga. She said she smoked joints laced with mandrax — a sedative that was banned in 1977 and is one of the most widely used drugs in Cape Town. Phoenix also said that every time she travelled back to Cape Town she would go to trance parties with her mother. Sometimes they would drink and use recreational drugs together. Janine said sometimes the "mom looked more high than the kids."

It was close to this time that Phoenix met Kyle, and she said she "fell deeply in love with him." Kyle had been using tik for a while by then. When they moved to Rosemary's place in Clovelly, they found the house in a mess. Dirty dishes were piled up in the kitchen and clothes strewn across the floor. Phoenix said it was obvious that her mother was on something.

In Phoenix's version of events, that afternoon on March 7, after the fight with Rosemary, is when Kyle came up with the plan to kill her. At first Kyle claimed he couldn't remember anything about that day because of his excessive drug use. The weekend before the murder, he said he felt ill and couldn't sleep and had lost his appetite. The only lucid memory is days after, of him standing in a hole with a sheet lying next to him. The court sent him for psychiatric assessment at Valkenberg Hospital, and it was found that he "does not suffer from a psychiatric disorder. His memory loss for the days preceding and including the period of alleged offence was not due to any psychiatric or pathological cause." He later admitted that he did say to Phoenix that "it would be better if Rosemary wasn't around."

According to Phoenix, after Rosemary left to go to her casting, Kyle was angry. He said he was going to hog-tie her when she came back. "We'll have to run away from everyone for the rest of our lives if we do that," Phoenix said. To which Kyle said they would at least have each other and they could take Willow with them.

In the guilty plea bargain she signed, Phoenix claimed Kyle had said he was going to kill Rosemary, but he couldn't do it alone. He needed help. The plan they came up with was that Phoenix would distract her mother and Kyle would come up from behind and strangle Rosemary. In the evening they put Willow to bed, and Kyle got the rope, duct tape, and black plastic bags.

When Rosemary came back that evening, she was in a good mood because of a man she'd met. Phoenix walked up to her and gave her a hug. "I'm sorry for fighting with you earlier," she said to her mother. As planned, Kyle came up from behind and strangled Rosemary. He strangled her for four minutes. When he finally let go of the rope, Rosemary "emitted a huge sigh" before she lost consciousness.

It was Phoenix who cleaned up her mother's blood, which had dripped from her ears as she died. They covered her body in a blanket and black bags and moved the body to the backyard. The backyard was littered with garbage, and they hid the body under a tarpaulin. Two days later, they moved the body again. This time they dug a hole in the ground and buried her.

The trauma caused by Rosemary's disappearance and the discovery of her body nearly destroyed the Theron family. Two weeks after Rosemary's memorial service, her sister, Angelique, hanged herself. Rosemary's mother also sank into a severe depression and is now permanently institutionalized. Willow had to undergo therapeutic counselling and is now living with foster parents in Knysna.

Judge-President John Hlophe, who handed down Kyle's sentence at the Western Cape High Court in December 2015, described Rosemary's murder as a "brutal killing" and sentenced Kyle to the same prison term as Phoenix: eighteen years' imprisonment with five years suspended on condition that he not be found guilty of a similar offence to the one he has been convicted for. The sentence would have been twenty years in prison, but the judge reasoned that Kyle had already spent two years under house arrest.

The tragedy of Rosemary Theron first caught my interest when I saw a photograph of Phoenix standing in the dock at the Western Cape High Court. In the photograph she's wearing a beige hoodie, and she looks lost and completely alone: a lone survivor washed ashore after a shipwreck. I wanted to find out more about the world she had come from. To find, as Didion says, the social or moral lesson.

The penultimate paragraph in the letter Julan wrote to Rosemary reads: "I am so sad Rosie, so sad to lose you as a friend and so sad to have you murdered this way and with your beautiful girl helping to kill you. I feel so much sadness and pain; I don't know when it will go away." Maybe that is the lesson, and there is nothing more that needs to be said than that.

DREAM CHASERS: MSINGI SASIS'S NAIROBI NIGHTS

INTRODUCTION
by Otieno Owino

In daylight hours, downtown Nairobi bustles. The streets are filled with pedestrians, traders display goods on shop windows, hawkers sell merchandise, and matatus jam the roads, with music blaring from built-in speakers and crew loudly beckoning passengers. There is urgency in the movement, as if everybody is chasing something that they *must* get in order for life to continue. It is not possible to live in this city and not be caught up within or moved by this rhythm. But the urgency sometimes only reinforces the fleeting nature of urban existence. Nairobians chase dreams: mostly opportunities for a better life. If the city, then, is a collection of individual dreams, then every individual's dream must remain important for the city to stay important.

As night encroaches, Nairobi slows down, the frenetic city retreats into itself, reclaiming its spaces so that any human presence appears to disrupt the emptiness. At night, only the bold and courageous venture out. It is these people whom Msingi Sasis's camera captures. A security guard looks on as a man fixes a broken-down car; a matatu crew chats as they wait for the vehicle to fill with late-night passengers; a lone man carries a heavy load on his head. These images capture the individual truth of our collective endeavours, that in the pursuit of our dreams we are severely alone. Despite the bleak monochrome, there is every shade of humanity here: in the shared umbrella, in the heads bowed in conversation. Sasis captures a quality of night that is both sinister and romantic. Within this interplay of shades of grey, figures lurk just beyond the glare of the street lights; they are hooded against the cold and are seen taking cover from the rain. They are what is left behind when the bustle has died down. They are a reflection of the enduring spirit of the city, pushing through long nights into the early hours to keep its rhythm alive. And if the subjects reveal the elements of human nature, then the buildings that form the background convey the mood and the atmosphere of city life. There is a subtle beauty that lingers despite apparent solitude.

Sasis' work captures a side of Nairobi that is not often part of mainstream narrative. He wanders through every corner of the city in the depth of the night till dawn. His photographs bear witness to a quest for the truth hidden in the city's silent hours and to his ability to capture continuous motion and rhythms in unexpected places.

1°17'S 36°49'E. It's twilight. I'm out on the Nairobi streets. Follow a shapeshifting instinct. Searching between shadows and silhouettes. 50-millimetre f1.4 lens distilling truths. A certain solitude within crowds affords me the luxury to penetrate into the metaphysics of this city. And suddenly my eyes are opened childlike to the wonders of a whole new world. This sprawling city glitters like thousands of diamonds scattered upon an edge of the Great Rift Valley.

Cityscape mise-en-scène. Asphalt jungle. Struggle for existence. Survival of the fittest. A street hawker's wisdom whispered in my ears, "Man, blessed is the rat that thrives in this place." Once only the seed of an idea, many distant nightfalls ago, is now fully grown into a metropolis. Trafficking in versions of abyss and paradise. Parallaxes. Acts of ontology. Fields of vision. Optical intimacies.

These Nairobi nights. Strangers playing out their innermost dramas in public. The seduction of electric lights upon the senses. The nights all look the same. You'll be lost in an eternal gaze that intoxicates the eyes. Perhaps a formula for the hypnotic.

Msingi Sasis
Nairobi, 2015–2016

BORDER CROSSINGS

Sarita Ranchod

In my first year of formal schooling, at an Indian primary school, *Janet and John* was our first prescribed text. I was five years old and already reading by then, thanks to my mother, Ba, sourcing early learning reading and writing materials via the school where she worked. I was intimately familiar with *Hansel and Gretel*, *Goldilocks*, *Snow White*, *Cinderella*, *Rupert the Bear*, and *Noddy* — all of the characters in these books coming from bedtime reading or storytelling by one of my aunts, or from library books. Gollywog from *Noddy* was the only Black character I encountered in these stories from my early childhood.

It was the 1970s, and we lived on the Cape Flats, a dusty, windy part of Cape Town, in a small Indian township called Gatesville, situated between various Coloured townships that together made up Athlone. The Black African townships of Gugulethu and Nyanga were nearby — all of us located somewhere along Klipfontein Road, an arterial road linking Black and white, working-class and middle-class Cape Town.

Aside from Ba and Bapu, Dada (my paternal grandfather), Ma (my paternal grandmother), and me, our household also consisted of Maya foi, Bapu's youngest sister, nine years older than me and more of a sister than an aunt, and Sarla foi, Bapu's second youngest sister, who was an education student at the university reserved for Indians in Durban and only came home during holidays. There was also Arvind Kaka, Bapu's youngest brother, a medical student at the University of Cape Town. My sister, Amisha, ten years my junior, was not yet born. We all lived in the same council house owned by my paternal grandparents, the first and only home that Ma and Dada would ever own. They had lived in many houses, moving their nine children often over the years, always as tenants.

This was home, and it was filled to the brim.

At that time Gatesville was a working-class neighbourhood populated with uniform council houses and blocks of social housing–type flats. On the streets of our neighbourhood, the ever-present South African Defence Force soldiers and their Casspirs — mine-ambush defence vehicles — patrolled in search of the slightest sign of trouble fomenting. During the early 1980s it wasn't unusual to find high school students hiding behind the vibracrete boundary wall of our house, safely out of sight, having outmanoeuvred police chasing them.

Ba, one of eight children, had grown up in Kensington, a working-class Coloured neighbourhood in Cape Town. Her father, my Ajabapa, ran a small shoe repair shop in their neighbourhood. Ajima, Ba's mother, was not a talker, and my most abiding memories of her are my fascination with the freckles on her face and the delicious, spicy chicken soup she would make and send over when I was sick.

Although it was unusual for women of Indian origin in Cape Town to hold down full-time jobs at that time, Ba worked around the corner from home, first as secretary and later administrator at Rylands High School, a progressive state school where both students and staff were actively involved in anti-apartheid activism.

As a small child, before I was old enough to go to crèche, I would sometimes escape Ma's attention and wander off from home to visit Ba at school. All the staff knew me from an early age, including the cleaners, caretakers, teachers, and senior staff, whom I would greet individually by name, prefixed by aunty or uncle. Along with the adventure of escaping Ma, there was the thrill, once I was at the school, of sometimes being allowed into the fascinating bulk stationery supply room that adjoined Ba's office: a space whose contents were full of promise and possibility.

My grandmother, Ma, had nine children. Bapu, my father, her fifth and middle child, was born when she was just twenty-one. Between her large girth, her strong, clear views, and her determined presence, Ma was hard to miss. She was intelligent and loved paging through women's magazines — especially the kind that had knitting patterns and recipes. She always had the radio on in the background, listening to radio dramas while she cooked and baked.

Ma wore a sari and a large, vermilion kanku dot on her forehead below the sharp middle path of her long, thin black hair that never greyed, thoroughly oiled, gathered together by a bun-making accessory that suggested more hair than she had, the bun completed by a hairnet to keep it all in tidy order. For as long as I knew her, and in pictures that preceded my birth, Ma never changed her hairstyle.

Ma was willing to sacrifice everything to ensure that those of her children with academic leanings were able to access higher education so that they would have a better life than hers. From the rented homes the family lived in while in Port Elizabeth and in Cape Town, she made savoury Indian snacks — gaathia, chevro, sev, and samosas — that Bapu and Arvind kaka sold door to door to supplement the family income and to ensure that her two high-achieving oldest sons were able to take up places at university with family support.

While Ma loved her children fiercely, and they her, it always seemed clear that my father, Bapu, was her least favourite child. He was born dark-skinned in a family of siblings who reflected an incredibly wide colour palette, from pale skin and light eyes to his own definitively dark shade of coffee. Family members described him as Ma's black sheep or her kaaryu, black child.

After completing school, Bapu trained as a photo-lithographer and worked at printing presses for most of my childhood. It was a world filled with letters, typefaces, the thrilling magic of Letraset transfers, typesetting, beautifully textured paper, and the language of layout, design, and artwork. My childhood was punctuated with mysterious darkrooms, terms like positives and negatives, kerning, bromides, pixels, fonts, and Pantone — words not heard in everyday language — and the heady smell of hot ink burning onto paper, creating magical printed works through massive hot, loud printing presses at the factories where he worked.

Bapu often did unpaid overtime at Esquire Press, laying out and designing underground and banned anti-apartheid materials, including posters and leaflets. Esquire was also where community-based newspapers such as *Grassroots* — publications that frequently attracted the ire of the government — were laid out and printed.

For his time, Bapu was relatively progressive. He vocally opposed the caste system in a community where it was so normalized that the local mandir — a Hindu temple — had been funded and built by the Mochi caste, traditionally shoemakers, the largest Gujarati caste in Cape Town and the one into which we were born. Being opposed to the prevailing social system, however, meant that Bapu was somewhat ostracized. This had its advantages. My parents' social circle, not defined by caste, religion, or race, meant mine was an uncommonly open and diverse childhood for the time and place.

Bapu refused to set foot in the mandir. On the few occasions he attended, such as on Diwali, he opted for us to attend the other Gujarati mandir in the area, the one that had been created by an amalgamation of several minority castes. But there were inconsistencies between Bapu's caste politics and what he required of me as his daughter. Despite his refusal to set foot in the local mandir, he expected me to attend so I would grow up with an understanding of

Hindu religious and cultural practices of the kind my parents had grown up with.

I was my father's daughter and shared his refusal to conform, constantly questioning not only the concept of religion itself but also the hypocrisy of Bapu expecting me to attend a mandir he refused to set foot in. If I had to be there, I needed explanations for all of the various rituals and ceremonies practised in Sanskrit or Gujarati. But few congregants were able to explain why we did certain things or their significance, at least, not in ways that would help me understand why they or we did what we did. My questioning of everything only served to infuriate Bapu, and as I grew older it became the source of many of our clashes.

It took me years to make sense of this. Perhaps the truth was that Bapu was unable to respond because he himself did not always know the answers. Those around me followed religion and ritual because that was what their parents did, or that was what they had always done, what they had been taught or raised to do, often without knowing or understanding the meaning and significance, other than creating and sustaining a sense of community.

The cultural instruction my parents required of me included after-school classes in Gujarati, held in a block of classrooms at Ba's school. On weekdays, I would walk there and back with friends who either attended language lessons with me or went to the after-school madrasa that was held in a different block of classrooms at the same time. On weekends, the school served as a Christian church.

Despite the school being close to where we lived, my friends and I sometimes took a shortcut through a hole cut into the fence. We would cut through the series of social housing blocks of flats and enter through the hole in the fence that served as border between the flats and the school. On hot days, if I was alone and the opportunity presented itself, I would walk through fresh-smelling, damp bed linens on the washing lines of the flat-dwellers to cool down.

At Gujarati school I was supposed to learn to speak, understand, read, and write the language. My teachers were women volunteers from the local community who were not always comfortable speaking English, and were certainly not trained as teachers. I was not a focused student and would rather have spent my after-school hours reading books or lying in the sun by my mother's sister Madhu masi's pool — halfway between Ba's school and home.

Several children in my Gujarati classes spoke the language at home, and as a result were better students. But my grandparents, colonial British subjects from India who had arrived in South Africa as little children with their parents, were fluent in both English and Gujarati and largely engaged with us, and the outside world, in English. They also spoke and understood some Xhosa, the language of the African population of the Eastern Cape where they had both grown up and raised their family before migrating to Cape Town in the 1960s.

Ma and Dada spoke to their contemporaries in Gujarati, but Bapu and most of his siblings, with the exception of his two older sisters, Kanta Foi and Bhanu Foi, despite having gone to Gujarati school, had not learned to speak Gujarati, although they understood it sufficiently. This, despite their father leading religious Hindu ceremonies in Gujarati and Sanskrit as an unofficial priest.

As girls born in the 1940s, and unquestionably destined for marriage, my two oldest aunts, Kanta Foi and Bhanu Foi, were forced with the assumption that they would need to converse with their in-laws in Gujarati. Ma's other two daughters were born much later, in the late 1950s and the 1960s, part of a younger, more modern and anglicized generation for whom speaking fluent Gujarati was less of a life requirement.

Gujarati school life was one I compartmentalized from other parts of life. I enjoyed being able to read and write an entirely different script and language system. I enjoyed that when I went to the mandir I could choose the Gujarati prayer books to follow mantras and Bhajans, but it felt like more of a "nice to have" than a cornerstone. It was more important to my parents that I behave respectfully towards my elders, folding my hands together and greeting them with a "Namaste" on arrival and departure.

And, of course, there was the added bonus of being able to understand overheard conversations between Ma and others, in person or over the phone, and the shared moments of us lighting the lamp and singing devotional Bhajans and mantras at home. Even with my limited Gujarati I understood that the Bhajans praised nature's elements, giving thanks for the universe, the moon, the sun, and the stars, speaking directly to some of the magic and wonder of childhood.

My love of reading went far beyond schoolbooks and bedtime stories. For much of my early childhood, the library was a cream-coloured single-decker bus that arrived one afternoon a week and parked in a lot across the way from Ba's school. Its arrival was the highlight of my week: the specially outfitted bus my gateway into wider worlds, its contents my refuge. I never missed a single visit.

The books I borrowed transported me to fascinating, sometimes disturbing, worlds, enabling me to journey into realities more interesting than my own. I could do anything, go anywhere. There were no rules, boundaries, or borders. There were no entry requirements, passports, or visas for this form of travel, and I needed no permission to read what I liked.

Through books I could find others who saw the world through similar lenses, confirming that I was part of something more, something bigger. My gateway to exploring the unknown and understanding the world, reading fed my desire for something much more than my immediate reality of living in ironically named Gatesville.

It was around the age of ten, driven by my mother, that I first visited a brick and mortar library. Athlone library, the closest to where we lived, was newly built and situated in a working-class Coloured township about five kilometres away from our neighbourhood, along the straight line that was Klipfontein Road, close to a busy transport hub, the street corners overflowing with fruit and vegetable hawkers selling their wares, enticing customers with their specials. The most common cries were "Aartappels-uiwe-tamaties," potatoes-onions-tomatoes, called out as if it were one word in a very particular Cape Flats Afrikaans dialect.

Early on I figured out a way to borrow more than the stipulated number of books from the library, sufficient to feed my voracious appetite. I signed up both my parents to Cape Town libraries, tripling the number of books I could choose from, officially giving me access to the adult and children's libraries.

Although the lives I encountered in books afforded me wide horizons, the confines of an education system bound by the ideology of apartheid ensured that the rest of my formal education was constrained.

I attended Coloured schools. With the apartheid-defined Coloured population being the majority population of Cape Town, there was a wider range of Coloured schools to choose from compared to the one Indian primary school that was close to home. I spent my first year of school at the Indian Rylands Primary School, after which my parents decided to send me to a "better school," Turfhall Primary, where subjects such as ballet and music were available. The local Indian school offered neither.

At the beginning of my third year at Turfhall Primary, I was eight years old and in Standard Two. One morning my class teacher asked that all the Coloured children in the class stand up. I sat. She counted the children standing. She then asked them to sit down and requested all the Indian children to stand up. I sat — neither of those labels described how I saw myself. I don't know whether or how she counted me.

It was only sometime later that I found out the reason for the exercise.

The school, under the direction of the Department of Coloured Affairs in making its annual allocations, provided one roll of toilet paper per Coloured child per school. The Indian children were not included in the allocation. Teachers were obliged to fill in these forms for planning and distribution purposes. I was one less roll of toilet paper for my school.

Turfhall's school library was a small space adjoining the needle-work room, its shelves spanning three walls with another row of shelves through the middle, dividing the space. The range of available fiction was limited. There were mostly reference books and other nonfiction that did not hold the same appeal. My bus library was more interesting, and I stuck to my other sources.

I progressed to Livingstone High School, another middle-class Coloured school, named for the colonial missionary "explorer" David Livingstone and situated in Claremont, an area where Black people, many of them descended from slaves, had been forcefully dispossessed and removed when the area was declared white. The school had somehow, inexplicably, escaped forced relocation.

Livingstone's school library reflected the school's left-wing Trotskyite and Marxist leanings. It was well stocked with books by Russian male writers, the likes of Solzhenitsyn and Dostoyevsky. Reading these authors transported me to faraway, snowy places: places I could relate to. Marxism made sense of how I saw and understood the world then, and presented a far more appealing, egalitarian possibility compared with the everyday forms of institutionalized racism I knew so well.

In spite of the school's political philosophy, the library at Livingstone contained mostly the writings of white authors, including South African writers such as Alan Paton and Nadine Gordimer. Later, as I realized the massive gaps in what was available, I hungrily sought out the work of writers of African, Asian, and Latin American descent, along with the writings of women, most often African-American women whose words spoke to me intimately.

These writers became lifelong friends in my mind and imagination.

I travelled the world from my bedroom, lying on my bed, on my side, reading, my legs roasting in the heat-drenched late afternoon sun that on the barren, sandy Cape Flats burns strong and harsh, regardless of season. The only interruption to that burning sun came on rainy and grey-weather days. My bed, adjacent to a large, west-facing window in the renovated room I came to share with my only sister, Amisha, made the perfect spot for languid, sun-drenched late afternoon reading when I came home from school.

At school I was bored and unchallenged by the formal syllabus that was prescribed, but eager to learn; I was curious to understand the world more, but the lessons themselves felt like a waste of time. It seemed clear to me that the required syllabus had little reference or relevance to my life or any likely paths I would take — the content felt disconnected from real life. I did as little homework as I could get away with, and precociously believed that my reading life was providing me with a better education than the tedium of school.

I habitually practised routine acts of subterfuge, placing a novel inside a textbook while in class, and doing the same at home when I was supposed to be studying. At other times I would hold a novel out of sight, below my desk, reading the likes of Milan Kundera, Simone de Beauvoir, or Anaïs Nin, books found in the Rondebosch Library — another stop on my expanding library travels — while a teacher was doing something dreary at the blackboard or asking us to read our textbooks.

Because Livingstone was situated in a white area, none of its students lived near the school. We all had to use some form of transport to get there and back. There were six of us, two of us girls, from my immediate neighbourhood who got off at the same bus stop on College Road, Rylands. We would all walk through a pedestrian lane that connected to Shaanti Crescent, continuing on from there to wherever we lived.

I had to walk past Amma's house to get home. Amma and Appa, "mother" and "father" in Tamil, were an elderly couple — or so it seemed from my child's worldview — and they and their three children, Gona, Tim, and Nasan, each between six and ten years older than me, were neighbours and friends. I loved Amma's South Indian–inspired food and would often stop in to see what she had made for lunch. Amma's food was different from Ma and Ba's cooking, not only in taste and flavour but also in texture. Some of my favourites were her spicy hot fish curry that included tamarind as an ingredient, providing a nuanced sourness to the dish. It was also a lot drier than Ma and Ba's fish curries, containing little tomato. Amma's braised potatoes, a simple dish of onions, potatoes, and dry spices, was my favourite comfort food from early childhood, when Gona, Amma's eldest daughter, would mush it up together with rice and butter, creating little balls on my plate, then indulgently popping the balls into my mouth.

After stopping at Amma's for my first lunch, I would make my way to Ma's — the council house now extended, the two houses linked by a door — to see what she had cooked for my second lunch. Ma loved to bake and cook and was famous for her superb food, including several complex, savoury Indian delicacies. She also made Indian sweetmeats such as jalebi, barfi, and magaj, most often close to Diwali, the Hindu festival of lights. Her recipes were in high demand, and, coming home from school, I was often met with the heady aroma of freshly baked biscuits coming from her kitchen. My favourites were a buttery shortbread dipped in chocolate and a delicious chocolate and mint biscuit that included peppermint crisp, always made in large quantities and stored in generously sized biscuit tins or Tupperware containers.

Because of her lifelong practice of sharing food with her neighbours, and having lived in mixed communities before apartheid enforced segregation, Ma had been exposed to many cuisines including Cape Malay and traditional Xhosa foods. A favourite of mine was her fantastic samp and beans dish, known in Xhosa as wmnqwsho, served with lamb. One of Bapu's favourites was trotters, which she always served with freshly baked white bread.

Another South African favourite was her baked gem squashes: the round, green, hard-skinned vegetable halved, seeds removed, stuffed with mixed vegetables and butter, covered in cheese, and baked in the oven.

Amma and Ma both hailed from Port Elizabeth and were of similar age. They also shared the remarkable ability of always having food to share regardless of how tight money was or how many mouths there were to feed. This sharing was part of community life on Shaanti Crescent. Ma often sent me out to make deliveries to different neighbours when she made something special, which happened often. Similarly, neighbours' children made food deliveries to us. My favourite, boeber — a combination of milk, sago, cinnamon, and cardamom with a thick, creamy consistency, eaten as a sweet dessert — was made and shared by Aunty Saida next door during Ramadan.

My last and third stop for lunch would be at home, on the other side of the dividing door. By the time Ba got home from school I would already have dipped into leftovers, continuously feeding my voracious teen appetite.

Ba, addicted to the spicy Indian tea we called cha, would start a pot — a mix of Ceylon tea, infused with fresh lemongrass, cinnamon, cardamom, ginger, clove, and black pepper — the moment she got home. In later years, her cha recipe changed to comprise equal amounts of Rooibos and Ceylon tea. She also dry-roasted her pre-mixed, aromatic tea spices to release their flavour before adding the other ingredients. Over cha, I would make my way through a pack of Marie biscuits or Eet-Sum-Mors, dipped in the deliciously satisfying spicy cha.

Before and after cha with Ba, I would read. My parents had a busy social life, making it easy for me to go on my library escapades using public transport. Library hopping was not an activity that they could legitimately refuse me, and I took advantage of this freedom and often went on solitary wanderings through second-hand bookshops and book exchanges in Claremont and the CBD, in the process exploring Cape Town.

If I could look after myself and keep out of their way, avoiding trouble, I could live under the radar, avoiding Bapu's moodiness, which resulted from his persistent headaches and insomnia, and his short temper that would surface unpredictably. Bapu was overly involved in my and Ba's lives, in every decision, no matter how minor, including those decisions ordinarily made by mothers.

It bothered me that he made all decisions at home and that Ba had to ask him for money that she herself had earned. Her income was paid into Bapu's bank account, one that she had no access to, and so she would have to ask him for money even for buying food or making discretionary purchases. The unfairness of Ba not having her own bank account and unmediated access to her own salary — and the very fact that this was considered normal and acceptable — was one of many inequalities at home that I found disturbing as a child.

Other clashes came when I asked why Ba always seemed to be in the kitchen once she got home from work and over weekends. She went from her paid job into her job at home, and often would not sit down to eat with us at mealtimes because she would still be busy in the kitchen ensuring rotis came to the table straight off the pan as Bapu liked and as he wished guests to experience her food, or because Bapu only ate his food steaming hot, requiring her to leave the table often to reheat food while the rest of us were eating.

Along with asking uncomfortable questions that inevitably led to confrontation with my father, I reacted by refusing any work that involved anything to do with the kitchen. I would not assist in preparations, cooking, heating food, clearing dishes, washing dishes, or any of the things that were expected of daughters. In my childhood and adolescent fury, my intent was to make a clear statement that I was not one of those women. My place would never be in the kitchen. At family and other social gatherings, when women automatically gathered in the kitchen, I made it my business to sit with the men, inevitably being the only girl among them.

I understood early on that the personal *was* political, and my parents, unwittingly, were my teachers. I was determined that I would never have a relationship like the one my parents had. I would not serve or be dependent on anyone. I would earn and control my own money.

I was twelve or thirteen when I got my first job, helping Tim, Amma's younger daughter, at her food stall in a Claremont pedestrian shopping lane that then linked the busy working-class Main Road Claremont shopping area to the considerably more upmarket Cavendish Square Mall. I worked on weekends and during school holidays, selling Indian snacks — bhajias and samosas — that she fried on the spot.

Later I worked again for Tim selling clothing and some of my own handmade clay jewellery at the then bohemian Green Market Square, originally a slave market from the 1690s, frequented by tourists and hippies alike in Cape Town's CBD. I continued with this weekend and holiday work throughout the 1980s until I reached the legal working age of sixteen, when I started working at Edgars, a large department store, variously on the sales floor, the fitting rooms, and in the accounts section, where credit checks were performed, accounts opened, and installments paid.

Throughout my adolescence, through the rebellion at home and my determination to learn independence, I found the spaces outside of formal lessons to be far more stimulating and engaging than anything we did inside the classroom. In unspoken defiance of government policy, Livingstone High School officially sanctioned regular political education sessions, which were run mostly by senior students in assembly format or in smaller groups based on interest, during school hours and breaks. During assemblies the Student Representative Council made announcements about upcoming protest actions, marches, and the logistical arrangements involved, even though the school did not officially sanction missing classes to attend protests.

But these were not ordinary times. If we were to miss school to participate in protests, we were required to have parental permission. It was a stipulation that was rarely enforced. At a large student march demanding equal education that took place on a school day, Black students from all parts of Cape Town converged on St. George's Cathedral, Cape Town's Anglican cathedral in the CBD. Desmond Tutu, then Archbishop of Cape Town, led the march. Armed riot police were out in full force, ready and waiting for us. Water cannons, barbed wire, tear gas, and rubber bullets were used in an attempt to disperse the gathering. Chased down the historic Company's Gardens, adjoining the cathedral, I made a narrow escape, crossing over a small stream and scaling a fence I would never ordinarily have been able to climb.

Returning to school the next day, I discovered that school officials had decided that on this occasion the rules were to be applied. All students who had attended the march were suspended. I made my way home expecting serious trouble with my parents but was surprised that when the school contacted Bapu he claimed to have given permission for me to attend, ending my suspension.

It was an unexpected and rare moment of support from my father. Whether it was to avoid any shame associated with suspension or whether it was an expression of his understanding and support for a legitimate cause that I supported, I cannot say. But he came through for me that day, and I suffered no negative consequences.

It was through the political education I received from students outside the classroom, and continued participation in other resistance activities, that I came to know, to understand, and finally to find the words to describe and clarify what I believed. I had the privilege of being able to think about the world I wanted and to begin to define my place in it.

I was finally receiving the education I longed for.

After school, I would often head for Claremont station, a fifteen-minute walk from Livingstone, to take a train to Rondebosch, the closest white suburb to us in Gatesville, with the Rondebosch Public Library about a hundred metres from the train station. Rondebosch was home to the University of Cape Town, which meant the area was somewhat more racially mixed than the rest of the city.

If I took the train to Rondebosch to use the library, Ba would sometimes collect me by car after she had finished her workday. If not, I took the train from leafy Rondebosch to the busy Mowbray transport terminus, where I would hop on a bus or minibus taxi that would drop me on Klipfontein Road, at a stop a five- to ten-minute walk from our house.

When my reading range expanded to the Cape Town library at the Cape Town City Hall, Ba did not feel confident enough to drive there. The CBD was outside her limited driving radius. So for visits to the City Library I took a bus or minibus taxi from Klipfontein Road to Mowbray, changing at Mowbray terminus to a bus, train, or another minibus taxi to the CBD. There was no single transport route for getting from Gatesville to the CBD.

Public transport felt safe to me then, and I knew my way around the bus, train, and minibus taxi routes that took me to the places I wanted to go: the Claremont library, the Rondebosch library, and the main City Library in the CBD.

Growing up on Cape Town's streets, as a pedestrian, a public transport user, and a brown-skinned girl, I quickly became accustomed to enduring harassment and name-calling. I wanted the freedom to traverse my city and so forced myself to become inured to this base reality. Comments made in passing, whether sexualized or not, referring to my little girl's body, my skin colour, my "Indian" otherness, or any other factor that resulted in whistling, catcalls, and other mouthy sounds by entitled adult men — whether builders, street sweepers, garbage collectors, or men driving by in cars

— was a fact of life. An independent, street-smart girl could not allow herself to be affected by these behaviours. So I ignored them.

Over the years, my legs and back had permanently darkened into a milk-chocolate brown thanks to the hours I spent soaking up the sun, not only on my bed but also lying on the hot bricks beside my mother's sister, Madhu masi's, swimming pool. I loved the feeling of those hot bricks against my body, immediately after or before braving the icy cold swimming pool.

While I was aware of skin colour, and how "darkness" was received and perceived, I did not much consider my own shade of brown, or the fact that I was making myself progressively browner. My love of the sun and the pleasure of it on my skin outweighed anything else. I was simply enjoying the deliciously lazy sensation of soaking up its heat, sun worshipping — my own take on the obeisance of the Surya Namaskar, a yogic salute to the sun.

At various points in time my legs became vertically stripy according to how they rested over each other while I lay on my side in the sun, reading and napping. The exposed parts were a deeper, darker shade. I would also have horizontal stripes according to the length of my school skirt and the exposed flesh between my skirt and socks on days when I read on my bed before changing out of my school uniform.

It was only after a holiday spent almost entirely on the beach on the gorgeous, unspoilt Wild Coast, part of a Bantustan "homeland" designated for Black Africans, that I started noticing comments about my "dark skin," becoming aware of how my increasingly deep shade of brown was, in certain quarters, being perceived as unacceptable for a girl. I had failed to know and act on the rule, spoken or not, that a girl of Indian descent should keep out of the sun.

Preserving paler skin was paramount to notions of beauty, and deliberate exposure to the sun was pure idiocy. Dark was ugly.

I had never given my own colouring much thought. I was brown. Fortunately for me, Ba had not taught me the rules of Black beauty. If anything, by not teaching me to stay out of the sun, or that the sun was an enemy and potential source of downfall — as good Indian mothers of daughters apparently ought to — she had encouraged my sun worshipping, reading on my bed on those hot afternoons or lying on the hot bricks beside Madhu masi's pool for hours on end.

Post-apartheid, Klipfontein Road still spans the length of racially segregated townships. My parents are the only ones still living at the now extended, transformed, conjoined council house on Shaanti Crescent. Ma and Dada have passed on, and my aunts and uncle live in vastly different contexts with their own families. My young sister too is married and lives in a new, middle-class, increasingly racially mixed neighbourhood.

Despite my relatively open and diverse upbringing, I challenged the limits of Bapu's openness through my relationship choices, which extended far beyond the boundaries of religion or caste. My curly-haired, pale-skinned Coloured boyfriend in high school, followed by a deep-brown first language Xhosa speaker and a blond, blue-eyed Nordic man at university and beyond, and now my long-term partner with her brown-skinned, dreadlocked femininity, resulted in many clashes. Though now, with the passage of much time and distance, Bapu has come to accept, and even embrace, my life choices, which, unsurprisingly, have never been points of contention with Ba.

In journeying beyond and through my own insider-outsider identity, in making sense of myself beyond the confines of self, community, or country, in travelling the world through books and in person, finding myself in places I could not have imagined, I have come to know that my communities, my ways of being, are fluid, constantly changing, creating and recreating a world without borders: a world that defies the policing of borders or boundaries.

A WOMAN'S SMILE

Barbara Wanjala

The first time I saw Ndeye Kebe she was standing on her balcony with her eyeglasses tinted in the sun and her mobile phone held close to her ear as she waved at Babacar and me on the street below. Babacar, not to be confused with my regular taximan, Boubacar, spoke very little French and was not familiar with the northern outskirts of Dakar. Noticing that we had driven past the Leopold Sedar Senghor stadium three times, I called Ndeye, who patiently guided him through the streets of the sprawling Parcelles Assainies commune in Wolof. Babacar had agreed to CFA2,500 prior to setting off, but because the trip had been more circuitous than anticipated, he wanted 500 more francs. Ndeye was waiting; there was no time to quibble. I paid and thanked him cheerily, "Jerejef!" then quickly exited the yellow Renault.

Changing taximen was a precautionary measure. Le taximan is a Dakar fixture. The currency of the glaringly English word "taximan" in what was once one of the major cities of the French empire struck me as a clear indication of the defeat of French linguistic purism against the onslaught of globalization. The relentlessly aggressive taximen of Dakar ply the streets in their yellow Renaults, Peugeots, and Toyotas, hooting and slowing down at the sight of any potential fare. At the Leopold Sedar Senghor airport a week prior, I had been besieged by five taximen who formed a ring around me as they called out, "Sister! Sister!" I had elbowed my way out and headed to the taxi rank, where I met Omar, who proceeded to rip me off mercilessly. Luckily I met Boubacar soon after. His prices seemed reasonable, and we rapidly established a certain level of trust. Boubacar's parents were originally from Guinea, but he had been born here and felt fully Senegalese. He was Fulani, the West African ethnic group known as Peul in French, believed to be the largest nomadic group in the world. I liked Boubacar, but because he was extremely inquisitive, I could not trust him on this sensitive mission. Instead I flagged down Babacar to take me to the one person I had come to Dakar to meet.

Ndeye Kebe heads Sourire de Femme, the only non-governmental organization that lobbies for the rights of lesbians in Senegal. Sourire de Femme translates as "Woman's Smile" in English, but it is not just women who fall under the purview of the organization's advocacy. "Sourire de Femme believes in human rights for all," Ndeye told me. "I started this organization because I have always believed that everyone is equal regardless of their social status. Whether one leads a comfortable life or is merely a street vendor, whether one is a man or a woman, I believe that we are all equal."

She ushered me past the apartment's entrance area, where a portrait of Sérigne Touba hung on a wall into the dark, cool living room. The curtains on the windows overlooking the street-facing balcony were closed, keeping out the afternoon heat. We settled in our respective sofa chairs, and she placed her feet on the table, her long blue and green waxprint boubou slipping to reveal a beaded ornament on her right ankle. Dark-hued, bespectacled, and elegant, she wore her hair braided in an elaborate style that wound up in a chignon at the back of her head. I had been told to expect a woman of a certain age, but I was discovering that Senegalese women were deceptively ageless. She spoke in a low voice that was younger in real life than it had sounded on the phone and that was occasionally drowned out by loud vehicles roaring past.

Understandably cautious, she declined my request to record the interview in order to reproduce her words as faithfully as possible. "I'll speak in French and you can take your notes in English," she suggested. I tried that at first, but as we progressed I found it easier to write down directly what she was saying. I translated her words into English when I sat down to write this story.

Finding Ndeye Kebe had not been easy. Sourire de Femme does not have a website but comes up often on Senegalese news sites in articles from two years ago. On November 9, 2013, five women were arrested while celebrating a birthday at Bar Piano in the populous Grand Yoff neighbourhood and charged with "crimes against nature." The bar was closed soon after following complaints from the community for "being too popular with lesbians." One of the five alleged lesbians was Sene Dieng, Sourire de Femme's assistant director. At thirty-one she was the oldest member of the group, which also included a sixteen-year-old who, being a minor, had not appeared before *le tribunal des flagrants délits de Dakar*, Dakar's court for flagrant offences, with the rest two days later. Ndeye Kebe came to their defence in an interview with *l'Observateur*, the country's leading newspaper, owned by world-renowned musician Youssou N'dour's media conglomerate, Groupe Futurs Médias, saying, "Lesbians are human beings. When the rights of a minority are violated, what must we do? We must act to give them back their rights." The suspects were later acquitted.

Arrests like these are regular occurrences in Dakar. When I met her on a Friday afternoon in July, Ndeye told me that Sourire de Femme dealt with at least one major incident every month. Currently they were lobbying for seven men who had been arrested that very Tuesday in Guédiawaye, a working-class suburb to the northeast of Dakar. The arrest had found its way into the papers despite the media's preoccupation with the trial of former Chadian leader Hissène Habré for crimes against humanity. The newspaper *Le Quotidien* reported that the seven men had been caught in the Guédiawaye police dragnet following phone calls from exasperated neighbours who complained about questionable nocturnal goings-on, including the smoking of Indian hemp. "The newspapers here like to sensationalize," said Ndeye. "I know what really happened there. I was the first person they called when they were arrested. People turn to me whenever such incidents occur, whether men or women. They know that they can reach out to me for help."

But being there for everyone is not easy. Ndeye had hardly slept over the past week as she had been shuttling back and forth between her house and the Guédiawaye police headquarters, raising funds to buy food and looking for legal counsel for the seven suspects in custody. Her sense of humour was intact despite her fatigue. "People say that my phone number is like that of a sex worker. It gets around," she joked. Our three-hour interview was punctuated by frequent phone calls and conversations of varying length, some in Wolof and others in French or a mixture of the two. She would apologize after each interruption, flipping the phone's pink cover shut and placing it back on the table. This last caller was an activist from an NGO for the rights of gay men calling to inquire about the seven men who were scheduled to be arraigned in court the following Tuesday. They were to be charged with "*actes contre nature.*"

Senegal's legal provisions with regard to same-sex acts are addressed in Article 319 of the Penal Code, which states, "Whoever will have committed an improper or unnatural act with a person of the same sex will be punished by imprisonment of between one and five years and by a fine of 100,000 to 1,500,000 francs. If the act was committed with a person below the age of 21, the maximum penalty will be applied." The earliest conviction under this law was in January 2009, when nine men were arrested on December 19, 2008, in a flat in Dakar on charges of homosexuality, among them Diadji Diouf, who worked for AIDES Senegal, an organization that provides treatment to MSMs*. The Court of Appeals would, in April 2009, overturn their convictions for indecent and unnatural acts

---

* MSM: Men who have sex with men.

and for being members of a criminal group and order their immediate release.

There is plenty of debate around what constitutes *un acte impudique ou contre nature*, an indecent or unnatural act. Some cynical observers say that the clause is deliberately ill-defined in order to be all-encompassing. Ndeye explained, "The law is ambiguous. Technically speaking, it is not illegal to be a gay person in Senegal. It is the so-called unnatural acts that are prohibited. In order for the offence to be punishable, the unnatural acts have to be proved in court." For one to be penalized for being gay, one has to be caught *en flagrant délit*, in flagrante delicto. But it is often more complicated than that.

In a 2012 case, two girls (aged between seventeen and twenty) were arrested after a compromising video of them was posted online. A young man was going through the files on his girlfriend's mobile phone when he stumbled across an eighteen-minute-long video of the two girls "giving themselves to practices of pure lesbianism under the eye of a camera," as reported in one online exclusive. "The degradation of values has attained a point of no return in Senegal," stated the site, which decided not to show the video. The angry boyfriend posted the video on his Facebook page, and it was quickly circulated across websites and mobile phones. Some enterprising individuals made a CD version of "the Lesbians of Grand Yoff" and sold it on the streets of Dakar.* Coming to the women's defence, Sourire de Femme cited the penal code's anti-pornography laws, which criminalize the distribution of objects of a pornographic nature. If the two young women were to be punished for same-sex acts conducted behind closed doors and not intended for public viewing, Ndeye argued, then the young man had to be punished as well, for he had committed the crime of disseminating the video. All parties were acquitted.

---

* *African Realities: Body, Culture and Social Tensions*, edited by Josep Martí, 2014.

* * *

Ndeye's extensive knowledge of the law is her foremost weapon in the war for justice and equality. One of Sourire de Femme's staunchest allies is Association de Juristes Sénégalaise, the association for Senegalese jurists. "We discovered that there is a severe knowledge deficit on human rights issues among legal practitioners. This is why our workshops are important," Ndeye said. With funding from various donors such as the Canadian embassy and the Paris city council, Sourire de Femme has conducted several workshops to raise awareness on LGBTI issues, with workshop topics ranging from human rights to sexual health. Workshop participants have included sex workers, LGBTI individuals, religious leaders, doctors, legal practitioners, and members of the National Assembly.

But lack of funding greatly hampers Sourire de Femme's initiatives. When funding is available they are able to hire venues for meetings, but most of the time they arrange with fellow NGOs who are able to accommodate or meet in private homes. The one upside to not having an office or a web presence is that like all moving things, Sourire de Femme becomes difficult to target. The organization also struggles to raise funds for legal fees. "Lawyers are not affordable," said Ndeye. "This is a huge obstacle because we are fighting on multiple fronts. We work within the community, but we also do battle in court. The law and the constitution are there to protect everyone's rights, but many of the people we fight for are unable to access justice because they are poor." Everyone is equal under the Senegalese constitution, but in reality homosexuals have seen their personal freedoms gradually shrink over the last two decades. To illustrate how much things have changed, she shared a recollection of her childhood in Medina, one of Dakar's oldest and most populous areas, which one American had advised to steer clear of because it was "full of thieves and pickpockets." There was nothing to see in Medina, he said. I would soon discover that I had been lied to.

* * *

Medina was created as a "native quarter" by the French colonial authorities in 1914 following a plague epidemic in order to separate the African and European populations in a bid to contain the disease. In another quarter of Dakar known as Sacré-Coeur, I had met a journalist from Liberia and shaken his hand. A friend of his joked, "You know there is Ebola where he is from, right?" I would also meet a journalist from Gambia who had travelled to several countries in the region to cover the Ebola epidemic. He had travelled to the remote village of Meliandou in Guinea, which borders Sierra Leone and Liberia, where the first case had been reported: a two-year old boy called Emile Ouamouno. The disease had taken Emile's mother and sister as well. Emile's father did not know how or why he had survived. I wondered where in Guinea Boubacar's parents were from and whether he was in touch with his distant relations there. Upon his return to Dakar from Freetown, the Gambian journalist had quarantined himself for twenty-one days, monitoring himself for any symptoms. His meals were delivered to his doorstep. "I told myself that if I had it I would kill myself. I did not want to be known as the Gambian who had brought Ebola to Senegal," he said. On the plane back to Nairobi, I found myself between two men of West African provenance, both of whom would lapse into long sneezing bouts from time to time throughout the ten-hour flight. I struggled to reconcile my pan-Africanist ideals with my hypochondria. I had left Dakar resolute in my conviction that love ought to transcend all barriers of gender, colour, religion, and origin, but in the face of a steady wave of indeterminate germs I found the love I had for my two African brothers beside me wavering. "The diseased African" stereotype of the French colonial authorities in 1914 was alive and well a century later, fanned by American news outlets.

Medina, which is home to the Grand Mosque of Dakar, gave birth to some of Senegal's most renowned artists, such as musician Youssou N'dour and rap group Daara J., as well as painter Fodé

Camara. It is within this tolerant and progressive artistic milieu that Ndeye grew up. She evoked a community that was accommodating of unconventional sexual proclivities. "When I was a child, there were three houses right around where we lived which everyone knew were inhabited by MSMs. This was around 1980. There were many famous *gouines* in the neighbourhood as well," she said, the use of the French word for "dyke" a departure from her usual politically correct NGO-speak ("sex worker," "MSM"). "P.N. was known as *la plus grande lesbienne de Dakar*, Dakar's biggest lesbian. Her female lover, A.F., visited her often. We would be playing outside when A.F. drove up at around 5:00 p.m. and entered P.N.'s house. She would stay a while and leave after thirty minutes or so. Everyone knew about their liaison, P.N.'s husband included. They were not on talking terms, but he gave her a daily allowance."

The existence of varied and fluid sexual identities was acknowledged by various Senegalese I encountered, both online and offline. One commenter on an article on gay identities in Senegal on a popular pan-African website asked, "Why is Western thinking so obsessed with creating [mutually exclusive] labels and categories?" Another commenter, an American-based Senegalese academic with whom I would later have several email exchanges, wrote, "The Senegalese do not have a term for 'homosexual' for the same reason they do not have a term for 'heterosexual.' People are simply not categorized based on sexual orientation." She would explain further later, "People were not identified in terms of straight versus gay. What was most important was what kind of a member of a family or community the person was. Sex, for heterosexuals as well as homosexuals, was just not openly discussed or flaunted in public." These conversations prompted me to reflect on my own ingested prejudices and unexamined biases. I was reminded of a public lecture on gender that I had attended back home in Nairobi where the scholar Wambui Mwangi had urged us to view gender and sexuality as continuums instead of binaries.

* * *

A word that I would come across often in my inquiries was "goorjigeen." Of the recent arrest, one online headline proclaimed, "Gay scandal in Guédiawaye: 7 'goorjigeen' arrested in full frolic by police." Goorjigeen is a Wolof word that translates as "man-woman." It is often used pejoratively to refer to effeminate men and to insinuate homosexual tendencies. But there had been room for goorjigeen within the rigid heterosexist confines of traditional Senegalese society. One older woman from the northwestern town of Louga told me that during her childhood, conducting any ceremony without goorjigeen would have been unimaginable. They were consummate hosts, wowing the entire village with their elaborate attire and mouth-watering dishes during weddings, birthdays, and christenings. She brought to mind the "gay uncle" trope when she recalled one uncle whose tchep bou djen, rice with fish in Wolof, was especially accomplished. An entry in the Routledge *Handbook of Sexuality, Health and Rights* corroborated her account: "Some decades ago in the cities of northern Senegal, goorjigeen also used to organize traditional dances and ceremonies called tannber that were well attended by the whole community." The handbook further stated that goorjigeen had close friendships with women leaders and played an important political role, reportedly welcoming Senegal's first president, Leopold Sedar Senghor, into the city of Saint Louis with song and dance. Marriage between younger and older goorjigeen had even been allowed.

If goorjigeen had formed such an intrinsic part of the societal fabric, what brought about the virulent intolerance towards them, to the point of blaming them for lack of rain? Ndeye attributed the shift in attitudes to the confluence of a variety of factors, key among them the rise and spread of HIV/AIDS.

At less than 1 percent, Senegal has one of the lowest HIV/AIDS rates on the continent. Its effective HIV/AIDS-prevention campaign has been lauded as an African success story. The disease was first detected in the country in 1986, prompting a proactive response from political and religious leaders as well as the scientific community. However, later reports would reveal higher infection rates among at-risk populations: around 20 percent for female sex workers and MSMs. Dr Ibrahim Ndoye, who was head of Senegal's National AIDS Council, told VOA in 2012 that taking the taboo out of prostitution and homosexuality would help fight the higher rates of infection among these communities. Unlike homosexuality, which is criminalized by law, prostitution is legal in Senegal. Ndeye believes that the higher prevalence of HIV/AIDS within the gay community led to associations between the two and contributed to stigmatization.

Another reason is religious conservatism. "Senegal is 95 percent Muslim," a tour guide by the name of Ibrahima told me as we contemplated a mural of marabouts on Gorée Island, where I had gone to visit the House of Slaves. "This is Sérigne Touba. He is my spiritual guide," he said, pointing to one of the men on the mural, a dark man with a white cloth wrapped around his head and draped over his body. It was the same man I would see on many paintings around Dakar, on the walls of shops, on stickers in taxis, and in Ndeye's house.

"Is he still alive?" I asked.

"No, he died a long time ago. He was a very small man, but he performed many great miracles. He was placed in a cage with a lion and it bowed down in front of him. He was banned from praying on a boat, but he took his mat and placed it on the water and knelt on it to pray. He did not sink. The French were so afraid of him that they exiled him in a forest in Gabon for eight years." Marabouts abound in Senegal. I struggled to comprehend Ibrahima's explanation about Senegal's Islamic brotherhoods and marabouts. There was a famous marabout down the street from where I was staying in the relatively affluent southern neighbourhood of Mermoz, but going by my frequent sightings of his portrait, Sérigne Touba appeared to be the most prominent of all.

* * *

I had arrived in Dakar one week to Ramadan's end in mid-July, fully aware that one of the challenges I would face would be the reluctance of LGBTI persons to open up to a stranger from the other side of the continent. My plan was to meet both queer and non-queer people willing to engage in conversations on sexual orientation and gender identity in Senegal, but this would prove more difficult than I had imagined. Brick walls stood at the end of many avenues of inquiry. Carefully worded emails met with no response, calls went unreturned. TV debates about homosexuality in Senegal on YouTube were in Wolof and thus incomprehensible to me. Nobody I met had heard of Ndeye Kebe or Sourire de Femme. It was during one of many such moments of frustration that I committed the egregious faux pas of broaching the LGBTI question during la fête de la Korité, the Eid festivities marking the end of the holy month. "I'm with our president on this. We are not ready to decriminalize homosexuality," one young lady told me after recovering from her shock at my question. She was quoting President Macky Sall's response* to American President

* "Now, on the issue of homosexuality [...] you said something very important — general principles which all nations could share, and that is the respect for the human being and non-discrimination. But these issues are all societal issues basically, and we cannot have a standard model which is applicable to all nations, all countries — you said it, we all have different cultures. We have different religions. We have different traditions. And even in countries where this has been decriminalized and homosexual marriage is allowed, people don't share the same views. Senegal, as far as it is concerned, is a very tolerant country which does not discriminate in terms of inalienable rights of the human being. We don't tell anybody that he will not be recruited because he is gay or he will not access a job because his sexual orientation is different. But we are still not ready to decriminalize homosexuality. I've already said it in the past, in our Cabinet meeting, it is Senegal's option, at least for the time being, while we have respect for the rights of homosexuals — but for the time being, we are still not ready to change the law. But of course this does not mean that we are all homophobic. But the society has to absolve these issues. It has to take time to digest them, bringing pressure to bear upon them, on such issues." White House Press Office, June 27, 2013.

Barack Obama during his 2013 visit. During the two presidents' joint press conference, a Western journalist cited the historic United States Supreme Court's ruling, which had occurred on the previous day, and asked the two presidents what efforts were being made to decriminalize homosexuality in Senegal. Obama had expressed his firm conviction in the fundamental notion of universal justice and equality for all, a sentiment shared by Ndeye and a core principle of Sourire de Femme.

By framing lesbian rights within wider contexts such as human rights or women's rights, Sourire de Femme has been able to champion its cause on various platforms, even engaging in fiery debates with conservative imams on national television. But not everyone views lesbian rights as a human rights issue. One male activist from a major human rights organization with whom I spoke said that his organization did not work in the area of lesbian rights. This is not the case for all the human rights organizations in Senegal, however. "Aboubacry at RADO is a very courageous and vocal defender of everyone's rights. Human Rights Watch is also an important ally of ours," said Ndeye. But more support is needed. While Sourire de Femme is the only lesbian advocacy group in Senegal, there are around seventeen groups that lobby for the rights of gay men. "In Senegal when we talk about homosexuality we are usually talking about men, and we forget about the women," Ndeye told the *Washington Post* following the Bar Piano incident. The disparity affects the amount of resources allocated towards alleviating the plight of vulnerable lesbians. Ndeye cited the example of HIV/AIDS initiatives focusing primarily on the MSM community, whereas the sexual health needs of lesbian women are underserved. "One doctor told me that prior to our workshop he had not been aware that it was possible for lesbians to catch sexually transmitted diseases," she said.

This marginalization of lesbian women exposes deeply entrenched patriarchal values and ideas that continue to render women vulnerable. "Women struggle to access the same rights as men, whether it is access to health, justice, credit, or property. And yet women are *les maîtres du monde*, masters of the world. So why are they being left behind?" asked Ndeye. The recognition of widespread inequality and the need to collectivize the struggle in order to obtain everyone's liberation was what prompted her to form Sourire de Femme. She had been fighting for women's rights in other ways before deciding to get together with a few like-minded individuals to create a solid formal structure that would facilitate organizing and mobilization as well as function as a support system for activists and a point of contact for allies engaged in the struggle for the equal valuation of all lives. "It was not easy given the environment we are in. But we fight because everyone should be able to access their rights be they an albino, a lesbian, a minister, a street vendor. We are all equal." Because sexual minorities often find themselves at the intersection of multiple oppressions, Sourire de Femme believes that it is especially necessary to amplify their voices. "The poor are most affected. Mechanisms need to be put in place so that LGBTI people are able to get paid work and escape poverty," she said.

Ndeye does not believe in silence. She says that dialogue and debate have a vital role to play in changing hearts and minds. "*Il faut poser le débat*," she said repeatedly during our conversation. "*L'important c'est de poser le débat*." You have to set the debate. Her words echoed those of South African "visual activist" Zanele Muholi, who said in a BBC interview, "We are doing this in order to be counted. We're speaking on the edge and challenging all forms of silence. It's a painful situation, of course, but it helps many others." Muholi's photographs documenting South African LGBTI lives were scheduled to be part of a 2014 exhibition by the Raw Material Company, an arts centre in Dakar. "Precarious Imaging: Visibility and Media Surrounding African Queerness" had aimed to shed light on homosexuality and homophobia in Africa and to examine the media's coverage of queer issues. But a religious mob had stormed the centre and broke windows and lights. The government closed the exhibit after the mob threatened further attacks. According to the French newspaper *Le Monde*, the head of one Islamic organization had referred to the exhibition as "propaganda for unions which are against nature" and said it was "detrimental to our morality and to our laws." Ndeye had spoken out in defence of the exhibition, and it was through following up on news reports about the arts centre that I finally managed to obtain her contacts. I believe that their gratitude for Ndeye's vocal support contributed in part to their support of my quest. However, harassment of homosexuals does not come only from conservative religious groups or the enthusiastic police vice squad "*brigade des moeurs*," the morality brigade. Stigmatization often begins at home.

Accounts of the persecution of homosexuals by members of their own families abound. In January 2013, Global Gayz reported that a gay couple had been assaulted by their parents. An asylum-seeking Senegalese lesbian known by the name Marianna was featured in the "When Love in Africa Costs your Life" project by the Toxic Lesbian group in collaboration with the Belgian LGBTI rights group Merhaba. In her shocking account, Marianna revealed that her parents had her circumcized to "cure" her of lesbianism. Her girlfriend had been beaten by a mob and had succumbed to her extensive injuries.

In the face of such hostility at home, were there any safe spaces for queer *dakarois**? Where did one meet others with whom to share experiences and ideas? Where could a queer person find love in Dakar? Bar Piano, the infamous meeting point of gays and lesbians, had been shut down for good. A journalist I spoke to told me that all nightclubs were closed during the holy month, and even after Ramadan's end I would have difficulties

---

* dakarois (m.), dakaroise (f.): French word meaning inhabitant of Dakar.

meeting any members of the LGBTI community. Because of widespread stigmatization, they had slowly been pushed out of Dakar's nightlife.* Although a few openly gay individuals could be sighted at the VIP nightclub in the upscale Almadies area on the Atlantic waterfront, most of the parties had moved out of the capital into the outskirts of the city. The other alternative would be to get invited to an exclusive house party, similar to the one the seven men in Guédiaway were having prior to their arrest, but I had not met anyone who could grant me access. A Senegalese friend in France suggested creating a false online persona masquerading as a lesbian in order to meet other lesbians. Out of curiosity I perused the listings on various websites. Most ads were over a month old but nevertheless revealed the universal human desires of love and lust: a young lesbian in search of "*complicité*," an African lesbian asking where she could meet a European lesbian, an invitation to a hot lesbian soirée, a clean and curvaceous drianké** lesbian at your service.

The ad by the anonymous drianké provided a new dimension to my inquiries. Until then, I had not stumbled across anything about lesbianism among older women. It had seemed as if the Sapphic tendencies among *dakaroises* were a frivolity of youth that was cured definitively by marriage and respectability. Anonymous testimonies on online "news" websites of sensational bent recounted romantic sexual awakenings in all-girl sports teams at school or in same-sex university dorms. One woman

---

* On an online article titled "Mbathio Ndiaye, Dancer: 'Dakar is infested with lesbians,'" the celebrity expressed her disgust at this phenomenon, which was rotting the city especially the upscale neighbourhoods of Dakar. One commenter responded: "S21 is a militia whose goal is the eradication of all forms of homosexuality. Goorjigeen and lesbians, you have been notified. If you want to continue with these morals is better to leave the country because HERE IN SENEGAL YOU WILL NEVER HAVE PEACE!!! S21 Watch."

** Also "diriyanké": "Women of high social position with a particular physical appearance (strong and corpulent with big buttocks) and an associated sense of elegance and generosity." Routledge *Handbook of Sexuality, Health and Rights*, edited by Peter Aggleton, Richard Parker, 2010.

told of a flirtatious older woman who kept touching her a little too meaningfully during a networking event, while another woman recalled an older woman stopping her big car and asking her to get in. I was told that young unmarried women who were renting apartments together in Grand Yoff and Ouest Foire in order to save money were destined to become lesbians and therefore eternally doomed. The gossip website Dakar Match reported that affluent older lesbians met in downtown apartments owned by a grande dame of the jet set, or in a big white villa in Almadies belonging to a divorcée, or in sumptuous villas in the seaside resort of Saly Portugal. The Internet had emerged as hospitable terrain for African women who loved women. I browsed through numerous online spaces ranging from personal blogs to e-zines that claimed voice and countered invisibility, but where did the less digitally savvy or less financially empowered African lesbian go to meet fellow lesbians?

I had been reflecting on the lack of spaces for women to express their sexuality fully and freely when I stumbled across a most unexpected sight during an evening walk in Mermoz. Chairs had been lined up along both sides of the street and a red carpet spread out in the middle. Women of various ages sat waiting in their finery, long mermaid-tail dresses in expensive fabrics whose bright colours and bold prints were replicated in matching headwraps that had been wound elaborately around freshly coiffed hair. Feet were encased in glittering high heels, and beautifully made-up faces were kept intact by languidly waved hand-held woven fans. A male musician stood in the middle of the red carpet wearing a long off-white tunic and matching trousers. He did a microphone check, his mbalax ensemble warming up behind him. A tall, dreadlocked man held a small drum underneath his armpit. There were two other drummers, both seated, each with his own set of drums; one used his hands and the other a pair of sticks. There was another musician holding a stringed instrument in his lap. I asked an excited bystander what was going on. "It's a wedding!" he screeched.

The singer belted out a few plaintive tunes in Wolof, his powerful voice beckoning curious onlookers from the whole neighbourhood. After three or four tunes of moderate tempo, the drummers picked up their pace and the singer segued into an upbeat song. All of a sudden, women old and young and large and small kicked off their shoes and leapt onto the red carpet, hiking up their skirts and making rapid jumping motions with their bare legs. Some danced in pairs, at quarters a prudish eye would deem too close. Their unrestrained exuberance, sensuality, and skill were a joy to watch. When I showed Boubacar the footage I had shot on my mobile phone he snorted derisively. "Look at these old women behaving like young girls. They can't go to the club, so weddings are their only chance to dance. That is why *elles en profitent*, they take full advantage of the opportunity." I showed the video to Ndeye and she provided a detailed explanation.

"This is *la danse du sabar*, the sabar dance. It is a women's dance." All-women ceremonies were a common occurrence in traditional society and have been the focus of some of Ndeye's research into women's sensuality within the Senegalese context. Prior to becoming an activist, she had once worked as a *psychosexologue*, a psychosexologist, a profession that had allowed her to put her psychology studies to use. "The small drum under the dreadlocked man's arm is called le tama. The dances took place in a women's only house. No men were allowed; it was strictly *entre femmes*, between women. The tama drummer would be allowed occasionally, but he was there to play his drum and nothing else. The sabar usually took place in the late afternoon, between 3:00 and 5:00 p.m. The husbands knew about it, but there was no jealousy. They understood. What is remarkable to me is the amount of preparation that went into these dances. The women would consume aphrodisiacs, light incense, wear beads and phallic toys around their waists, and style their pubic hair into moustaches, beards, or braids. Some even went completely bald and sprinkled glitter. You have to wonder why they went to such great lengths for other women."

During the sabar, women would sing songs known as taasu,* which formed an important part of the Senegalese oral tradition. Ndeye gave an example:

> Prête-moi ta marchandise jusqu'à demain,
> Je te paierai par la pochette et la culotte.
> (Lend me your merchandise until tomorrow,
> I will pay you from my purse and my knickers.)

"If you study our history and anthropology, you will see that everything is linked to sex. Despite the inherent eroticism of some of our traditions, there were very strict codes on what was permitted and what was not. For example, one was not allowed to mention sex organs in front of older members of society. Also, premarital sex was frowned upon. Young girls were expected to stay chaste until marriage," said Ndeye.

The sabar was immortalized in Joseph Gai Ramaka's 2001 film, *Karmen Geï*, a Senegalese film adaptation of the popular opera *Carmen* by the French composer Georges Bizet. The film tells the story of the bisexual female prisoner Karmen, who seduces the female warden of the prison on Gorée Island. The warden would later commit suicide, and her burial was accompanied by Mouride chants. The film had been highly acclaimed at Cannes, but its Dakar screening was met with protests from the powerful Mouride brotherhood, who condemned the burial scene as blasphemous, and many mouridistes gathered outside the CICES cinema in Dakar

---

* "Wolof dances are associated with poems, frequently bawdy, which are called taasu. These poems are often associated with a particular dance step, so that its performance evokes the companion taasu whether or not it is spoken by the dancer or one of the drummers before the dance begins. The taasu provides women with a vehicle for social control, as well as creative word play." Deborah Heath, quoted in *Hip Hop Africa: New African Music in a Globalizing World* by Eric S. Charry, 2012.

threatening to set the building on fire. "In Gambia it's the law that catches you. In Senegal, it's the mob that catches you," said Ndeye.

Ndeye had been attacked by strangers on her way back home after returning from a conference abroad. She told me that her hip was still painful and she was only able to wear flat shoes. A prominent female intellectual had refused to collaborate with Sourire de Femme on a report on LGBTI rights in Senegal, saying, "I'll never work with homosexuals." Ndeye herself has been referred to as *"la plus grande lesbienne de Dakar,"* but in the *Washington Post* interview she said, "This is a private matter and not part of the debate. What people say is irrelevant to me. What matters are my personal beliefs and my personality." Verbal assaults pale in comparison to the traumatic experience of witnessing a personal friend being exhumed from a Muslim cemetery, his putrefying body dragged and deposited before his parents' house, who then reburied him only for him to be exhumed a second time. "People say that Senegal is tolerant. What is tolerant about exhuming someone simply because he was gay?" She asked why religious leaders utter incendiary words that lead their followers to kill, instead of simply guiding the so-called lost sheep to the light. She said that the prophets encouraged open discourse about sexuality. She quoted a Hadith from the Koran in which God says to man that it is not man's duty to forgive; forgiveness is God's domain. I asked her how she was able to forge on under such trying circumstances. "Commitment," she replied. "I am committed. Strength as well. And conviction. Do you know how long women fought in France simply so that they could wear trousers or smoke cigarettes? Why are Saudi women fighting for the right to drive? Why did Malala win the Nobel Prize?" The pain in her hip flared up again. Her phone rang; the UNHCR was calling about the seven men in Guédiawaye.

It was time for me to go, and for Ndeye's work to go on.

Part III

THEN AND NOW

THE LIFE AND DEATH OF ROWAN DU PREEZ

Simone Haysom

A MFULENI FAIRYTALE

Cape Town and its suburbs sprawl across a peninsula that juts out into cold and fierce seas, flanked by dozens of beaches — tiny crooked shores, long windswept banks, and bays festooned with boulders. On the Indian Ocean side, which the poor can reach by train, there are fishermen, tidal pools, and discarded plastic bottles; the models and their mansions are found beside the Atlantic. October ushers in the summer with fits and starts of warm weather, and legions of tourists and locals visit these beaches, sunbathing, swimming, kite flying, and surfing. The beach sand of the Cape is soft, fine, and pale, thanks to the beating it receives, day after day, century after century, from two relentless oceans.

This same sand also lies beneath the Cape Flats, the vast archipelago of poor suburbs that stretch back into the hinterland at the base of the peninsula's stem. Mfuleni, like many of the city's poor townships, has been reclaimed from dune fields. It is not clear that this reclamation is permanent, that the dunes will not try to take the land back. The wind can be ferocious. On the streets on the edges of Mfuleni sand fills up the gutters, is whipped into ghosts, into last exhalations of breath, into djinns that swirl up and disperse.

In the middle of an October night in 2012, a twenty-two-year-old albino man called Rowan Du Preez was found by one of these peripheral roads, naked and covered in burns. The remains of a tire smouldered nearby, the only light in the dark verge of the dunes. He cried out for help and was eventually found by two police officers from Blue Downs station who stood above him and asked questions, then radioed for help. In the ambulance Du Preez thrashed and swore in agony, but soon after arriving at hospital he slipped into a coma, finally passing away that night.

In Cape Town the murder of the poor is commonplace, yet this case attracted attention. Not because the man had been "neck-laced" — murdered by having a tire placed around his body and set aflame — and not because such a brutal murder was seemingly merely revenge for a petty theft. Rather, the murder of Rowan Du Preez was reported in the newspapers because the woman charged was Angy Peter, a local activist, well known as a crusader against police corruption, police negligence, and mob justice. "Rowan was a *skollie* [thug] who used to steal our things," an unnamed Mfuleni resident told a *Mail and Guardian* reporter in the immediate after-math. "But Angy used to say that you can't take the law into your own hands."

Angy Peter, the face of the criminal justice campaign for a vocal Cape Town NGO, the Social Justice Coalition, presented a novel defence. Many vigilante murderers perform the paradoxical ges-ture of publicly defending themselves with an admission of guilt — we killed because we had to, or we killed because, unlike the state, we seek to defend our community. But Angy Peter's not guilty plea stated, "Killing or hurting [Rowan] was the last thing I wanted ... The very real probability exists that the charges against me have been fabricated by policemen."

Her husband, Isaac Mbadu, also an activist for the same organ-ization, was charged too. Their co-accused were an acquaintance,

Azola Dayimani, a man who sometimes worked as a driver for their organization, and Christopher Dina, a Coca-Cola factory worker whom they said they did not know.

All these people came from Bardale, a neighbourhood in Mfuleni, and lived within a few streets of each other and the victim and his family. Because of the case many of them moved to safe houses in other parts of the city. After sixteen months they were able to put their accounts of the matter before the Cape High Court. The trial would run for over a year.

SELF-HELP

When I returned to South Africa after four years abroad, what struck me immediately was how the public execution of criminals had shifted from being a shameful hangover from a bitter past to almost a matter of pride. It showed our can-do attitude in the face of government inaction. Even the prosecutor in Rowan's murder trial referred to vigilante murder as "community self-help."

In the week of my arrival newspapers carried photographs of jubilant residents of Khutsong, a township attached to a mining town near Johannesburg, celebrating the deaths of four teenagers and a sixty-one-year-old man. The boys had been local tsotsis (gangsters) enacting a reign of petty robbery and assault in their town, and their neighbours had had enough. After a short community meeting on a soccer field one Saturday, a determined crowd marched out into the town. The teenagers were dragged from their houses and killed in the street. The crowd burnt two and stoned the others. The adult victim, also burnt, was a sangoma (traditional healer), alleged to have given the younger men muti, magic concoctions that helped them to carry out their crimes.

I had moved to Johannesburg, and the Khutsong killings, less than ninety minutes' drive from the city, were all over the news, for a day or two at least. "It's just like a fairy tale," someone said to me.

"Like the villagers banded together and defeated the ogre." News coverage dealt with the residents' frustrations, the inadequacies of policing, the difficulties posed to the police by laws to protect children's rights, and so on. None of it named the victims or provided any background to their lives before the murders.

A few weeks later a friend said to me, "I've just come back from Cape Town, and the craziest things have been happening to a woman I know ..."

That woman was Angy Peter. I would spend the next two years following her trial, and also the concurrent Commission of Inquiry into Policing in Khayelitsa for which she was supposed to have testified.

That story presented me with more mysteries than I could ever have expected, and certainly more than I wanted. But the mystery that bothered me most was the matter of Rowan Du Preez. How did he come to be so loathed by his neighbours, yet so loved by his family? What did it mean that this social outcast ended up in the middle of such a large political intrigue?

Desiree Jack, his aunt, seemed to shake with anger on the stand. More than one of his friends said they were haunted by the last time they'd seen him, calling for help. The policeman who transported the family to court told me that John Ndevu, his grandfather, so nervous that he would be late, would wait from dawn by a lamppost in the informal settlement of Strand for the police van to arrive. Then John Ndevu would sleep the whole way to court, and cry the whole way back.

It was not easy to understand this man who had died young after a life on society's margins, especially as his closest family members would not grant me an interview. For a long time, all I had were the public traces that Rowan Du Preez left of himself in the world, most of them bureaucratic, official, and traumatic. Ten arrests and three successful prosecutions in his twenty-two years, including a spell at a youth reformatory. Documents in which he is also sometimes known as Simphiwe Ndevu, sometimes simply as "Roy." There is one picture of him in print, taken at a distant, odd angle and out of focus. He is carrying a backpack and wears a zip-up jacket and a white bucket hat. He is either scowling or straining to hear what a companion is saying. It looks like a surveillance photo rather than a remembrance, and staff at the newspaper that ran it can no longer remember where it came from.

Eventually, I found an aunt, Veronica, who hadn't been a witness at the trial and was prepared to talk, and some of his former friends, who demanded anonymity. The more time I spent in Mfuleni the more I realized that there, like the rest of Cape Town, my hometown, elemental forces of history and place bear down heavily on each story. I hoped that where the record of Rowan's own life was scant, the record of his family's passage to that corner of the city might stand.

THE "NATIVE LOCATION"

Mfuleni is one of Cape Town's most far-flung neighbourhoods, a thirty-kilometre drive out of the city bowl along the highway until, on the northern lee of the N2, opposite Khayelitsa, it is laid out on the east bank of the Kuilsrivier. Established in 1950, it was originally a tiny government-initiated settlement for a handful of black labourers employed in Somerset West, Strand, and Gordon's Bay, small towns along the southeast curve of False Bay. The Union government founded Mfuleni with a few stands on wild state land, notwithstanding the objections of the European Property Owners Association of Eerste River, who objected because they had no police station. "How much less safe we will feel," the Association complained, "with a large native location established in our midst."

John Ndevu, Rowan's grandfather, father to Veronica and Yolanda and key witness in the murder trial, arrived in Cape Town around this time. Born in the Eastern Cape around 1935 and educated up to the seventh grade, he was a young man, perhaps even a teenager, when he left his rural Xhosa village to find work in the city or its peri-urban farms. Then, as they would be for the next five decades, black workers like Ndevu were treated as a necessary evil by the Union government: a quantity whose labour and movement must be tightly controlled, but who must never be allowed to feel rooted in Cape Town. For hundreds of years various administrations refined the ideology that cities were for whites. Blacks must be kept in rural areas, the overpopulated, underdeveloped areas that played a central role in policies of forced family breakdown. Since the colonial period, black men had been required to have written permission to enter the Cape, and in the 1920s the Union government made it a national requirement that black men carry a Pass, their passport to urban areas, where their presence had to be tied to formal employment. Their families were forbidden to join them.

In Cape Town the majority population was Coloured, a group which colonial racial typologies had marked out as distinct from both whites and blacks and which today celebrates a distinct cultural identity. Descended from settlers, slaves, and dispossessed local people, they had no ancestral rural area to be remaindered in. For the white supremacist administration this was a problem that could only be solved by ghettoization.

John Ndevu's family life showed the scars of these policies. In 1960 he returned to his village and married Adelaide Ngqola, with whom he had three children, including Veronica Ndevu in 1962. Veronica did not know if he was present continuously for their births, but he left the family again for the city when they were all babies. According to Veronica, she next saw him again at the age of eighteen, at the time of her marriage.

At some point in that absence, Ndevu took a second wife, a Coloured woman whose name may have been Sylvia. For most of his adulthood, many of the fundamental aspects of John Ndevu's life were illegal. For a black man to move to Cape Town without an offer of employment, and so official sanction, was illegal, as was any job he did without a Pass, though he may have secured one later. I was unable to find out if his second marriage was kept a secret from Adelaide, but marrying a woman of a different race was certainly a transgression against the country's colour bar laws. Finally, to make matters worse, they lived together. The Group Areas Act had gradually divided the city into racial zones and made it illegal to reside outside of one's racially designated area. Manenberg, where he lived with his wife, was scheduled as a Coloured-only neighbourhood.

Living in Manenberg meant having to pass as Coloured, which Veronica says meant her father changed his name. This too was a detail I couldn't pin down. Perhaps he took a month — September, January, October — surnames common amongst Coloureds; names given their ancestors by white settlers who didn't understand or care what their slaves' and workers' real Malaysian, Indonesian, Madagascan, Khoi, or San names were. Jonny September — with a complexion on the pale side and the Afrikaans he learned at the workplace, he could've gotten away with that.

It is unlikely John Ndevu came anywhere near Mfuleni in the 1950s or '60s, when it was just a handful of households, out in semi-rural land. In the 1970s and '80s it began to grow, at first through the process of racial cleansing instigated by the Group Areas Act. In Strand, Somerset West, Waterkloof, and Eerste Rivier black households were shunted off prime land, their shanties razed or homes sold, and deposited in rental stock in central Mfuleni. Workers' hostels were built nearby for single black men who had a sponsored Pass from their employers. The hostel dwellers, up to ten in a single room, were construction workers employed by Ovcon and Concor and Triamic, Vianini's concrete pipe production workers, and Superocla men who laboured with asbestos. In time, as the townships became powder kegs of frustration and anger at the apartheid regime, their employers were obligated to pay insurance against fire, riots, and riot fire.

In the 1980s it was Khayelitsa, across the road from Mfuleni, and Crossroads to the northwest that burnt more than anywhere else in Cape Town. And it was Site B, in the middle of Khayelitsa, where John Ndevu moved at some point when, Veronica says, he couldn't cope or wouldn't put up with his Coloured wife's drinking problem. He took with him the children he'd had with Sylvia: Desiree, Yolanda, and Alistair. He raised them alone, trying to provide stability. Around him Khayelitsa was bearing the brunt of apartheid's endgame chaos. People filed into Khayelitsa, fleeing violence from state-sponsored militias in the townships of Crossroads and Nyanga. At a moment's notice, four-wheel-drive mine-resistant vehicles would pour out riot police. Strikers and protesters would close off the exit routes if the police didn't do it first.

REPEAT OFFENDERS

The dream was that after democracy there would be no need for violence, either on the part of the state or on the part of the people. The police force would be transformed, and it would serve citizens, not politicians.

John Ndevu stayed in Khayelitsa through the 1990s, and around him the township became dense and vast as migrants trickled in, mostly from the rural Eastern Cape. Unable to afford life any closer to the mountain, they concentrated in outskirt suburbs, which consistently swelled with informal settlements and backyard shacks. John Ndevu's adult children from his first marriage were amongst them.

The Ndevus lived in many of Cape Town's suburbs, and only her most dangerous ones, struggling to gain a stable foothold. In Khayelitsa, leaving the house at night in the informal settlements frequently cost people their possessions or their lives. In Mannenberg, the hold gangs had over daily life tightened, and schools closed for weeks at a time when gang wars flared up. By the mid-2000s Cape Town had become the most dangerous city in the country, with the highest murder and rape rates and the most drug-related crimes, though these conditions observed the city's strict spatial distribution of poverty and insecurity. Vigilante violence was an increasingly banal fact of life. By 2012 only exceptional cases got front-page coverage: known instances of mistaken identity, or those involving multiple victims.

The police force, too, failed to become the democratic institution once hoped for. Instead it functioned uneasily with the mandate of a civilian police service that cherishes human rights, which stood at odds with the inherited culture of militarized force aimed at containing a violence it didn't control. In poor neighbourhoods the ratio of residents to policemen remained impossibly high, and detectives worked with dozens of serious violent crime dockets on their desks at one time. Courts and prisons were similarly overburdened.

Places like Khayelitsa possessed the right conditions to create young men who were terrors to their neighbours, and none of the resources to reassure residents that those same men would be arrested, convicted, or rehabilitated.

Mfuleni itself was no exception. Having been a rather small peri-urban settlement until the 1990s, it then grew rapidly as it absorbed migrants from the rural areas and people displaced by conflict, flood, or fire in other parts of the city. In the process it met the expanding outer edge of Cape Town and was absorbed as one of its suburbs — except, not quite. Some public housing was built, but mostly different administrations organized shack settlements into huge low-density extensions. In the last few years this has entailed the slow razing and colonization of the dunes into marked plots by the City, which also fitted them with piped water, an outside toilet and sink, and enough space for a shack, spanned above by geometric webs of low electric wires. But the houses on these plots were built by their owners' hands, with plywood, cardboard, and zinc. They are gimcrack and precarious, and the contrast between them and the squat concrete toilets and sinks reinforces the feeling that the suburb is not wholly accepted by the city. This extends to services such as security too.

The Mfuleni police station is big and newly renovated, but it is also ten minutes' drive from the suburb, where very few people own cars. Residents complain at community meetings that they cannot get a van to arrive when they are the victim of a crime, and they hardly ever see the police patrolling. The small satellite station at the taxi rank is manned by two people who can only radio for help. While they are not completely neglected, when it comes to crime the people of Mfuleni feel they have to make their own arrangements in order to get either safety or justice.

Bardale is the very newest corner of Mfuleni, named for the farm it gradually encroached upon. It was laid out by the City in 2009 right beside the Klipfontein Road. A sandy field was left bare in the middle of the neighbourhood, most probably for future development as a park or sports ground. About half of the sites were given to people from Khayelitsa who had been forced to leave their shacks because of the expansion of the railway or the building of a power plant. The rest went to people who had been living in an informal settlement, squatters from Strand. Amongst the latter was Veronica Ndevu.

After years living as a slum tenant and a squatter, Veronica may have felt lucky to have a tenured plot, if not a house, and running water on site. But Bardale is still a place where, with 44 percent unemployment in Mfuleni, few people have jobs. Groups of laughing children play on every street, and so they may do it safely residents take picks and hack deep troughs into the roads to slow cars down. Young men idle. Everyone knows where the meth houses are. On weekend evenings shebeens (unlicensed bars) blast house music, on Sundays shacks shake and rattle with the noise of ardent worship. On Mondays those with jobs walk down to the Mfuleni taxi rank. There Toyota Quantums jostle for spots next to women turning glistening meat on coals, and the minibuses leave when they are full, heading at an urgent pace towards Table Mountain, which sits sturdy and flat in the distance with the rich suburbs of the city at its base.

In the minds of the residents of Bardale the sandy field marks a division between the people who were moved from Strand and the people who were moved from Khayelitsa. On a bad day this means a division between an honest person and a dishonest one, a selfish person and a generous one. If you stepped out of the Ndevus' shacks in 2012 you could peer through a gap between other houses at the end of their cul-de-sac and see, across that field, Angy Peter and Isaac Mbadu's house.

Angy had been one of the founders of the Social Justice Coalition when it was set up in response to the 2009 spate of violent xenophobic attacks on migrants from the rest of Africa. Her colleagues were fellow activists, most of whom had cut their teeth in the HIV/AIDS treatment struggle. Since then she had been assigned to the criminal justice campaign. Most of her work — attending trials, accompanying victims to the police station, arguing with policemen and prosecutors in meetings — was in Khayelitsa, but she was also working on expanding the SJC's work to other townships. She started a branch in Mfuleni and began mobilizing members.

Many of the recruits for the SJC Mfuleni branch were young people, and one of them was Rowan. Not everyone was happy about this — Rowan was known to be a criminal, and weren't they supposed to be fighting crime? Angy persuaded them not to judge him so quickly. She wanted Rowan to join the SJC for two reasons. As a repeat offender, he knew the criminal justice system back to front. Also, she saw him as a leader who would bring other thugs with him, beginning a process of rehabilitation in the neighbourhood.

THE CHILD OUTSIDE THE HOME

Veronica told me that when Rowan was born, on January 28, 1989, Yolanda, her half-sister, was dismayed to find out her baby was albino. She wanted to leave him behind at the hospital, but their sister Desiree wouldn't let her. In Cape Town's townships albinos are known colloquially, and without affection, as ingawu — monkeys. Some people believe their condition is the manifestation of a curse. During her pregnancy with Rowan, Yolanda had lived in Site C in Khayelitsa, next door to an albino woman whom she was always teasing. Much later the family would joke: that's the reason you had one.

Veronica never knew who Rowan's father was, and, no matter how often she asked his mother, Yolanda would always deflect the question. Throughout his childhood Rowan too tried to get his mother to tell him his father's name. She never did. Du Preez was the name of the husband she had left before she even got pregnant with Rowan. She kept the surname for her own reasons and also gave it to the two other boys that came later, Monde and Nathaniel. At times, frustrated with Rowan's questions, she'd point at her own father and say to the boy, That man cares for you, he looks after you, feeds you. He's your father.

When Rowan was a child, the family would be told by neighbours, again and again, that Rowan did "silly" things on the street. They dismissed this as the normal behaviour of an energetic boy. The first time they *knew* he stole was after his mother's boyfriend, who had for a time been the family breadwinner and had provided for her children's needs, left. Rowan took an armful of his mother's clothes, sold them, and bought himself a new outfit.

Some time later John Ndevu and Rowan ran into a neighbour, the father of another albino boy, at the spaza shop. The neighbour took John aside and said, "How is your boy doing? Because mine — he's stout, he's up to all kinds of mischief."

"Mine too," Rowan's grandfather replied. "He's up to nonsense." But he was reassured that Rowan's behaviour was just a characteristic of albino boys. It makes them silly children, doing silly things.

In court his grandfather and aunt Desiree referred to Rowan's behaviour as "naughty." They denied knowledge of the true extent of his crimes. Whether they were lying primarily to themselves or to the court wasn't clear. Even Veronica, who doesn't deny his criminal history, was adamant that Rowan was a sweet, loved son. He cooked for them, made jokes, had charm. He chastised his younger brother if he was disrespectful to Ndevu. He was easy to be around, dutiful like a child, and even when he grew up you could still send him on errands and he would go without complaint, return, and help with the chores. "One child inside the house, and another out-side the house," the judge offered, as a compromise between the family's evasions and the version already on record.

CRIME AND PUNISHMENT

I have wondered long and hard about Rowan's sense of belonging. Cape Town has not stopped being a place where you are asked to declare a fixed identity, lest you make other people uncomfort-able. On his mother's side, he was part-Xhosa, part-Coloured. On his father's, unknown. His skin colour a blank that was filled in only by insults. He moved between several suburbs: Manenberg, Khayelitsa, Westbank, Strand. When he reached adolescence what beliefs about his identity could he seek refuge in?

Veronica says Rowan was twice suspended from high school, and finally expelled. The first suspension was for stealing from other children — "silly things like that" — and the second was for stabbing an ex-girlfriend with a ballpoint pen. "But she didn't die," Veronica noted. By the age of fourteen he had been expelled for slashing the school principal's tires after his teacher had con-fronted him in front of the class about the ballpoint pen incident. His criminal record indicates that at fifteen he was arrested for theft and sent to reform school.

After reform school released him, Rowan continued to get into trouble with the law. At sixteen he was charged with the rape of a teenage girl. Veronica thought the police had gotten the story wrong. Rowan's friends came to the family after his arrest, claim-ing he had been with them at the time of the alleged attack. But perhaps they didn't take this information to the police. Several years later, when the case finally came to court, Rowan was con-victed and given a suspended sentence of five years. Yet Veronica remained convinced that he'd been unfairly treated, as the case had relied on the testimony of a witness she called "half-minded," mentally disabled.

Rowan's criminal record notes he went by two nicknames, though really they were one, given to him by other boys in Manenberg: White/Nigger. His post-mortem revealed that the latter was inlaid on his skin, probably through makeshift methods, along with two other tattoos, a $, possibly gang insignia, and the name of his mother, Yolanda, by then deceased. She had died of food poisoning when Rowan was sixteen.

In 2010 Veronica secured a residential site in Bardale. Independent, no longer married, working as a domestic for a white family in Somerset West, and now commanding a precious resource, a title deed, she invited her father and his grandsons to come and live with her.

John Ndevu was already in his seventies when Rowan and Nathaniel came to live with him. (The middle child, Monde, it was implied in court, was sent to live with his grandmother.) He was retired, and he probably received a state pension of, at most, R1,200 per month in 2012, and a child support grant of R270 for Nathaniel's upbringing. Sisters Veronica and Desiree, who often visited to help with cooking and cleaning, had part-time jobs. A family primarily living off one or two welfare grants would not have been unusual in Mfuleni. Regardless, getting by on around R1,400 a month would not have been easy for the family.

Right from when Rowan was a child up until adulthood, John Ndevu couldn't put up with anyone beating the boy. Rowan's skin was pale, almost translucent, and his grandfather imagined it was stretched thin, too delicate to protect the child within. With the move to Bardale, Ndevu's protectiveness continued. If Rowan stole, his grandfather let it be known that the injured party should come to him first and he would find a way to resolve matters.

The problem was that once you get a reputation for being stout, Veronica told me, it doesn't matter what you actually did or didn't do — people will always come for you. Nomawethu Nombewu, who may or may not have been on the Street Committee for Bardale, depending who you believe, was the story's only true agnostic on the subject of who murdered Rowan. She told a similar story to Veronica's. Rowan's problem wasn't just that he looked different but that, to make matters worse, he couldn't draw on a female harangue to shift blame and argue down the crowd when they came for him. "Mamela," Nomawethu said to some of Rowan's old friends in my hearing. "Who of you has a mother?" she asked them. "And I won't beat you if your mother is standing behind you, ne? But an old man? What can he do?"

No one ever mentioned Rowan, educated only up to eighth grade, having a job. In Mfuleni he had soon developed close friendships with a group of other boys, many of them also known to be dropouts and tik (meth) smokers. These boys explained they would do "piece jobs" for their neighbours, small tasks involving manual labour, and they would skarrel, which meant asking people for cash, or occasionally mugging them to get it.

They were not quite a gang but a group of skollies, in which Rowan stood out. Whenever anything went missing, it was always Rowan who would be dragged out of his grandfather's yard to account for it. "And the people here," Nomawethu said, "when they beat you they really *moer* you."

In late 2010 Rowan met Angy Peter. This is how she describes their first encounter: Rowan was being pinned down in the sandy field outside her house, and men from Bardale were kicking him. She told them to stop, and they told her to get lost. "What did he do to you?" she said. "Let the police handle it." But the men were convinced that Rowan had broken into one of their homes, and the goods were still missing. Angy told them if they continued she'd call the police herself — and that the authorities might be more interested in the assault than the theft.

"Fucking impimpi!" one of the men said to her, and the beating continued.

Making good on the threat, Angy walked to the satellite police station at the taxi rank and told the officer on duty what was going on. By the time she'd walked back to Bardale the police still hadn't arrived, but John Ndevu had. He told the men he'd pay for the goods Rowan had taken. The group dispersed.

A few months later Rowan came to her house. He wanted to know what so many of his friends did there, once a week. A few of them had already been convinced by Angy to join the SJC, and Rowan probably had more of an idea of what happened there than he let on. Nomawethu described the SJC as the best thing that had happened to Rowan's fellow skarellers in a long time: "They loved it." Angy explained what the Social Justice Coalition did and what the meetings were about. If he wanted to join, though, he'd have to live clean. She got annoyed when he started to say he didn't have a choice. "Crime is not like tik," she told him, "you can change."

Each week the SJC Mfuleni Branch met in Angy's living room. The three-room shack she lived in with Isaac was simple. They didn't own expensive furniture or objects, except for a television. The branch members crammed onto and around a worn pink leatherette lounge suite. If the household was exceptional it was because it had the rare structured calm of a home with two parents, both of them in full-time employment, owners of the land the shack sat on, landlords to the woman next door, and able to send their three little girls to schools outside the township. Inside that room their visitors were told that social movements of people just like them — poor, badly educated, without obvious prospect — had changed the world.

In court, the family gave away little of what they had thought of Rowan's involvement with the organization. Rowan's aunt Desiree described the SJC's work as "that anti-crime business" and said she had hoped it would help Rowan. John Ndevu thought about the SJC as a group that "taught young people how to carry themselves." He said he was able to identify Isaac as one of the culprits behind his grandson's murder because he remembered meeting

Isaac in his yard one day, so well mannered, speaking in a very nice voice, introducing himself politely before collecting Rowan for a meeting.

THE COMING STORM

An urban planner working for the City told me that he had heard rumours of men who hunted waterfowl through the Driftsands wetlands and up the Kuilsrivier. He told me the landscape around Bardale had not accepted all modifications. The water table is high and the winter rains are hard. Engineers strive to route flooding through faceted concrete culverts, but even a minor squall channels tons of detritus onto open spaces. Huge tubes of concrete lie by the side of the Old Faure Road waiting to be set into the earth. The City abandoned its plan for a cemetery when the first bodies came back up.

In the year that Rowan was killed, was it obvious to anyone that a storm was brewing that Bardale would never be able to contain? Early portents should have been the company he kept with Cheese and Caras, more organized and experienced criminals. In high summer they invited him on one of their escapades, which started in Atlantis with the hijacking of a bakkie. They drove it to a string of Somalian-run spaza shops in George and, brandishing guns and crowbars, demanded airtime and money. Shortly afterwards Rowan was arrested for armed robbery and murder.

Angy was a powerful presence in the neighbourhood. She was a woman who spoke out, stubborn and formidable, who "wouldn't mind your face," as Nomawethu put it, to tell you what she thought. She made her views heard at every community meeting. Her neighbours came to her when their children went missing, when the police wouldn't let them open a case, when they found weapons in their tenant's shack. She had a dozen senior policemen's personal mobile phone numbers, and only used them to complain.

Awaiting a bail hearing, Rowan called Angy from his prison cell in Polsmoor and asked for her help. She said she wasn't sure what she could do. It was a busy time, preparations for the Commission of Inquiry into Policing in Khayelitsa were underway, and every day Angy was occupied with collecting affidavits. She forgot about Rowan's call. By the time she did try to get in touch with him, the number was disconnected.

Later, when his grandfather paid R1,000 to the bondsman and he was released, Rowan found out he had been expelled from the SJC branch. He wanted to rejoin, and Angy instructed him to write a letter to the Branch asking for forgiveness and another chance. It isn't clear what happened, but Rowan never again attended another SJC meeting.

Later Veronica would hear that when the police had questioned one of the Somalian shopkeepers, he had picked up a piece of fruit from his counter and said, "Like this — one of the robbers looked like this." The police had come straight for Rowan.

"Why do you rob when you're so identifiable?" she said to her nephew at the time. "No other thieves here are the colour of a peach." Veronica's neighbours were beginning to lose patience with her nephew. She couldn't go out on the street without someone bringing Rowan up. They told her they wouldn't chase her away, because they knew her, because she'd been in Bardale since the beginning. But Rowan had to go. John Ndevu arranged for Rowan to stay with someone in Delft, but within three weeks Veronica found him back in her house.

"Hayibo, Rowan," she said. "Why are you here?"

His grandfather had called him back.

In the weeks that followed Veronica began to panic. Afraid she'd be caught up in whatever backlash was going to come, she packed up her things and went back to the Eastern Cape.

It was raining on August 10, 2012, when Angy and Isaac's TV went missing. A hard winter rain. Perhaps this is why they didn't hear the break-in. There are township rumours that some robbers use muti to induce a deep sleep in their victims. But Rowan had once given Angy a more earthly explanation for the number of times victims would sleep through a robbery. Thieves knew to push smouldering CD disks into cracks in the wall before they robbed a house — the resulting smoke was a supposed sedative.

On the shelves of the TV stand in Angy and Isaac's shack were pictures of their daughters, six-year-old Hope's face pressed up to her mother, with sisters Tumi and Ntobokeng in matching pink outfits on the lawns of the Company Gardens, the city centre's public park. There was also a framed picture of Isaac as a teenager with two of his hip hop crew. The family portraits now surrounded a gaping absence, less than a square metre of negative space where their flat screen plasma had been.

It was 2:00 a.m. Angy and Isaac were sure of one thing — if Rowan hadn't done it, he would know who had. So Isaac set out to look for him.

THE MISSION AT VERONA

Beatrice Lamwaka

This is how the war starts for me. I am eight years old and in Primary Three at Lacor School. My father is a doctor — at least, that is what everyone calls him. Dakta. I find out much later that he is actually a medical assistant. He treats people from home, early in the mornings before he goes to work on his bicycle and when he returns back in the evening. Our home smells like a hospital.

My mother, whom we call by her first name, Rosa, is always at home. Most of us, her children, call her Rocha. It's my father who pronounces Rosa with "sa." He was taught by white men, he always reminds us.

My mother cooks eggs for my father before he goes to work. She boils syringes when he needs to administer an injection.

I have many brothers and sisters, but I will not talk about all of them. Two of my sisters have moved away from home. Ocili works in the Uganda Commercial Bank in Kampala. While in Kampala, she realized that she wasn't fit to be called Ocili anymore, and every time she came for a visit and I called her Ocili she corrected me, Cecily. But I soon forgot again. My sister Acayo is a midwife who works in Matany Hospital in Moroto. Both these sisters send me dresses that are way too big — that way, I can wear them a little longer till they fit.

My brother Odong is the third born and the quiet one, until you start a fight with him; for him a fight never ends. There is my sister Flo. She is friends with everyone in the village, and she is also secretive. When people were only just suspecting that she was pregnant, she gave birth to a baby boy.

My brother Richard is two years older but he thinks he is the boss of me.

Our home is near the main road that goes to Anaka, and if you go in the opposite direction you will get to Gulu Town. The main road is parallel to the railway line, and the train passes through every morning and again in the evening. If we want to catch the train, we walk three kilometres to the station at St. Mary. Once our neighbour tried to jump off as the train slowed to pass our village. He broke his leg.

Today, my father has returned early. I see him on the road, coming home on his bicycle. Sing:

Ligi ligi Baba oo (Ligi ligi Daddy has arrived)
Ligi ligi Baba oo (Ligi ligi Daddy has arrived)

This is the song I sing with my half-sister Adyero who is one year younger than me. Father always brings something home for us all: lagalagala, boiled maize, sim sim melted with sugar.

The path leading to our homestead is wide, so you can always see whoever is coming towards the house and anyone on the path has a clear view of our home.

My father brings seedlings and the seeds of different plants. We have giant pine trees, bamboo, and eucalyptus. Fruit trees — mangoes, avocadoes, banana, oranges, lemon, jack fruit, jambula, durian, adunnu — and flowers — frangipani, jacaranda, cassia, jasmine. The trees surround our homestead, and we are woken every day by the loud chirping from the trees. Sometimes we incorporate our words in the bird's song:

Agakakak meni otedo ngo? (Raven, what has your mother cooked?)

Boo boo boo boo boo, the bird answers.

My mother has planted boo as well as eggplant, malakwang and otigo around our home: vegetables she sends me to pick whenever she needs them. Our farmland is a kilometre away. That is where we grow sweet potatoes, maize, lapena, beans.

In 1986, when Yoweri Museveni became president, he brought peace to Uganda. During the coup there were rumours that he was going to kill all the Acholi because Acholi had killed people in Luwero, a stronghold for his rebel activities. But since we don't hear of any killings or reprisals, we have begun to relax and hope there will be no retribution.

That evening when my father returns from work, he seems tired. There are no patients waiting for him with their chickens or goats, so I bring his chair, rwot onino — the chief is sleeping — and unfold it under the mango tree. He brings his radio from his room and sits listening to the news.

"Lamwaka, go get me water," my father says. I was going to get his water even without him asking, but he always asks anyway.

My mother is cooking lapena with sweet potatoes. The smell of the food wafts across the compound. The kitchen is full of smoke from the burning wood and I don't want to stay in there for long. Our kitchen is directly at the end of the path leading home, only blocked by a metre of the main road. I look up and I can see men walking on the road, but because of the smoke I don't pay much attention.

"There are men coming," I tell my father when I bring his water.

"Are they carrying a patient?" he asks.

Before we can say more, the men arrive and walk straight to my father. My mother comes out of the kitchen.

The men have guns slung over their shoulders. They are wearing lacaka caka trousers but no shirts. They wear sapatu, not shoes or boots, on their feet. All the soldiers I have seen before wear lacaka caka trousers and matching shirts with heavy boots.

When we see them we sing:

Lacaka caka meno bongo lweny (Camouflage clothes are for fighting)
Lacaka caka meno bongo kolo (Camouflage clothes are for provoking)

The men who come today to greet my father as he sits under the mango tree are friendly; they greet us as if we are old acquaintances. My mother offers them water to drink and chairs to sit on. They refuse the seats but accept the water. My mother goes back to the kitchen, but I am sure that she is following what is going on. I sit on the ground beside my father. I want to know what is going on here.

The men stand around as if their mothers never taught them that when you stand around someone seated, you suck their blood. My father begins to look uncomfortable in his chair.

"Mzee, itye maber?" They ask over and over again as if they have not just greeted him.

There is a play on the radio. If these men were not around, we would have listened to this play without interruption. The men introduce themselves: Okello from Laliya, Otim from Anaka, Larem from Koch Goma, Nyeko from For God, and Mwaka from Lacekocot. Although it was years ago, I remember the names of this first group of men. Their faces have never faded from my mind.

"My daughter is Lamwaka. She was born on the first. What about you?"

"Lamwaka, you must give me chicken, since you are younger," Mwaka tells me. Then, to my father, he says, "I don't know when I was born, my mother never told me."

I am not allowed to stand around my father or any adult. I am afraid to suck their blood. If I want something from him, or if my mother sends me to ask him for something, I have to kneel and then ask. Seeing the men standing there makes me wonder what they are really saying.

"Lamwaka, come into the house," my mother calls to me.

I quickly follow her voice into the kitchen.

"Why do you want to listen to adult conversations? This child of mine!"

I am not in the kitchen for long when my father calls me to catch one of the chickens walking around the compound. My father has never asked me to catch any chicken; that is my mother's responsibility. She is the one who knows which chicken is ready to be eaten.

I go straight to the bamboo trees where I know there will be more chickens and I can sneak up on them. They all run in different directions. I have always hated running after chickens because they never stay still when you need to catch one. My brother Richard joins and finally he is the one who catches one.

"Why are we giving them a chicken?" Richard asks.

"I think the men with the guns want it," I tell him.

"I saw some men at Korina's also getting chicken."

"Eh." I do not know what else to say.

When we return with the chicken, my father's friends Apa and Orub are seated with him. The other men are still standing. Now they seem anxious to leave. Richard hands the chicken to one of the men and the bird squirms as the man holds it away from his body and gun. It defecates on the ground.

"Apwoyo," he says. The men thank my father and then they are leaving, walking back along the path before turning to the left towards Bwobo.

Richard and I stand there for a moment, neither my father nor his friends saying anything.

"Things might be getting bad," Apa says after a while.

My mother appears from the kitchen. She is excited. Earlier in the day, the women at the well had said there are many men in Bwobo and many more are joining now. We must be careful now. Where is Flo?

I have not seen Flo since I returned from school. For now, she is not going to school until her son Oringa is older. Wherever she is, I know she will come home with stories that she will tell us.

The next evening, and again after that, the men came back, guns slung to their backs, lacaka caka trousers and shirts mixed with civilian clothes. Each time there were different men, but each time there was the same friendliness. They would introduce themselves and say where they came from. The evening of the second visit, I recognized a boy from my school. He was in Primary Seven. He looked away as I watched him; maybe he never even recognized me.

That time one of my own chickens went. I had a number of chickens that patients had given my father in payment for his dakta services. He had given them to me to look after. My chickens were mine in name; I never really took care of them. They became part of my mother's flock, but I knew I was supposed to be in charge of them.

The men kept coming, and sometimes they would come during the day and my mother would have to give them a chicken. We also started eating chicken more than we normally did. My mother said there was no need for us to continue keeping chickens if they were going to be eaten by someone else. When the chickens were all gone, the men started asking for goats. At this point, they were still humble and polite.

The neighbours were also complaining about the loss of their chickens.

"Every day they just come and take and take," our neighbour Korina complained to my mother one day after the men had left.

"They are protecting us from getting killed," my mother said.

"But who is killing us?" Korina asked.

My mother kept silent. I wanted her to say something. I knew that she knew more. Nobody wanted to say anything, but I wanted somebody to explain so that I would know what was happening.

At school, my classmates also talked about the men with guns and the food that their families had to give them.

Then one day the men came again, and this time there were more men with guns, and they were not speaking in low voices anymore.

"All of you sit down," they said. My sisters, brothers, and mother — herded under the mango tree where my father was already seated in his usual spot, listening to the radio announcements.

"Where is the gun?" they asked. Maybe because I was young and was carrying my sister's nine-month-old son, they didn't ask me to join the rest of the family. When I tried to sit with them, one of the men urged me to move on. I walked over to my half-brother's house, which was built ten minutes away from our homestead. Nobody was home. I didn't stay. I tried to hide in the obia grass, but I couldn't stay there. The obia was taller than me and nobody would see me. My nephew was quiet in my arms, as if he knew there was something wrong.

I went back to where my family was gathered together, with the men pointing guns at their heads. I tried to sit again but couldn't. In the end I just kept moving between my half-brother's home and back under the mango tree, still not sure where I should stay. I was afraid that they would be shot and I would remain alone. I didn't know what to do.

"Bring the gun," one of the men shouted.

"Get it from wherever it's hidden."

"We don't have any gun," my mother protested. "There is no gun in this home."

"Do you want us to check for it, and if we find it ..."

Everybody seemed worried. Flo was crying. I had never seen a gun in our home. Flo had never showed interest in joining the army or any group with guns.

The conversation went on for a long time. For me, it seemed like forever, and I didn't know what to do. Then, I heard someone shout.

"You, child! Where is the gun?" There was silence.

"There is no gun here," I said.

I was known to say whatever came into my head without any thought of the impact. One time, my mother had saved food for my father and then my father unexpectedly returned home with several friends. My mother wanted to keep the food until later, but I went out of the kitchen and started singing loudly for everyone to hear, while swinging on a tree. I sang:

Ki kano dek (They have hidden the food)
Ki kano dek (They have hidden the food)

My mother had to serve the food, worrying all the time that it would not be enough, and she later pulled my ears. I was already used to her telling me, "You and your mouth!"

But this time there was no need for me to hold my tongue. There was no gun. I hadn't seen one at home. The only guns I had seen belonged to the soldiers or the men who always came home with them.

It took a long time of begging and pleading before my family was let go. The sun was already setting when the men walked away. They left us with a warning: "Ci lil."

Go and tell them.

That is what the men with guns were called in the beginning. Ci lil. The *them* they referred to were government soldiers. Of course we wouldn't tell them. The soldiers were mainly in St. Mary, Lacor, and the men in mismatched lacaka caka were in Bwobo. We were in the middle.

Later there were rumours that if you went to Bwobo you would find ci lil roasting chicken and goats' meat. There was a market in Bwobo were we used to buy food, and suddenly we couldn't go there anymore. At that time I do not think any of us ever imagined that the ci lil in Bwobo and soldiers in Lacor would meet. My school, Lacor Primary, was about two kilometres away from home. We, the children from the village, walked to school and returned home together. On our way back we would climb fruit trees and pick whatever was in season, not caring whose homestead we invaded. Mango season was my favourite. The trees would be yellow with ripe fruit. And the trees were everywhere. We had two mango trees at home, but other people's mangoes always tasted better.

Next to our homestead was Verona and Alokolumh, which had started off as a seminary before it became the country's national seminary. This is where we prayed on Sunday and this is where most of the villagers gathered for events. Verona was run by two Italian priests, Father Umberto and Father John.

Father Umberto had a full beard and spoke Acholi with an Italian accent. He loved to take pictures. Most of my early childhood pictures were taken at Verona: playing kwepena with other girls, dancing in church, practising dancing on Saturdays when there would be choir practice or evening classes for First Holy Eucharist or Confirmation.

The mission at Verona became our refuge when the war began. I don't remember why we decided to run there when gunshots started, but I remember my mother, my sisters, and I, and the rest of the villagers, running to Verona. We picked up some of our clothes and carried half-cooked lapena and ran to the mission.

The Fathers welcomed us. The two huts that were in the middle of the parallel buildings that housed the priests and the seminarians became our home.

Verona kept us safe when there were gunshots at night. My elder brother, Odong, never came with us, and most times my father spent the night at home. He talked about mosquitoes biting in the bush but never mentioned exactly where he went. That is when I realized that the men found their own refuge, and for the women and boys around my age, Verona was ours.

During the day we went home and some of us still went to school. Some went to poto to plant maize, lapena, beans, and sweet potatoes. In the evenings, if there were no gunshots, we carried our bedding to the mission, and some food for the little ones to eat. By around 7:00 p.m., the women would be seated on the verandas of the two huts where we slept as the children ran around Verona.

When the gunfire started, it did not stop for a long time. Children were being abducted on their way to school. There were stories that they were being trained to fight. Rumour had it that the children were more vicious than the adults. They had no mercy and they followed orders of their leaders. These were stories that were coming from distant places like Kitgum and far away villages in Gulu district.

I developed a keen interest in these stories and I would try to imagine them in my mind, but however much I tried the stories didn't ring true. There were stories of soldiers running away from ci lil who reported that these men were strong and that they could fight for hours. Whatever they wore, they got from the bodies of soldiers they had killed. I remembered the polite men we had given chickens, and I couldn't imagine that they were capable of such activities. Yes, I could imagine the men who had wanted the gun, those could kill. But not the ones who had only wanted chicken.

Just as Verona became our home, our family homestead became a place of refuge for many people. First distant relations, fleeing all-out war in their own villages, came and asked my father for a spot of land to build their houses. My father agreed. Soon others who weren't relatives also came, then, during the harvest season in 1999, the government gave the refugees seventy-two hours to enter into internally displaced people's camps. Because our homestead had become a home to many people, it was declared a camp, so yet more people still moved in.

The camp stretched from the fence of Verona to gang pa Alo to Korina's home. Every spot of land had a house on it. My father insisted on keeping a small compound of paspalum, but eventually, as the conflict wore on, many years of being walked on by thousands of people daily made the grass die.

In Verona, the huts were large enough to house up to fifty people. Since we didn't carry our mattresses or beds as time wore on, we slept on the floor and covered ourselves with whatever we did manage to carry from home.

One day, at about 8:00 p.m., when the women were seated on the veranda of the huts telling stories, we heard strange loud voices coming from the dining hall where the seminarians were having their supper. They may have come in from the back door where we couldn't have seen them. The air was still. It was clear that something was wrong. We quickly crept back to our beds. Lay still as if we were dead. Suddenly the voices were nearer to our hut. The door was opened. We never locked the door, just in case anyone needed to leave at night to use the pit latrines. A bright torch shone on us. We remained silent, even the children were quiet. Nobody moved. Then the door closed and I heard someone sigh.

We didn't stay long afterwards at Verona. It no longer felt a place of safety. Everybody was asked to leave. We went back home, where we found about a hundred elderly women and young children living on our land. My father still slept in the main house, but the rest of us chose to sleep in huts built around the compound, which weren't so exposed to the main road. I slept in one hut with my mother. Flo stayed with my aunt in another hut. My brothers were in another hut. The good thing with the huts is they are usually cool, especially in the dry season.

During the day I played with new friends, the children whose families had moved onto our land. My mother started using her big saucepans — nywal ber — to feed my cousins. Fetching water was fun because we all carried jerry cans, and the pots would be filled fast but then again they would be empty sooner.

Our hut now also doubled as the kitchen. It was divided into two: one room worked as the kitchen, with shelves for pots, saucepans, plates, and a pot for drinking water. Then the other was the bedroom where we kept our clothes and bedding. Whatever my mother could hide was buried in the ground.

My father broke one of the doors to our four-bedroom house and filled the hole with bricks to keep away unwanted guests, but they came anyway. Any time they wanted.

A group comes one night while we are sleeping. The banging of the door wakes me and my mother.

"Funguwa mulango," one of the intruders shouts. Our door is so useless. The man pushes and pushes until it opens. A bright torch is pointed at my mother. The man tells her to pull up her mattress and he checks underneath it for money but doesn't find any. He then searches throughout the hut. He finds a jerry can of waragi and takes it for himself.

"Where is your father?"

I look at the gun he holds. "In the main house," I reply.

He points the gun at me and says, "Let's go." He orders me to carry a bag of my clothes and my mother's gomesi.

Outside there are more men with guns.

"Call your father," he says as he knocks on the door.

"Baba, Baba, Baba!"

"Who is that?"

"It's me, Lamwaka."

"What do you want?"

"Tell him, there are sick people who need treatment."

"Some people need treatment."

"Tell them to go to a witch doctor."

I hear the bed ruffling and then footsteps. The main door opens, and the men grab my father and take him to his bedroom. One man, with a gun pointing at me, stays behind.

"Sit down."

I sit down.

He continues to point his gun at my head.

"Hail Mary, full of grace, the Lord is with thee, blessed art thou amongst women and blessed is the fruit of thy womb, Jesus. Holy Mary," I say.

"Our Father, who art in heaven," I say.

The gun stays pointed at me.

Inside the house, the men ask for money, and when my father says he doesn't have they insist that since he pays my school fees he must have some money.

I say, "Hail Mary, full of grace ..."

I hope that they don't hurt my father. I pray that somehow I find myself somewhere else. Nothing happens. I am on the veranda and a gun is pointed at my head.

They pick whichever drugs they can lay their hands on.

"Carry the things and follow."

I carry the bags and follow.

Somewhere, not far off from home, the men take the bags from me.

"Run home without looking back or we will shoot you."

I run home and I don't look back.

My mother opens the door as soon as I reach the threshold. My father is in the kitchen too. He leaves. My mother hugs me. We stay in that position for a long time. I lie in bed hoping that this has all been a dream, but when I wake up in the morning the police are there.

My father has been speaking to them. My mother too. I am asked to tell what happened. I do so.

The police say, "These men were thieves." It seems ours is not the only homestead that has been robbed. They went to many homes and robbed people of their belongings.

"You should have run," my brother Odong whispers to me.

I don't tell him I froze. That I disappeared and my body was just there.

"You should have run," he whispers again. "They wouldn't have shot you."

Flo and my aunt say they heard something but they couldn't come out. My brothers did too. They sneaked out of the hut and slept in the bush.

I am in school. The teacher is telling us something, but I am not paying attention. I am thinking about the boiled cassava in my bag. The spot where the sunshine hits the cement through the classroom roof is still behind Akongo, my classmate, this means break time is far. I move my butt on the bare floor. I still have to pass two classes to sit at a desk. Only Primary Six and Seven have desks to write on.

Then there is the sound of gunshots. It may be far or near. I cannot tell. Then there are pupils jumping out through the windows. The teacher is still talking. We are trying to get to the door. I finally manage to push through. I am out of the classroom. Some of my classmates are still trying to get to the door. Some are screaming. Others are crying. Then we are running and running.

I am running towards home. I have to get home to my mother. I stop. The sound of gunshots is coming from the direction of our homestead. I have to run to my father. I have been to the hospital only once. I run on the main road towards Katikati, to my father.

I run. I run.

I don't have my bag anymore.

I run. I run.

I find Gulu Hospital. I find a spot under a big tree where I can see my father through the window. *He will see me*, I tell myself. He is still busy, but he will see me.

I sit under the tree, still afraid, knowing I have to wait. I gather some pebbles and play seven stones by myself. I greet people as they pass. They greet me. I move and sit in a different spot when the sun begins to burn me. I wait. My father will see me.

"What are you doing here?"

"There were gunshots and I ran here."

He tells me to wait, he will be back. I wait. He will be back. I play seven stones again. He comes back with his bicycle. We will go to my uncle's home in Layibi, close to Gulu Town. It is safer there than going back to Alokolum.

My father rides, and I am perched behind him. People are moving around as if nothing has happened. This is the life we have learned to live. At the sound of gunshots people lie still for a while and then soon after they are back to doing whatever they need to do. The attacks are usually short-lived. The rebels shoot and the soldiers respond and the rebels run away. People pick up their dead and life continues.

We get to my uncle's. My cousins are happy to see me, and my father says he will leave now before it gets dark. He will come for me.

He returns the next day and we go back home. All is well, my mother also heard the gunshots but she was at the market buying food.

"I was at the market. I stayed there until it was quiet again, and then I came home," my mother explains. She cooks chicken and gives me my favourite part, the gizzard plus liver with big kwon kal.

My sister says, "No, that is mine. I always eat the gizzard."

"Let her eat," my mother says.

We are home. My father is showering. Soldiers approach our compound. We can tell they are soldiers. They are dressed in lacaka caka.

"Where is your father?"

"Bathing."

"Tell him to come."

"He is bathing."

The man with the gun goes to the bathroom, tells my father to come out. He comes out in his towel, soap lather on his back and shoulders. The soldiers order him to dress.

"You are feeding and giving drugs to rebels."

"They took them by force."

"You have to come with us to the barracks."

The soldiers lead my father away. At home we sit, waiting and waiting. At last, in the evening, he comes back.

"What did they do?"

"They asked me so many questions."

That is all my father says. We don't ask him again.

Another day, men with guns, dressed in lacaka caka with civilian clothes, come to our home.

"You people have been telling the soldiers where we are."

"No. We've said nothing."

"Give us some Panadol, Aspirin ... we need medicine."

My father gives him the drugs.

My father continues to treat the people in the village, those who couldn't go to hospitals. He also continues to give drugs to the men in lacaka caka.

One night we are woken up by villagers carrying a man who was cut by the rebels. He had refused to give them his goats. They attacked him and left him for dead. The villagers walked from Paminya, about ten kilometres away, in the middle of the night. My father gives the wounded man first aid, and he and his companions wait until dawn before travelling on to the hospital. The man survives.

"Get dressed," my mother says. "You are going to Matany." I quickly dress up. I pack my three dresses in a hand-sewn bag. That is all I have. Richard will take me to town, where there is a car going to Matany Hospital where my sister Acayo works. I have never been there, but I have always wanted to visit. I am glad that the time has come now.

The trip to Matany takes almost twelve hours. I get sick and vomit in the car. It's the first time I have travelled such a long distance. I am the youngest in the car. The rest are Italian sisters who work at the hospital with my sister. They speak fondly of her.

"Margaret," they refer to my sister Acayo, "she will be happy to see you." I smile.

They speak mostly in Italian, but to me they speak in English. I have never spoken English, except during English lessons. I am silent for most of the trip.

"We have arrived," Sister Bruna tells me. I look up; the hospital is beautiful. There are lights everywhere. My sister is wearing a blue dress with a white cap. She looks different but seems happy.

"Thank you for coming," she says over and over again. "We cannot see the school that you are going to from here, but it's very nice."

I smile. I am too exhausted to ask questions.

It is ten years before I return home. When I reach what was our homestead, it's almost impossible to find my mother's hut. There are too many children, too many huts. There is hardly space for me to walk.

"That is Nyapa Dakta."

"Ah, she works for World Food," people say behind me. Children run after me. Others call out that they heard that I was recording the details of orphans and widows so that I can help them.

When I finally find my family, it is my mother I see first. She is frail. Her hair is grey. She looks older, but her dimples and smile come easily. Flo has had three more children whom I have never met. My father sits under the mango tree listening to the radio. All these years, the mango tree has not been cut down. Nobody has built his or her house under the tree.

"My daughter, you have come," he says.

There are graves close to the huts. When I ask why people have buried their dead here, he says, "They will take them home when the war ends."

THE SEARCH FOR MAGICAL MBUJI
Neema Komba

THE ROCK DOESN'T LIKE ME

When I first heard about Mbuji — a mystical treasure hidden deep in the middle of Mbinga — I was skeptical. "The rock has secrets," my uncle Alexander, who lives just a few hours' walk from the Mbuji rock, told me. "I have passed the rock many times, but I do not pay close attention to it. I figure if I mind my own business, the rock will leave me alone."

He spoke about Mbuji as if it were alive. I tried to picture it in my mind, something like the rocks I had seen in Mwanza, giant formations floating in the blue waters of Lake Victoria, but Uncle insisted that Mbuji was much more majestic. Some locals claim it to be the second largest rock in Africa. Some claim that you do not climb it if you are in your right mind, for it has already killed two people — an American explorer who slipped on his way down and a local man who threw himself off the rock. They say it was the rock's residents, evil spirits, ibuta, that caused these two tragedies. I wanted to see it for myself, to prove these people wrong. *Spirits don't live inside rocks! A rock cannot kill people!*

I hopped into a bus and travelled sixteen hours to Mbinga, the birthplace of my parents, which sits on steep Umatengo hills that extend south, all the way to the shores of Lake Nyasa, some thousand kilometres from the city of Dar-es-Salaam, where I live. I love Mbinga. I love the "I am standing at the edge of the universe" feeling that the place gives me. I love how the air is thin and crisp, and how calm and serene it is. I love gazing at the endless panorama of meandering hills.

I went on this journey with my parents, who, despite being born and raised in Mbinga, had never seen the rock up close. After the bus, we hired a taxi and travelled south along a dirty, unpaved road from Mbinga town towards Mbuji. It was mid-April, near the end of a six-month rain season, kifuku. The air was fresh, a mix of red earth smell after the rain and pine and eucalyptus fragrances, whose forests cover parts of the hills. The hills were green, decorated with maize, beans, wheat, peas, and ngoro, which are holes that form a honeycomb pattern to prevent soil erosion, making the hills look like bao, a local board game, from afar.

From a distance we could see Mbuji. The huge grey stone stood erect on top of wheat fields, the tip of this imposing rock slightly kissing puffs of greying clouds. It didn't seem as big as they'd said it was. As we neared Mbuji, in the village of Myao, we pulled over in front of several houses lined up by the road. Michael, our taxi driver and tour guide, dramatically got out of the car, sat down to greet the men sitting in front of the houses, and asked for an elder to give us permission to go to the rock safely. One house in particular resembled my grandfather's house, with arched brick pillars on the front porch of the house, a relic of German missionary architecture. Two long mats made of maloulu, a plant that grows by the river, lay in front of the house, drying maize flour used to make ugali, a kind of stiff porridge. The villagers looked at us suspiciously, as though we had stepped from a different planet. I wonder whether it was our interest in seeing the rock that intrigued them or the way we were dressed, my mother draped in a big maroon Masai sheet and me wearing tight trousers unlike most women there. The elders told us they had no cultural authority over the rock. We had to go to Mbuji village and meet the elders there. They warned us, however, that the rock was not kind to strangers.

We passed by the Mbuji village council, a ramshackle baked brick building with a row of rooms that serve as offices. Two wooden flagpoles with no flags stood in front of the building. Kornelius Ndunguru, an elderly man in a brown jacket and a Kufi cap, commonly known as barakashea, sat on a wooden bench in front of the office. Few people went in and out of the office as we got out of the car. We sat down to greet the elderly man, who was kind enough to call someone to take us to the rock, which was about half an hour from the village council offices. The young man, a mganda dancer, warned us about the rock. He said we had to be "complete" to be able to climb, although in what ways he didn't say. He was reluctant to talk about the rock, so we asked him about mganda instead, which he seemed happy to talk about. Mganda, a Matengo dance for men, is a fusion of traditional Matengo culture in rhythm and British colonial culture in dress. The men dress in crisp white shirts and shorts, polished black shoes, and long white socks. They wave a ponytail-looking mpukii, made by tying cow tail hair on a stick, and step in slow, poised movements to a chant and drum beat.

Grey clouds formed above us as we neared the rock. Michael, a fearless Matengo man, forged through dirty, slippery roads to the village at the foot of the rock. The village was something out of a painting: an expanse of cool, green grass towered over by two enormous rocks, with houses lined around it and a heavy mist hovering above. We stepped out of the car in slow motion, lost in the allure of the place. It wasn't just one giant rock, as we'd seen from afar, but two mountains of solid rock. A skinny black dog ran from one of the houses and barked at us, as if to tell us we were not welcome there.

A man, possibly in his late thirties, wearing green gumboots, faded blue jeans, a sun hat, and a rainbow-coloured jacket, approached us to answer our questions. He identified himself as Olaf Komba, the traditional guardian of the rock, the man responsible for conducting all the rituals relating to the rock. He said there are several caves around the rock, and ancestral spirits reside in them. He said the climb was difficult, that the weather had to be dry and clear, and one had to be physically fit to make it to the top. Another man, with dishevelled hair, reddening white trousers due to the red soil, and a fading green jacket, walked up to me as Olaf was explaining his role to my parents (guiding people along safer paths and appeasing the spirits of the rock). He grabbed my arm and locked his brownish-grey eyes with mine. With a slurred speech, he told me to give him some brew money or else there would be no way out of the village. His words left an unsettling feeling in my belly, even though I knew they were probably untrue. I bravely detached myself from the grip of his dirty, chapped-from-hard-farm-work fingers and walked away without giving him any money.

The sky, as if to heed his threat, turned a violent shade of grey, almost black. The whole of Mbuji was covered in fog. The rocks were no longer visible. Olaf told us to hurry out of the village if we wanted to make it out before nightfall. If it rained, the roads would have been too slippery to pass. We left Mbuji, attempting to speed down a rough road. The car was bathed in red mud as we struggled out of difficult spots. We got stuck in the mud three times before we made it back to Mbinga town. I felt like I was in some horror film, trying to get out of a haunted village.

You know how some things don't logically make sense, and you know you shouldn't worry, but there is that little voice inside that says, *What if everything is real?* that makes you afraid? That's why I am going back, to conquer this absurd fear inside me that the rock doesn't want me there.

MAGIC IS IN THE EYE OF THE BEHOLDER

"Please don't climb the rock," my mother, who knows my stubborn nature, pleads with me as I drop the weight of my body into the seat of the waiting taxi. I don't understand the urgency in her tone, but it cuts through my bravado and a chill runs through my spine. They say mothers can sense danger that can befall their children. *This could be a sign.*

Going to Mbuji that first time, I was sure that I was a detached observer, an outsider. What could a rock, a mere geological occurrence, do to me? Today I am not too sure.

My heart thumps in my chest as we make our way through a now familiar road to Mbuji. It is just Michael and me. We speed down a winding road, leaving a red cloud of dust behind. It is just a little past noon, but there is no sun overhead. A thick, grey blanket of fog covers the top of lush hills with their browning fields. The weather is rather gloomy and cold for a dry season.

My mind drifts away from the loud *vroom* of the car engine to the disturbing gaze of the man we met on our previous trip there. I can still feel the pinch of his fingers on my arm. I want to immerse myself in the view around me and forget about the man and his threats, but I am too tense to pay attention to the details of the scenery. I look with disinterest at the people and the places we pass. Michael is quiet in the driver's seat, lost in his own thoughts. Within an hour and fifteen minutes, we reach Mbuji village.

It has been three months since my first trip to Mbuji. The village at the foot of Mbuji is still as picturesque as before; it hasn't lost any of its charm. The large green field is now a warmer shade of green, almost yellow. Children are playing on the field, some playing football, some walking on wooden stilts. Golden patches of sunlight peek through light grey clouds. A few trees grow in the cracks on top of the smaller rock, which I learn is called the Angongo, the female rock, the bride to Mbuji, the male rock. A white cloud of fog circles around the larger Mbuji rock. A small part of me is relieved that the weather isn't great for rock climbing, and another part of me, the more curious one, is a little disappointed.

Michael and I walk towards a group of people standing at the edge of the field and ask for Olaf, the guardian. A woman with a baby wrapped in a kitenge on her back and a pile of wood on her head passes nearby as we ask. The group calls out to her. She happens to be Olaf's wife. Olaf's wife looks tired, like many Matengo women I have observed. The burden to feed the family here lies on the women. They have to cultivate the farm, cook, clean, fetch firewood, and pick the coffee. As far as I can tell, the men have two important jobs: to slash the farms and get them ready for digging with nyengo, a handheld slasher made with iron fixed on a thin wooden pole, and to spend the rest of the time at the kilabu drinking local brew. From one end of the field, we can see the men crowded in a one-room kilabu drinking fermented maize ngelenge, or kipasula, cassava wine, brewed with fermented sorghum and soaked cassava flour. We can also see women working, some carrying timber to a building site and some spreading white maize flour on long mats. There are hardly any idle women around.

"We need to ask about the rock," Michael announces to the group after Olaf's wife goes to find him for us. The buzzing chatter of the group drops to an eerie silence. Just like the first time, no one wants to speak to us about the rock. The women walk away and go back to work. Girls listen in from afar, afraid to get closer, afraid to speak to me, just like their mothers. I walk up to a young man whom I peg to be in his early twenties, casually leaning on the brick wall of a house, chewing on a stick and looking down at the grass beneath him. The colour of his jacket blends so perfectly with the wall that he looks like he is a part of it. He tells me that his name is Gido.

Gido doesn't walk away when I ask him about Mbuji. He seems amused, a slight smile on his face when I ask him if he is afraid of the rock. He tells me he is not afraid, that most people there aren't afraid. A young boy in dark blue shorts and a maroon woven sweater jumps into the conversation. A mischievous smile brightens the black roundness of his eyes. He lowers his voice to share his important secret. "I climb the rock all by myself, I go there to hunt," he declares, pride evident in his face. He then runs away to kick a football made of plastic bags with his playmates. Gido tells me that a lot of small animals live around the rock, like rabbits, makupi (which look like oversized rats), and snakes. When I ask about spirits, he nearly chokes with laughter. "I don't know about spirits," he says in between chuckles. "I have heard of a large snake inside one cave. I have never seen the snake, though, and I wouldn't want to see it. Witch doctors come to the rock to find magic," he tells me. "I have even gone with them from time to time as a guide, not because I believe, but because of the meat."

"Meat?" I ask.

"Traditional healers take a male goat to slaughter and offer sacrifices in the caves or on the rock. They are forbidden to return with the sacrifice meat. If you want to eat free roasted goat meat, you simply go with the witch doctors and have your fill," he finishes with a laugh.

Gido thinks that I could go to the rock if it weren't for the fog. I wouldn't need any special ritual, just a guide who knows his way. "The rock is a bit treacherous, especially on the way down," he says. "There are many paths, but only few lead down safely."

"I have already called Olaf," I tell him. Gido shifts his position but says nothing.

Olaf appears from a little corridor between two houses. He is dressed in the same faded blue jeans, rainbow jacket, and a sun hat. It must be his work outfit. His friend, the weird man from last time, tags along too. He has the same intimidating look and the same green jacket, but this time it's paired with brown cadet trousers, off-white sneakers, and a panama hat the colour of milk tea. His name, I learn, is Isaac Kawonga, born and raised in Mbuji.

CIGARETTES AND RITUALS

Olaf inherited the role of guardian from his father, who also inherited it from his father before him. Someday his son will be the guardian too. Their family was the first to live in Mbuji, at the foot of the rock. His ancestral spirits are the ones that live in and around the rock. He invites us to go up close to the rock, like a father of the house would invite his guests.

Olaf leads the way. While I knew the rock to be a little further from where people lived, I didn't anticipate that we had to climb several hills to get there. We walk past a beautiful house with blue pillars, towards coffee fields with ripening coffee fruits, past a loud buzz of a chainsaw cutting down trees, past pointed rocks and a stream, up a very steep hill.

"It's just a little further," Olaf calls to me as I stop yet again to catch my breath. We have been climbing the hill for what feels like half an hour, with Olaf leading the way and Michael and Isaac on my tail. We reach the top of the hill and start walking down. We pass more houses and coffee farms; it looks just like any other hill. Olaf tells us we are now on the Angongo, which is regular earth on one side and sheer rock on another. The Mbuji rock is a mountain in itself, surrounded by smaller hills.

"What does Mbuji mean?" I ask Olaf questions in between my heavy breathing.

"It is the name of a tree, a very big tree that was somewhere at the foot of the rock. It is no longer there," he answers in a clear voice, unaffected by the hike.

We make our way down the Angongo. I can see Mbuji from the right corner of my eye. I want to stop and look at it, but I know we have to move closer to it, so I keep walking. We cross a stream, near the place where water falls from a rock, forming a small water-fall. We don't stop at this place either. We walk past cows with big humps on their backs and hides grazing near the river, their shiny black coats contrasting the cool green grass. We start climbing the hill that is right next to the Angongo. We have to go to the very top of it to be able to climb Mbuji. My breath catches and I shiver from both the chill and the hike. My heart pounds from such heavy exercise; I can hear it beating in my ears.

We stop underneath a grove of eucalyptus trees. There is a cave. We walk to the mouth of the cave, a narrow slit in the middle of a raised rock that appears sharp and dangerous. Michael and I marvel at the strange structure. Water flows from the mountain to the rock and goes underground into the cave. We climb on top of the little rock in front of the cave and peek inside. Olaf pulls out something from his jacket pocket, cassava flour wrapped in a piece of old newspaper. He starts talking to himself, and I realize that he is performing his ritual.

I had expected something more elaborate — the sacrifice of a white chicken or a male goat — but this was too simple, the same ritual that the rest of the Matengo do when they go to clean the graveyard of their deceased family members. Sprinkling cassava flour on graves is like taking flowers to your deceased, showing them respect, love, and remembrance. I am too stunned to comment. Olaf sprinkles the white flour near the mouth of the cave, while talking. He seems certain that his ancestral spirits hear him; he prays to them, "Please look after us, we are only here to take a lesson. Receive the visitors, whatever they are looking for, help them find it. Help them see, and when they take pictures, if it pleases you, show yourselves, and give us a sign that you're there." As he finishes his prayer, I have a strong urge to say, "Amen," but I don't. I am not sure who we were praying to. As Olaf was praying, I noticed Isaac taking out a bunch of dried tobacco leaves, rolling them in a likapati, a dried-up maize husk, and lighting his cigarette. He didn't close his eyes or pay any special attention.

As if to answer Olaf's prayers, the white fog that circled the male rock disappears and the sun fully comes out, although it does not warm up. We can now climb to the top of the rock without any trouble if we want to. Was this the magic everyone talked about, the sudden disappearance of fog, or is it just a lucky coincidence that the grey clouds moved and the sun is shining brightly? It is still chilly as we walk away from the cave and keep climbing towards the top of the mountain. The cold licks my exposed skin like a wet tongue on an ice cream cone.

We stop halfway up the hill. It is 2:00 in the afternoon. Mbuji is close, but not close enough to touch from here. We can see the thorny cactus and aloe vera plants that grow on the rock. Birds of different colours, especially ones that have black and white patches, common in the area, fly above us. Olaf points to the place where the American fell. His face drops when he talks about the accident. "He fell on his way down. He lost the trail. It is much harder to climb down than to climb up. You have to crawl on all fours." A strong wind gushes through tall eucalyptus trees like a beautiful hymn as Olaf talks about the tragedy. Somehow the American's spirit lives there too, dauntless and curious, a sad reminder of our fragile lives even amidst adventure. I think of my mother's worried face when I left the house. My resolve to conquer Mbuji crumbles. I can't hike any further.

WHEN MBUJI CAUGHT FIRE

Olaf tells us the most famous legend of the rock before we head back to the village.

"The rock protected our people," he begins, tilting his head back as if searching for a distant memory. Isaac rolls another cigarette, tracing the trail of the smoke with his eyes. Michael and I listen.

"One year the Germans set up a camp at Nkongulela." Olaf points to the left, to a hill covered with brown maize ready for harvest. "They started building a fort there. They wanted to blow up the rock and take over the land. The villagers were terrified. Then one day, as the villagers were losing hope, Mbuji caught fire, and the colonialists ran away." Olaf finishes, his eyes widening in wonder of his own story. Michael gives me a skeptical look, slightly tilting his eyebrows as if to ask, *Can you believe this guy?*

"How did it catch fire?" I ask.

"You see the grass around the rock?" Olaf asks, pointing at the green I thought was mould. "It caught fire, and the fire wasn't easily put out."

"And you think that this fire was started by the spirits?" asks Michael, who has been quiet most of the trip, sarcasm evident in his voice.

"Are you sure Mzee Manduta or one of the warriors didn't start the fire?" I ask again.

Olaf smiles, and the skin on his forehead creases as he thinks of the answer.

"I don't know."

Olaf's great-grandfather, Mzee Manduta, was a hero. He is honoured at a special place in Barazani, Litembo, with other heroes. During the Maji Maji war, he mobilized people to fight against German raiders and their allies. They used the caves around the rock as a hideout for women and children. The fighters climbed on top of Mbuji and threw stones and spears at the enemy. Olaf has been taught since he was a boy to guard the rock that protected his forefathers.

My uncle was right; the rock does have secrets.

THE ANCESTORS AND MY MOTHER

When she first warned me about climbing the rock, I thought my mother was afraid of the spirits of the rock or curses from people like Isaac. But my mother is not afraid. She doesn't believe myths and taboos are mere superstition.

My mother, a proud Matengo woman, was born in the village of Kipololo, part of the rocky mountain range that covers a large part of the Umatengo land. From her village you can see the gleaming night lights of Malawi across Lake Nyasa. Mama comes from the original chief clan of the Matengo, the Kinunda. Her great-grandfather on her father's side, Teka Teki, was beheaded at Barazani, Litembo, in front of his wives and children, during the Maji Maji war. His wives ran away to their natal homes and took their children with them. Their cousins, the Hyera clan, took over the chiefdom after the Kinundas fled and scattered all over the land. My mother thinks the ancestors were smarter than people give them credit for, that taboos have meaning beyond what we think, that because fear is easier to plant than understanding taboos serve better to protect the people.

She once told me of a pond near where she grew up that swallows people up. The topsoil near the shore is loose, and the land sinks when people step on it. Most mountain people, not knowing how to swim, drown. The elders, to reduce the danger of the area, told people that the evil spirits in the pond swallowed people that passed near it. People, especially children, being superstitious and afraid of the spiritual world, did not pass near the pond. Today the pond sits like an abandoned curse in a valley surrounded by green hills. In Rungwe there is a place called the Bridge of God on the Kiwira River. A big bed of rock swallows up all surface water in a powerful whirlpool on one side and then vomits it on the other side of the rock, taking anything and everything with it. To keep people away, there are all sorts of taboos and cautionary tales around the place.

The more I think about my mother's stories, the more I believe there is more to the magic of Mbuji than meets the eye. Besides being dangerous, Olaf's ancestors used Mbuji and its caves as a hideout during the war. They had to protect their secrets from outsiders. Yet when I look at Mbuji through Olaf's eyes, I can see his connection to the past, to the struggles and triumphs of his ancestors. As a child, I didn't think much about my forebears. I couldn't see why they should matter so much. Now I want to know more about them. I want their spirits to be engraved in mine, and to pass them on to the next generation. I envy Olaf's connection to his roots. I admire his unapologetic faith. I am ashamed that I was afraid of the perceived darkness garnished around traditional beliefs.

ORDINARY LIFE IN AN EXTRAORDINARY PLACE

"Are you sure you don't want to go further?" Olaf asks us calmly, not offended by our lack of belief. Michael and I shake our heads in unison. I can almost feel my mother's smile when we start heading back to the village. My shoes slip because of the steep slope; I land on my bottom. I imagine how precarious that little fall could have been on Mbuji. We climb back on the Angongo, up to a point where Mbuji stands directly opposite us. We rest. We can hear the splash of water falling from a small rock in the river below. A black cow softly lows from a distance. Children laugh as they dig holes, catching insects to eat. Tree branches dance to the silky rhythm of the wind. The camera clicks, Isaac poses, showing his browning teeth for the very first time that day as Michael takes his picture. All these sounds make the rock come alive.

"You have to climb to the top of the Angongo, at least, and see the view from there," Olaf tells us as we start going further up on the Angongo. A haggard woman with a big bundle of firewood walks towards us. "Jambo," she greets us, slightly bending her knees in habitual politeness. None of the men pay attention to her. The lines on her face tell me there is no magic in being a woman here. I have seen the struggles of the Matengo women all around. They work hard for their husbands' land, but after they are old and spent, the men marry younger women to keep things fresh. When I accuse Olaf of this, he protests, "I only have one wife, just like the church wants."

"Church?" I ask. "How can the guardian of spirits, the man in charge of rituals, go to church?" Isaac snorts, and Michael bursts into a fit of laughter.

"What church?" I ask again, sure he would tell me something like tambiko, a traditional worship ceremony.

"The Catholic Church," Olaf casually replies, as if this clash of beliefs is nothing to him.

We walk further up, to a house near the very top of the Angongo. Two elderly men and a woman are drinking cassava wine. They invite us to sit and offer us the wine in a green plastic mug called lobu. We take a sip out of respect, everyone drinking from the same mug. The wine is porridge thick, but tastes like beer. One of the elders is Mzee Kornelius, the man we met at the village council in April. He is not wearing his barakashea today. He wants us to buy him alcohol to show that we respect elders. Michael gives him a 1,000-shilling note, and he complains. As we leave the house, Olaf warns us that people sometimes use fear or respect to get free things from visitors. I steal a glance at Isaac to see his reaction to the statement; he lights another cigarette, he doesn't seem to remember the last incident. It takes us less than ten minutes to get to the top of Angongo.

We gaze at the beautiful world below, and for one brief moment we are all engrossed in the same view. Isaac even stops smoking his cigarette. We can see all of Mbuji and Mawono villages from the top, shiny aluminum roofs, green coffee farms, and wheat and maize farms looking like discoloured football fields from afar. We see Michael's car below, a small silver sedan glistening in the light of the sun. A soft wind blows, and I breathe in the cleanest air I have ever breathed. I ask Olaf what it is like to be on top of Mbuji. He smiles, a candid smile that lights up his entire face, and says, "It is the most beautiful thing I have ever seen. You can see all the way to Songea. You can see Lake Nyasa all the way to Malawi. Up there, the world isn't so small. You can dream of other things." Isaac nods his agreement to this. For the first time since I encountered him, I am not afraid of Isaac; he seems quite approachable.

It is now past 4:00 p.m., and the sun slowly descends west. We carefully make our way back to the house on the hill. I nudge Olaf to tell me about his double faith. He is certain that there is only one creator, but he thinks traditional rituals are as important as those of the Church, if not more. "I bet when the Catholic priests are on holiday, they go back to their villages and do their traditional rituals too," he says. Black and white don't always mix to form grey; sometimes the colours remain separate, like the stripes of a zebra. Back at the house, the elder who owns the house gives us some uncooked plantains to take as a gift. Mzee Kornelius still wants more brew money. I give him some money, and he doesn't utter a word of gratitude. I give the other elder some too, to thank him for his kindness. He thanks us profusely for almost two minutes. The lady walks out angrily, cursing us in kiMatengo about how there are supposed to be equal rights. "Why don't I get some money, is it because I am a woman?" she asks. She complains about how she is the other ritual person and guide, but no one goes to her. Her voice is all too familiar; another woman in a male-dominated field. I am only left with a 500-shilling note and a 2,000-shilling note. I don't know why, but to my shame, I give her the 500, half what I gave either of the men. She seems happy regardless, and walks downhill to the kilabu.

On the way down to the village, we meet Moses, a short fourth-grader sitting with his grandmother on their front porch. Michael, who is also my translator, asks them about the rock. I do not speak my mother tongue. I grew up in Dar-es-Salaam, the melting pot of tribes, where everyone speaks Swahili. Moses and his grandmother have never been to the rock. The older woman, possibly in her seventies, tells Michael she is afraid of falling. I can completely identify with her fear. Moses can't wait to be big enough to climb. Michael asks the grandmother whether the spirits from the rock reach their side. She says their lives are quite ordinary, and there are no spirits in the village. We walk past a group of women and children gathered around an open fire, roasting maize on the cob. Their happy laugher fills the evening air, and the aroma of charred corn fills our nostrils.

As we make our way back to the car a man calls that he wants to talk to me. I stop. He is Chunda, a middle-aged man who has lived in Mbuji most of his life. For him, the rock is neither sacred nor historically relevant. Yet it still fascinates him. "I climb up there often, I mean if the other people come from so far to climb, it is a shame for a local man not to know what is up there," he tells me. "If you wake up to it every day, Mbuji loses some of its majesty. You have to go up there to see it again," he admits.

"What is up there?" I ask him.

"Magic," he laughs, and leaves me to walk down the rest of the way by myself.

Meanwhile, I think of my uncle's fear of looking closely at Mbuji lest it do something to him. When I see him, I will tell him to pay attention to it, to marvel at the artistry of its creator, to reach out and touch its folds, to unveil the secrets it holds. I have caught a glimpse of Mbuji's magic; I have seen it come alive in Olaf's tales and in Chunda's claim. I have come to learn that if the lens with which we see life is magical, then we can see magic even in ordinary life. However, there is something mystical about Mbuji: its temperament, the way it demands attention yet fades in the background of day-to-day life. One day I will come to this place again, and I will climb to the very top.

FORGETTING LAMIDO[*]

Chike Frankie Edozien

I open my eyes, but I'm not moving. This siesta has probably lasted twenty minutes, and now I'm staring at the lanky body awakening beside me. It's midafternoon, and outside the streets are choked with crawling vehicles. The ubiquitous horn blaring over the past few days has been getting on my nerves. When did Ikoyi become so noisy? At least it's serene here inside the Moorhouse. The air conditioner is humming softly, chilling the room. The severe brown wood panelling décor evokes masculinity. Nothing's soft about the furnishings. This small boutique hotel may be tailored for busy businesspeople, but it's also an oasis from the chaos of Lagos. And it's in this oasis that I'm cozy and reconnecting with my childhood love. I stretch and see our naked selves in the mirror, legs intertwined on the crisp white sheets. All afternoon we've been canoodling. Then having furtive, furious sex.

After all this time, our bodies haven't lost that feral magnetism for each other. We tried to tamp down the sexual tension by staying out at the bustling Eko Hotel with others. But we failed. It's been ten years plus since we last met. In the end we just gave in. He

---

* Some names and identifying details in this essay have been changed to protect the privacy of the individuals.

stirs, spurring me to inch closer and put my arms around his waist and peer over his shoulder. He smiles, and I melt.

"You dey ok?" he asks softly.

Years ago, whenever we were alone, his deep voice softening to a whisper made me feel loved. It does so today. He still has dimples, and the whites of his eyes still shine against his ground-nut-coloured skin. He has no tribal marks, but still he turns to see if mine remains. Few people notice mine. It's hidden like a small scar under my right eye. He finds it and begins caressing it. Then he kicks off the sheet. And as my Fulani lover's sinewy naked body stretches into the X position, I touch his afro gently, marvelling at the thick head of hair that's still so soft. What sort of pomade is he using now? I gaze at this body that's remained taut, even though it's without the chisel of yesteryear.

"You look great," I say, now fingering his belly button.

"I no be fine boy again oh," he replies, adding, "Your hair still plenty." He always appreciated the hair that sprouted abundantly all over me. I shave my head and face regularly, but I love my hairy chest, legs, and arms, and rarely trim or "manscape." I'm happy it still thrills him, but I feel trapped. I can't even pull myself out of bed because I'm savouring the moment. Even his scent, a mix of cigarette smoke and musky cologne, holds me captive. I hug him tighter. That Diana Ross ditty keeps floating in and out of my consciousness: *Touch me in the morning. Then just walk away. We don't have tomorrow, but we had yesterday ...*

What am I doing? I think. I've just spent hours having sex with someone else's husband. And now we're in a silent post-coital afterglow. I remember him always talking, even after sex, but today he just smiles. We're content to look into each other's eyes. We both want to be here. Guilt isn't part of the equation. With this man, it never has been. Not when I was nineteen and not now, when we are both in our thirties. Nothing's changed. Yet, somehow, today everything is different.

* * *

Alhaji Lamido Gida and I first meet in the 1980s, when we lived not far from here. My brothers and I are Ikoyi boys. "Aje butter" children. Middle-class kids whose parents have multiple cars, homes with domestic help, and send them on holiday. Abroad. Lamido's twenty and, in my mind, an adult. He's friends with my older brothers, and we meet when he comes to visit them. I'm sixteen and on holiday from boarding school in Port Harcourt. During my years at the coed Federal Government College, I'm introverted, bordering on shy, but I come alive when involved with the Drama Troupe and the Press Club. It takes three years before I finally begin to enjoy boarding, and now I have friends from all over, not just the Lagos kids. I find that the boys' dormitory, where these lifelong friendships are formed and everyone strategizes about chasing girls, is also home to hidden but rampant guy-on-guy desire.

By sheer happenstance I'm seduced by a classmate whom I call Smiley. Although he's two years older, we're both going into Form Five and gearing up for the West African School Certificate examinations. After oversleeping one morning, I don't have a pail of water to bathe with, and I don't want to risk wasting more time with the long trek to the outdoor quadrangle where twenty-four communal taps are situated for students to fetch water.

I've already missed the bread and boiled egg breakfast. I ask Smiley, who isn't one of my friends but who is also running late, if he can share his full bucket with me. I expect a no, but he says yes with a little smile. And we bathe together, sharing every bit of the water, scooping just a little at a time so there is more for the other. I make it to class on time, and we become pals. When I go to fetch him one evening for night study, I'm surprised to find he's not ready. He has a brown cotton wrapper tied around his waist and no shirt, as if he's about to go to bed. He pulls me into one of the tiny inner rooms, locks the door quickly, turns out the lights, and whispers, "*Ssshh.*" We keep still while the prefects usher everyone out. I hear the clanging of the chains on the outer gates and know everyone's gone. Smiley gets back on the lower bunk and beckons. I lie on the thin foam, and in the darkness he begins giving me little pecks. His lips send shivers and sensations I've never felt before down to my toes and up along my spine. I'm contorting each time he licks someplace. Then the furious rubbing of his prick against mine, giving way to us removing our clothes. Smiley stops and whispers, *"Turn this way."* I'm confused, but he gently moves us into a comfortable position. And for the first time I'm having sex. Intercourse feels weird at first, then fantastic. There is pain, but that comes later. When in the deep throes of ecstasy I heave and ejaculate, I think I've just peed. Smiley calmly explains that it's just sperm.

That night kicks off moments with him about which I can't even tell my best friend, Paulie, back in Lagos about. At fifteen, this kind of sexual play is new. But not for Smiley, who tells me of others he's "gone out with." Boys having sex with each other surprises me. I didn't realize it was even possible. After I leave I feel great, but then the "good boy" in me is wracked with guilt. The term is almost over, thankfully. So the first thing I do when I arrive home in Lagos is to head to my parish on Saturday and get on my knees at the wooden pews, where my priest gives me his undivided attention. *Bless me father for I have sinned. Since my last confession ...* I have lost my innocence. During these years confession was often heard on the outer church verandah, privately but not in a wooden box.

The Church of the Assumption is a single-storey building next to a marble office tower and across from the Falomo Shopping Centre in Ikoyi. I'm a regular reader at morning Mass and have worshipped here with my family from infancy. The young priest knows me well and names my "sin" homosexuality. He acknowledges my internal struggle and encourages me to end this. He sympathizes, but warns of consequences. The priest makes me feel that this is "behaviour" I can vanquish if I just try harder. And if I am strong.

But I'm not. I'm never strong when I return to Port Harcourt. No number of Hail Marys will work. When it comes to Smiley, I'm constantly weak, acquiescing to every invitation. At some point I move into his room. We're seniors prepping for O Levels, so I'm not under the same level of scrutiny as I was in the lower classes. But then, unexpectedly, another classmate, Christopher, and I also begin to fondle occasionally, secretly meeting under the cover of darkness by the twenty-four taps when we can sneak off. But I know this thing is passing. It's puberty play, purely physical and devoid of real emotion. So I keep going to confession, and I pray. I pray for a good girlfriend. I pray to be like my brothers.

Lamido changes all this. By the time I'm in Lower Six, I have more freedom at home. I've aced my O Levels, but I flunk the yearly Joint Admission & Matriculation Board (JAMB) exam, so I can't get into any university yet. My options are to either take it again or complete A Levels. As I prepare to retake JAMB, I'm studying all day but partying with friends at night. And a familiar face begins popping up. On Friday evenings, Paulie and I usually head to Jazz 38 on Awolowo Road to listen to live music. Sometimes the Afrobeat King, Fela Anikulapo-Kuti, makes an appearance en route to his standard set at the Shrine in Ikeja.

Paulie and I have been close since primary school, when we eschewed football to worship Motown divas instead, particularly Diana. We were blissfully peculiar before we knew what it meant to be so. Taking turns at the microphone on the outdoor stage to belt out Sade's "Smooth Operator" is becoming our thing. Then Lamido appears. Though his parents are in Kano, he lives with his siblings in Ikoyi. He's always up to trying anything in the name of fun. He feels no guilt. *I'm a Muslim,* he tells me. *So I don't drink, but I'll smoke anything smokeable.* I admire him. He oozes charisma. He loves his brothers, reveres his sister, and dotes on his nephews. It seems his siblings are in charge of his education. There have never been sparks between us, he's really my brother's pal, not mine, but now, as my friends and I gallivant around Lagos, I start running into him often.

Strolling by the waterside near the 1004 residential complex in Victoria Island to gawk at folk, *gist*, and drink is something Paulie and I also do often. These heady days after high school, looking for palm wine or barbequed meat has become de rigueur. We stroll along the water on the road to Maroko, and sometimes stop first at the chop bars that dot Bar Beach. Victoria Island is upscale residential, but more and more nice joints keep popping up. We love to people-watch. Other times we retreat to the snooker room at Ikoyi Club. Our friends bring their girls along. We all go to the same house parties. Sometimes I have the girl who likes me and I invite her to tag along. At other times, I'm solo. I'm fine alone.

It's on one of these unattached night outs that I run into Lamido again near 1004. We leave the others and go get suya, near the Second Gate. I find these piping hot beef skewers, the peppers and the onions, irresistible. It's a cool evening, and Lamido's wearing one of his floor-length caftans, a brown one, with black leather slippers. He's enticing, and I'm only just noticing. Chopping suya, licking our fingers, and chatting with him alone feels nice. After our night out, he takes me home in a taxi. We get off at the Queens Drive junction to stroll to my gate. Once under the giant tree that provides shade during the day but blocks out the street lights at night, he leans in and sneaks a kiss. His tongue slides in and out of my mouth very quickly as he looks directly at me. No one can see. It's so unexpected but so enjoyable all I can do is smile. I'm seventeen; he's twenty-one.

Before tonight I'd not thought of him romantically. But this whole evening and the kiss gives me sensations that I've not felt since the first time I was with Smiley. Lamido smiles and says he'll see me tomorrow, and for many evenings he comes to fetch me to hang out alone. *Oya make we waka commot*, he says before our moonlight strolls. He's old enough to drive, but we take taxis everywhere. I've never seen him behind the wheel. When guys walk hand in hand it feels brotherly, but I get goosebumps every single time he touches my hand. I shudder when his hands meet the small of my back. He's tactile, and I like it. Lamido's a man-about-town, energetic, slim, with a thick head of soft black hair. I love touching his afro. I like his dimples. He's always elegant, and the scent of his cigarettes and cologne make him seem so adult. His body is toned, but I never notice him play basketball, football, or any other sport. He talks a lot, switching effortlessly from Hausa to pidgin when sitting barefoot on the floor with the house-helps. But at Ikoyi Club he'll discuss politics in Queen's English before going dancing.

He's a tough guy, but alone I see only a very tender side. He tells me jokes in a soft voice and is just full of gratitude for me. I love that his eyes light up when we meet. He loves that I'm not so butch and doesn't mind my sometime swishy gait. Gossip has little effect on him. He lives contentedly in his own space, and I enjoy being there with him. He only desires that we meet. Often. In the bedrooms reserved for overnight guests, we're constantly having life conversations, then having sex when everyone's at work, then more conversation, followed by more lovemaking. But we talk of our dreams too. Lamido encourages me to dress traditionally and gifts me a metallic grey brocade caftan. It has intricate embroidery with a thick white thread all around the chest area and the edge of the sleeve and ankles. It is obviously expensive. He thinks I can pull off the caftan with the kind of natural *savoir faire* of a Fulani man that he has, but all I want to wear are jeans and T-shirts from London. He seldom wears Western clothes, and when he does his outfits are more fashionable than anything I own. He's the first to use the "L" word. *You're my first love,* he says over and over.

I stop going to confession.

But sometimes I wonder: Is he just "toasting" me as we guys do? I'm not exactly sure how this love happened. Lamido is popular and has options, including all the girls who want him. I have just been going through the motions with the Warri girl who has decided I'm her boyfriend now that my brother is done with her. It seems the right thing to do. Before I left Port Harcourt I had a girlfriend who was interested in me. Most of the time we passed notes and met up to chat. It was fun and simple, but not electric. Now, in Lagos, I have this girl who, after flirting with my brother, settles on me. And it's fun to take her places, to hug her and hold her tight as we say goodbye, to show her off. But the truth is I have zero desire. But when Lamido looks my way, my heart beats faster and my smile grows bigger. It's a jolt, and I'm happy. I find Lamido has a whole circle of friends who are similarly peculiar, top and bottom, or "tB" guys. He's far along in his studies at the Ahmadu Bello University in Zaria and has a girlfriend there. I've seen her picture. He rarely mentions her to me, but often shows her photo to others.

After one term in Lower Six, I abandon school and focus solely on studying for JAMB. My brothers are already in universities, so I'm the only one at home. On the second try I pass, and months later I receive my admission to the University of Port Harcourt's Theatre Arts department. So back to the Garden City I go after nearly seven months of unfettered access to Lamido. I'm supposed to be thrilled, but my love isn't around. When we meet during one break, we chat about how we could disappear and get hitched … if not for the gender thing. *If to say you be girl, I for don marry you carry you go Sokoto*, he says.

In my first year at Uniport I'm a young man in love. But not with Janice, the girl I'm now dating. The Warri girl in Lagos moved on. I'm acting and even get a part in the lavish operatic dance-drama production *Woyengi* at the Crab Theatre. Still, I yearn for Lamido. I wish he could see the show. I long for his touch, his constant whispering into my ears telling me that I'm his bobo. I miss the way he pulls me close, his reassurances that all would be well. I ache for him.

I crave Lamido, even when my other high school romp mate, Christopher, reappears. We bump into each other on campus, and every so often he politely asks to visit. At Uniport dormitory space is tight; I've had to rent a room in Choba village. It's tiny, enough for one bed, an ironing/study table, and someplace to hang clothes. The wall has peeling blue paint. My room is next to the shared toilet in a bungalow that is home to a large polygamous family. Even though I miss the camaraderie of dorm living, I have privacy. My space is also a refuge for Christopher. He's discreet, visiting only late at night and staying over. Once we're in bed, we pick up on the frottage we had engaged in during our last year of boarding school. Afterwards we say little, and we never socialize. We simply hang out with our girlfriends and give a quick hello if we run into each other. We're barely friends. These encounters make me hunger for Lamido's full-throttle, passionate lovemaking and big personality. Christopher's fun and unsure, but Lamido's certain and simply knows how to fuck.

And live.

Now, more than a decade later, Lamido and I are luxuriating in this large bed at my hotel. I've rediscovered his touch and realize how much I've missed it. But he's been some woman's husband now for more than ten years. He's also a businessman running an import concern in one of the new office towers near Kingsway Road. The next evening, he brings along a strapping gardener from Suru-Lere whom he'd introduced me to the day before.

The guy's handsome, quiet but noticeable even when he's saying little. His arms are huge, and his body carved like the workingman he is. *This is someone to play with later*, Lamido says at the time. I feign appreciation then but reminisce about the old days. Then he would never have thought to share me.

Now Lamido's brought him to the room declaring we must "chop this yam together." We have a threesome. This is a first, and really all we do is take turns having furious intercourse with the gardener before turning to each other to make love tenderly. The gardener's a tall area boy with a shaved head and shaving bumps on his chin. His voice is mellifluous. It soothes me, and I find I like him. I enjoy chatting with him once the roll in the hay is over. His mother is Yoruba from Lagos, and his father is also Yoruba but from Benin Republic. Lamido isn't his boyfriend, but they have a "special friendship." Over some cold Star beer, I gather that he earns little and has a wife and young son. He helps Lamido out sexually, and Lamido helps him out financially.

When he goes to the toilet, Lamido derides him as an *ashawo*. I laugh, but I know he's no prostitute. He's just told me, with pride, of the flowers he's planted nearby and other gardening jobs he's done lately. He just hasn't earned enough to make ends meet. I give little thought to the seediness or morality of their arrangement. People use each other; that's life. I just notice the genuine affection he has for Lamido. But in my gut I know Lamido won't reciprocate. Love isn't in the air for either of us. It's clear that Lamido can't stay away from me physically, he's still caressing my tribal mark and rubbing my chest hair, but he has zero interest in rekindling the relationship. The gardener can't see it yet, but Lamido is moving on from him too. We can all play here before everyone has to return to their lives, their women. I wonder how Lamido could move on so easily after seeing me, especially since it was so difficult to leave him behind. But I did choose to leave.

After my first year at Uniport, things changed. The labour strikes and student unrests were constant. And when I was home there was no peace either. My parents' marriage had hit a rough patch, and things began to deteriorate when my two immediate older brothers secretly left the country and immigrated to America. Home was a powder keg. Mum left. At nineteen, I got so angry that my mother had gone that I lost my fear of talking back to my father. I blamed him. I no longer put him on a pedestal. I sneered at the woman he brought home and openly scoffed at his sister's insistence that I go to confession for being so rude. I, the normally obedient one, was done with that. I had an attitude, and it wasn't one of deference. So Dad refused to pay for school or anything else for me. And then one evening, in front of his new paramour, he told me I was no longer welcome in the home I'd grown up in. "You can't stay here," he said as she looked on. The thing to do would have been to fall on my knees and beg. But I just looked at them defiantly, shook my head at the usurper desperate to become the lady of the house, then went upstairs, packed my bags, and left. I have not lived in any of my father's homes since.

A friend of my mother's who lived close by took me in. Now I was constantly broke on campus, living off the generosity of my friend Fela, splitting his money to return to Lagos by bus. For years I'd taken the forty-five-minute flight, now it was a bumpy twelve-hour road trip. I was constantly brooding. I studied but didn't hang out. I auditioned and got bit parts on TV shows, but the payments never came. Fela kept me sane by pulling me out of my room and sharing everything. My mother was furious when she eventually found out that once she was gone Dad had withdrawn his financial support and I was starving on campus. She had not expected it to go this far. A year earlier I'd been promised a summer holiday abroad, and my mum, despite now having to make a new life for herself, didn't renege. She bought the ticket when I returned to Lagos for summer break. I was to go to my aunt's in London as usual. When we had one last meal with my aunt at Ikoyi Club, a friend of Mum's, Aunty Joy, casually gave me several hundred British pounds for my holiday.

During this difficult period, Lamido, the one who knew me inside and out and loved me, had little time for me. He was now about to marry his girlfriend. We would not be disappearing together. He'd graduated, begun working, and marriage and procreation were the next steps. He also went on pilgrimage to Mecca and was going to have a nice wedding. This was the reality. I, on the other hand, had nothing.

So I zapped. I left Port Harcourt behind. I left Lamido to his new wife, as difficult as it was, and I travelled abroad with no intention of returning. My first stop was London. I'd been there in happier times for summer shopping. This time I cleaned a bakery in

Willesden Green for three months to earn money before making my way to America. It was a struggle there. My brothers helped find a nighttime office cleaning job and a small room to rent so I could go to class during the day in Syracuse. Lamido and I had little contact, and then our communication withered. He showed no inclination to visit. I was determined not to return until I too had a degree. I wasn't going to be the one who dropped out. So I adjusted to a life of classes and twelve-hour shifts, but I did graduate and I began working as a journalist. Acting was out. I was twenty-five and unburdened.

After years of struggle, I lived an honest, openly peculiar but low-key life. No one in New York cared. My brothers made no fuss. They had gay friends by then. My sister and mother visited, at different times, the tiny apartment I made my home in Brooklyn, and they reoriented themselves to my reality. I never hid. And on my first trip home since I'd left in a hurry, Lamido was the first person I looked for. I began to come home more often, seeking out work in Africa. In those years many classmates and friends who had also fled the country for higher education or to escape political turmoil began returning. But it seemed every "tB" boy who returned home followed the Lamido model. Get married. Have babies. Then continue with secret boyfriends.

From my childhood best friend, Paulie, to Smiley and many in between, everyone fell in line. Was it simply the cost of living hassle-free in Naija that meant all these "tB" guys had to find wives? Couldn't they just be discreet and live without having to marry women they had little interest in? Of course the pressure for women is even more. At a certain stage all they hear are questions about getting hitched, as if all their accomplishments add up to naught if a husband isn't there to show off. I started to believe these men needed wives to succeed professionally. One friend said he would never have gotten that promotion to Senior Lecturer at the Ambrose Alli University in Ekpoma if he'd remained single. You're considered mature if you are married. That's the way it works. After having a career that was based on ability and luck, I wondered if I'd be able to work full-time in Lagos at a high level without these ersatz symbols of maturity. Folks who presented me with opportunities said yes, of course. But I wasn't sure this would be possible if I'd remained at home. I've had some good fortune and had a career where sexual orientation hasn't been an issue. And so I empathized with friends who'd had to join the marital bandwagon. Some insisted I was overthinking it. *Oh, you still spend too much time working in New York, when you move home fully you will marry and have someone too on the side. That's the way it is.* Everyone does it. No one pays any attention to their effeminate gait or preference for the company of men after they've paid some woman's dowry and put a ring on her finger.

My lecturer friend left Ekpoma, decamping to England to teach. He took his wife with him, but his charade continued. He couldn't find a solid relationship to have on the side. He isn't unique. From Manchester to Chicago, I meet successful Nigerian professionals happily in this boat. As long as they are perceived to be heterosexual, it's all good. Once, in London, a Delta-Ibo man with a thick beard and shaved head tried to pick me up at a pub on Rupert Street. I enjoyed the attention and found him very attractive. He reminded me of the late military leader Odumegwu Ojukwu. It was a plus that he had lived in Asaba, my hometown. As I downed my lager shandy, I sized up this potential mate. We flirted all night, even exchanging kisses at the end. It was fantastic — that is, until he began to give me details of his upcoming nuptials in Lagos. I stared in disbelief. "Don't you have the same pressure?" he asked, shocked that I found it incredible he was going home to marry. "She'll be there now! I'll do my thing, ah ah!" he said.

Is it just the career, or is it also parents pushing for grandchildren that leads these men to marry women they aren't in love with? Sharing a life with someone you don't love can't be easy. I'm not sure I could do this. I'm lucky. My parents have grandchildren already, so I'm not tasked with keeping the lineage going.

My father and I, years later, put love ahead of pride and have a good, open, and warm father-son relationship. We are proud of each other. I know I have uncommon freedom because my siblings love me unconditionally. Every family is different, and mine isn't the norm. Far too many men can't risk being cut off emotionally or financially. Not everyone is this lucky. I've known for years that Lamido's sisters and brothers wouldn't accept his gayness. Not back then, and not today.

Years after our initial reunion, I still make the effort to meet up with Lamido whenever I'm in Nigeria. He's since left Lagos and settled in Kaduna. And as he has aged he's embraced his softer side. Like when he tells me how he just missed being the "first lady" of one of the northern states. His ex-boyfriend lost the election.

One evening in Abuja, we go to his brother's home for dinner in Asokoro. The meal is an elaborate spread of tuwo shinkafa with goat meat and some fish soup. There's no booze, but conversation flows. I listen as his siblings talk about flying across the country in a private jet with their friends. His now grown-up nephews are preparing to head back to British universities and gab on about the different business class options. Lamido, his current boyfriend, and I have a swell time. And in this rarefied but intimate bourgeois circle, Lamido refers to his man as a friend.

When our hosts rise up from the table and are out of earshot I say to Lamido that his new boyfriend is really nice. He shoots me a look of absolute panic. "Na wetin I do you now?" he says forlornly. I'm not to use the "B" word while in the house. I apologize profusely. I thought it obvious that they are a couple. But if his relatives refuse to see his true relationship, then it doesn't exist.

Back in Lagos over some Chapman's at Bogobiri, Paulie isn't surprised. He tells me his own fear is not just his brothers but his in-laws. Should they ever find out about his boyfriends, he'll just deny it. I often wonder if Paulie and Lamido had a thing after I left. They both refer to each other as Lagos sluts and never hang out with each other. Now both are married to women they never spend any time with, pretending to the world not to love men. Smiley, too, who never left Port Harcourt, would be devastated if his family found out what really stirs his loins. He's been "happily married" for years.

One school friend who it seemed wouldn't deign to marry for society finally did, and it shocked me. Chidi Omalichanwa, after decades in Europe, returned to Lagos and pulled a Lamido. He was a class ahead of me. I had no idea of his gay adventures until the early 2000s, when we reconnected. Chidi told me that back then he was sexually active with some of our schoolmates. All boys. They are now all married with children. I've felt the electricity that passed though him and another classmate when we all bumped into each recently. Their hug was long and tight, and both seemed to get shy and momentarily at a loss for words. They hadn't seen each other in thirty years. After high school he got an engineering degree, then went to Europe for postgraduate study. His career skyrocketed. I admired his joie de vivre, and seeing his successes I wasn't surprised when he moved home to helm a multinational. Over the years he'd grown into this tall, broad-shouldered, handsome, dark-skinned man. Chic and bespectacled, he morphed into a macho guy from the geek I remember. Now he's a catch. And Lagos suited him. He was an Oga at the Top, good career, good home, upper-middle-class life. But I remained dumbfounded at how quickly he married a woman he'd met soon after resettling. Children followed.

Chidi is now forty-five and straight, after two decades of boy-friends. It made more sense to me for Paulie, who had never moved away, to get married. I was able to rationalize Lamido's marriage. But Chidi's remains a head-scratcher. The man returned to Nigeria with accolades, and his hiring was a coup. He already had the career and financial muscle, so why jump into forced heterosexuality? Over the years he's joked — or at least I thought he was joking — that I was lucky I got away from him in high school. He'd set his sights on me, but my sexual awakening happened later. I often thought he said this merely to be complimentary. So I'd flirt back and say, "Damn, if not for that oyinbo boy you have, we could have been together." Nowadays my response is standard: "Too bad! You've gotten married!"

One very clear evening, with stars shining brightly in the Lagos sky, we join other school friends at a swanky V.I. hotel rooftop for drinks. I'm swirling wine and having a good time. After Chidi's downed a few shots of Maker's Mark, I pull him away for some real talk. He whispers that even though he had male sexual contacts in school, at university he had three serious girlfriends. *Ah. Maybe he's one of those truly bisexual guys*, I think. But then, after moving to Europe, he fell in love with a man. He dated English and Irish lads only. I'm reminded of a difficult breakup he'd had a few years earlier, before he returned to Lagos. Even though it was raw, I hoped he'd get over it. I hated to see my friend, a really good guy, so hurt. But here he is now telling me that that breakup was the straw that broke this camel's back. Loving dudes afterwards was just too hard. His solution to healing was to tell himself, *It's time to settle down and get married.*

If he'd married after he left the University of Nigeria, Nsukka, might he have had his amazing career abroad? Or might he have soared all along in Nigeria, rising higher than he is now? Probably. He's that bright. I stare into his eyes and wonder how he is doing this. It's proving difficult. His attraction to black men is strong, so he's avoiding places where he could be hit on. But yes, he has flings. "Each time I travel to Europe. They're not lovers, just 'contacts.' It's not as if I'm looking, but if I travel it happens. I choose not for it to happen at home because of the situation here," he whispers, afraid the servers might overhear.

The "situation" is the criminalization of homosexuality and the prescribed fourteen-year jail term approved by lawmakers and the president in 2014 as a populist's gambit ahead of an election they ended up losing. The stunt unleashed a manhunt of suspected gays among the hoi polloi. But folks of means simply retreated indoors and carried on. Or went abroad.

Chidi refers to his interactions with his foreign fuck buddies as having *a coffee and a chat.* But even these trysts are becoming rare. It's as if he's weaning himself off men. It's a high price to pay for sanity in Nigeria. Before we rejoin the others, I pull him closer for a hug and mischievously whisper, "So does this mean there is no more hope for us?" Chidi pulls his head back, takes a good long look into my eyes, and bursts into a fit of laugher. And responds, "There's always hope for you! We'll have a 'coffee and a chat' when we're in London."

Months later, we chow down on some goat pepper soup, yam, and tender guinea fowl at Ikoyi's Casa D'Lydia. A giddy Chidi is explaining that life isn't terrible. He wanted kids and now has three. And he's finally found someone. Someone local. Someone safe. Someone married with children too. His companion is a businessman whose family lives in Sokoto. But he's alone on weekdays in Lagos. He gets Chidi. Chidi gets him. They are happy.

ABOUT THE AUTHORS

KOFI AKPABLI has twice been named CNN Multi-choice African Journalist for Arts and Culture. His travel column "Going Places" is published in the *Mirror*. He is the author of books including *A Sense of Savannah — Tales of a Friendly Walk through Northern Ghana*. A teacher of Communication Studies at Central University, he lives in Accra with his wife and children.

ISAAC OTIDI AMUKE lives and writes in Nairobi, Kenya. He was selected to participate in the 2014 Commonwealth Writers creative nonfiction workshop in Kampala, Uganda, and the 2015 Farafina Creative Writing Workshop in Lagos, Nigeria. He has written nonfiction for the literary journal *Kwani?* since 2012, and his literary journalism has appeared on the Commonwealth Writers website. He received the 2013 Jean Jacques Rousseau Fellowship from the Akademie Schloss Solitude in Stuttgart, Germany, and is working on a two-part memoir on student activism and life as an asylum seeker.

CHIKE FRANKIE EDOZIEN was raised in Lagos, Nigeria. An award-winning reporter, his work has appeared in the *New York Times*, the *Times* (UK), *Quartz*, *Vibe* magazine, *Time Magazine*, *Out Traveler*, the *Advocate*, and on various broadcast news outlets. He co-founded the *AFRican* magazine in 2001 to tell African stories overlooked by international media. When he is not teaching journalism at New York University, he's travelling across Africa.

KEVIN EZE was born in Nigeria, where he began writing and learning the piano at the age of seven. He studied Literature and Philosophy at the Jesuit Faculty in the Congo and Sociology at the University of Paris XII, France. His stories have appeared in *Writers, Writing on Conflict and Wars in Africa, Long Journeys*, and in the magazine *Actu'elle*. He is the author of *The Peacekeeper's Wife* (Amalion Publishing, 2015). He lives and writes in Senegal.

MARK GEVISSER is a South African writer whose books include *A Legacy of Liberation: Thabo Mbeki and the Future of the South African Dream*, which won the Alan Paton Award in 2007, and *Lost and Found in Johannesburg: A Memoir*. His work has been published in *Granta*, the *Guardian*, the *New York Times*, the *Observer*, *Foreign Affairs*, the *Los Angeles Times*, the *Wall Street Journal*, and all of South Africa's major newspapers. He has also written an award-winning documentary film, *The Man Who Drove With Mandela*, and worked as a heritage curator in South Africa. He co-edited the pioneering book *Defiant Desire: Gay and Lesbian Lives in South Africa* in 1994 and is currently completing a new book on the new global conversation about sexuality and gender identity.

HAWA JANDE GOLAKAI was born in Frankfurt, Germany, and spent her childhood in her homeland of Liberia, later living in several African countries when her family fled the civil war. In 2011 she published her debut novel, *The Lazarus Effect*, a crime thriller that was nominated for several awards. A sequel, *The Score*, was released in November 2015. She was nominated by the Hay Festivals as one of the thirty-nine most promising African writers under the age of forty, and an extract from her forthcoming novel appears in the *Africa39* anthology published by Bloomsbury. She works as a medical immunologist and health consultant in Monrovia.

SIMONE HAYSOM is a writer based in Cape Town. She is a recipient of a Miles Morland Writing Award and is working on a book of narrative nonfiction about a murder, a trial, and an alleged police conspiracy from which her story in this anthology derives. Her fiction has been published in the literary magazines *Prufrock* and *Carapace*, read at Liar's League

London, and anthologized by PEN South Africa. Her nonfiction has been published in South Africa and the United Kingdom.

ELNATHAN JOHN is a Nigerian lawyer who quit his job in 2012 to write full-time. In 2013, he was shortlisted for the Caine Prize for African Writing for his story "Bayan Layi" and again in 2015 for his story "Flying." He is a 2015 Civitella Ranieri Fellow and, since 2011, has written a satire column about politics and life for a major Nigerian weekly newspaper. His first novel, *Born on a Tuesday*, set in northern Nigeria, was published in 2015. He lives in Abuja.

NEEMA KOMBA is a poet and writer from Tanzania. She is the 2014 winner of the Etisalat Prize for Literature in the flash fiction category. She is the author of *See through the Complicated*, a book of poetry published in 2011, and is the co-founder and coordinator of La Poetista, a platform for poets and other artists to showcase their art and create a positive impact in the community. She is also the coordinator of the Woman Scream Festival in Tanzania, which is part of a worldwide movement to fight against gender-based violence using poetry.

BONGANI KONA is a Zimbabwean-born freelance writer and Contributing Editor at *Chimurenga Chronic*. His work has appeared in *The Mail & Guardian, The Sunday Times, Rolling Stone (SA), Chimurenga Chronic,* and other publications and websites. He is studying for an MA in creative writing at the University of Cape Town.

BEATRICE LAMWAKA is a recipient of the 2011 Young Achievers Award. She was shortlisted for the 2011 Caine Prize for African Writing and was a finalist for the South African PEN/Studzinski Literary Award 2009. The anthology of short stories *Queer Africa: new and collected fiction* (2013), which includes her short story, won the 26th Lambda Literary Award in the fiction anthology category in 2014. She was selected as one of the Young African Scholars for the Harry Frank Guggenheim Foundation's special program in 2009. Her stories have been translated into Spanish, Italian, and French.

SARITA RANCHOD is Executive Director of Under the Rainbow — Creative Strategies for Positive Change, an international development practice based in South Africa. She has worked for and with several international development agencies including UNDP, CIDA, Hivos, and GIZ on local and global assignments. She taught in the Journalism and Media Studies department at Rhodes University, South Africa, and was Commissioning Editor of the Rhodes Journalism Review. As a Nelson Mandela Scholar, she read for an MA in Gender & Development at the Institute of Development Studies, University of Sussex, UK.

MSINGI SASIS was born in Nairobi, Kenya. He is a multidisciplinary artist whose projects include "Nairobi Noir," photographs of Nairobi at night. The images form part of a growing body of street photography and multimedia work with strong influences from his filmmaking background. "Dream Chasers," which appears in this anthology, is a prelude to the first two Nairobi Noir books currently in progress: Vol. 1 "The Night Is Alive," and Vol. 2 "A Soft Dream."

BARBARA WANJALA is a Kenyan writer. Her story about a trip to Djibouti to conduct a (failed) survey on democracy was published in *Roads & Kingdoms*, an independent journal of food, politics, travel, and culture that was voted the Gold Winner for Best Travel Journalism Site by the Society of American Travel Writers in 2013. She was shortlisted for the 2015 Hailer Prize for Development Journalism. Her work has also appeared in *Kwani?*, Kenya's leading literary magazine, and several lifestyle magazines in Kenya and Ethiopia.